FURTHER WORDS OF WISDOM

Through Eileen Ellen Davey

CON-PSY PUBLICATIONS MIDDLESEX

First Edition
2001

©Trevor Paul Davey

This book is copyrighted under the Berne Convention. All rights reserved. No part of this book may be reproduced or utilised in any form or by any means, electronic or mechanical, including photocopying, recording, or by any information storage and retrieval system, without permission in writing from the publisher. Except for the purpose of reviewing or criticism, as permitted under the Copyright Act of 1956.

Published by

CON-PSY PUBLICATIONS

**P.O. BOX 14,
GREENFORD,
MIDDLESEX, UB6 0UF.**

ISBN 1 898680 23 X

FURTHER WORDS OF WISDOM
Channelled through the Deep Trance Mediumship of Eileen Ellen Davey
Edited by Matthew P. Hutton
With introduction and additional words of explanation by Trevor Paul Davey

NOTE & DEDICATION

Previously published titles by Eileen and Trevor Davey include **'Words of Wisdom'** through Con-Psy Publications. Also **'Go Forward to a New Millennium'** through the Olympia Press, 36 Union Street, Ryde, Isle of Wight, PO33 2LE.

This book could not have been written without the advice, assistance and information provided by the various communicators in this volume.

We would also like to thank John and Jean Webb for proof reading the original script, along with Pauline Hutton and Ray Taylor for their support and help with this project.

Further Words of Wisdom is dedicated to the physical life and work of Eileen Ellen Davey in bringing spiritual awareness to all who sought with the guidance, help and support of her host of companions from the Spirit Realms.

Eileen returned to Spirit on 22 May 2001.

CONTENTS

	Page
Introduction	6
Energy - a power beyond our comprehension	10
A special message at Christmas time.	12
Rescue work and helping those that need enlightenment.	14
Lucy - a success story.	17
Thoughts - your future.	19
Colour energy.	23
Colours in healing	26
Questioning makes progress.	28
Going forward with a vanguard of truth.	30
Energy recognition.	32
Colours in everyday language	33
Healing needs time to be effective.	35
Mind is more than brain.	36
The importance of the number 7.	39
Numbers worth a thought?	40
The energy of a single candle for concentration.	47
God of the granite and the rose.	49
Fingerprints more than just a human feature.	51
Looking at the energy behind the written word.	54
Ectoplasm.	57
Cause and Effect.	58
More to people than meets the eye.	60
Energy of the planet earth and our responsibilities.	62
A matter of theology.	64
Photographs with "extras".	70
Pendulums.	72
So why don't we know everything?	74
Special places.	75
The flower.	77
The light of spirit.	79
Do not judge a book by its cover.	81
Thoughts before words.	82
Spring is in the air.	86
Silence - a valuable commodity	87
Memories of an earthly existence	89
A matter of time.	93
Love is the most powerful energy.	97
Life in the spirit dimension.	99

Some examples of our spirit friends learning.	107
Energy linking with colour.	110
Visitors from spirit.	112
Spirit working in unison.	112
Fairies an explanation.	118
Thoughts at the beginning of a New Year.	122
Tasks we perform.	126
Clarity of communication.	128
The Age of Aquarius.	130
Communication on a thought level.	132
Energy - cause and effect.	136
Preconceived ideas - a problem.	139
New energy and the path of progress.	146
Linking and greeting spirit communicators.	151
Organisation of spirit - an insight.	152
Spirit children.	153
Blessings given by spirit.	154
Thought pictures.	156
Talking of energy.	157
An example of the "doorkeepers" role.	165
Learning to commumicate.	167
Knock, knock - is there anyone there?	170
More on children in spirit.	170
What is vibration?	174
The higher realms.	176
Advice on sitting for development.	179
Speed is relative.	181
A question of reincarnation.	183
Types of trance communication evidence.	185
Different attitudes to healing.	187
Protecting the medium.	189
Progressive Education	190
Learn by own experiences	192
A lost traveller.	196
Thoughts on the development of religion.	198
Helen Duncan - her thoughts.	200
Keeping types of communicion separate.	201
Music in the Spirit Realms.	202
Use of green light.	202
Blessing from Father Dominic.	204
A final blessing to you all.	204
The communicators.	205

INTRODUCTION

We are told that we come to the physical existence or dimension from our natural home in the Spirit dimension to experience particular activities and learning on a path of knowledge that we have chosen for our personal development. Exactly how this works is probably beyond our human brain's ability to comprehend at this stage in our individual development.

We do know from the history of ancient civilisations that people were more in tune with their ancestors and accepted the existence of the Spirit dimension in worshiping the Sun and Moon, icons of their interpretation of a higher energy. Our history may well be distorted from the true way of life of the Incas, Chinese, Japanese, Greeks, American Indians and many other cultures, but a glimmer of understanding survives today. We can accept that the truth has been distorted perhaps to make the story more interesting or acceptable before the written word evolved. The clues are in the mythology, the Old Testament, cave drawings, ancient burial sites and places of significant importance where the ancient civilisations worshipped a higher energy.

No doubt for good reason we have a culture that ensures we respect and look after ourselves and others until such time as our physical life is no longer and we return to our home in the Spirit Realms. If we accept that we are in this physical dimension to experience and develop our mind or you may term it the soul, then we must have a duty to ourselves and our fellow beings to live this life to the full. We may have realised what our path of development is. The knowledge from our past being blocked from our human brain to an extent otherwise it is suggested that we would be less focused on living this physical life. So many of our experiences seem on reflection to be unimportant but surely we need the "tools" to reach the total experience that enhances the mind.

Sometimes there is a very special once in a lifetime opportunity that we are given but so often we do not realise the significance to our personal spiritual awareness. We were privileged to enjoy an experience of a host of teachers from the Spirit Realms who came to talk and explain answers to questions on the understanding of life. This was generally given through the deep trance communication with a number of personalities. Some could be very serious and brought very advanced knowledge from the higher realms. Others came for a chat, often with great mirth and joy. but always with a degree of learning. Deep trance is defined as being when a medium or channel allows themselves to go into a state of suspended animation and allows the communicator to take over the body. The ability and developed trust of the medium in their spirit companions develops over many years and must only be allowed to happen in the right circumstances and environment, under the supervision of the mediums "doorkeeper" or "protector". In Eileen's case this was Mafra a Portuguese gentleman of great knowledge who Eileen had absolute faith in and the knowledge that while she was in a state of trance I was always there to ensure that all was well and had the knowledge and experience to deal with any difficulties. When undertaking any communication with the Spirit Realms it is vital that a process of opening up to the spirit energies is undertaken and every knowing medium will have their own way of doing this and equally as important to close down after the communication is completed and this can be as simple as saying, "Thank you Spirit Friends, God Bless". The knowledge held in the medium's physical brain is utilised by spirit to convert the thought process into a language that the sitters can understand. On rare occasions the spirit communicator is able to use words, either in their "mother tongue" or outside of the medium's vocabulary, to provide knowledge and names.

It has been noted that on occasions words in the English language do not exist that fully describe the thought being generated. In this case a more wordy explanation is given to ensure the message is fully comprehended. However, sometimes words slip out in the communicator's "mother tongue". Interestingly, questions have been asked in another language unknown to the medium and answered both in English and the language the question was asked in.

If we accept that thoughts come before words are uttered and that thoughts have no language we can understand how spirit communicates with us and with each other with no language barrier, then perhaps it's not so strange.

Perhaps a little background to our personal development that will assist the reader in accepting the words that are contained in this book are now appropriate.

Eileen was a late bonus child, her mother being in her 40's when she was born in the West London area known as Isleworth. Her parents were of the Methodist line of thinking and her father, after being offered successful spiritual healing for a serious condition, investigated the Spiritualist line of thinking and developed as a healer. Alas, Eileen's father passed to spirit when she was just 13, this of course being a traumatic event in her young life but gave her a deep understanding of people with similar experiences and made her a very strong character. My parents and grandparents were very involved in the Spiritualist movement and, in particular, the Lyceum movement which aims to bring spiritual awareness to interested people of all ages. True Spiritual Awareness is a way of life in the understanding of the interaction of the physical and spirit dimensions. Apart from the proof of survival element it can be a tool for opening up the mind to a greater understanding and development of one's own personality.

My first meeting with Eileen was at the Hounslow Lyceum and we became great friends and loving partners. We married in 1967 and our only daughter Judith came along in 1970.

Let me tell you of the early home circles organised by Eileen's mother with a lovely medium Muriel Miller who worked in trance bringing Eileen one of her companions Beda. Some 30 years later Beda would speak through Eileen. This was before Eileen had developed into an advanced trance communicator, psychic artist, mental medium and spiritual healer. This development did not really start to take place till the late 1980's and was not expected or strived for. We were just developing as healers. By a series of events, or was it urges and opportunities we were guided. We joined a healing development group which, apart from training us as accredited healers, became a very strong physical circle. In this circle of communication we were privileged to have demonstrations of spirit energy moving objects about, distinctive footsteps and raps, spirit materialisations of both human and animal forms being able to physically touch the sitters, sand prints, ectoplasm, aromas and much more and importantly we were able to converse direct with spirit teachers.

After a few years Eileen became aware of the presence of spirit and gradually she developed her own unique methods of communication allowing spirit to occupy her body for spiritual awareness for herself and others.

Eileen returned to the Spirit Realms on the 22 May 2001 at the age of 55 after a short but valiant battle against cancer. She was however able to work with spirit up to a few weeks before her passing and received a lovely communication titled The Flower which was used at her service of Celebration of Life.

This book has been produced as a non commercial venture in tribute to Eileen's spiritual awareness work of acting as a channel for the teachers from the Spirit Realms.

The words in this book are a mere selection of the many conversations held in the home circle and public demonstrations. This book complements the first book "Words of Wisdom" by (Eileen) Ellen & (Trevor) Paul and the second book "Go Forward to the New Millennium" by Eileen Davey.

The words recorded in these pages are direct transcripts on the words given by the spirit teachers with only the tense changed and where appropriate personal names changed to "friends". Some additional notes have been added for clarity and explanation without I trust detracting from the teachings that were conveyed.

As with all questions being answered by a knowing tutor the answer is given to suit the level of understanding and acceptance of the questioner. In some cases we have been told that the human brain can not comprehend a particular concept until a certain stage of our personal development has been reached. This is really as simple as trying to make a small child understand a complex mathematical process when they have only just grasped that two and two make four. It is the same with the inquiring mind. If you do not understand the basic concepts, the advanced answer will be unacceptable and disregarded.

I hope whoever reads these words will find some level of inspiration and answers to their particular needs in putting together this great jigsaw of existence. The answer may just be an opening for further thoughts and questioning but this is how we learn by development of our understanding. We all have to work through this knowledge development in some form to fulfil our reason for being in the physical dimension. It could be described as our path of life. Therefore what is acceptable to one and perhaps no one else will have an identical level of understanding, not dictated by others or whatever religion, creed or dogma we have grown with. It is our personal path of spiritual development and no one has the right to dictate to us. We have to find our own way. In the same way we have no right to dictate to others but we can lead by example, suggest ways of thinking and demonstrate an open mind in acceptance of others rights to their own views.

In the past years we have had so much investment from the teachers from the Realms of Spirit for ours and others development. We always said we had no right to keep this information to ourselves. It is hoped that through the pages of this book we can offer these teachings to anyone that wishes to investigate.

It is my personal affirmation to continue the work Eileen and myself undertook with great pleasure of interactive spiritual awareness events both in the U.K. and abroad.

To quote some of the great communicators :-

"Knowledge is of two kinds. We know a subject ourselves, or we know where we can find the information upon it" - Samuel Johnson

"It is not so much our friends' help that helps us as the confident knowledge that they will help us" - Epicurus

"Knowledge advances by steps and not by leaps" - Lord Thoms Babington Macaulay

"The empires of the future are empires of the mind" - Sir Winston Churchill

ENERGY - POWER BEYOND OUR COMPREHENSION

This teaching was given by Aramday who when on earth was an Arab of high standing. He poses the question as to where does energy begin. You are then invited to experience energy, created between your hands, within a circle type environment.

"Energy is important.
> Energy is eternal.
>> Energy is creative.

Where does energy begin? You are energy. You come from Creative Source which is energy. Energy flows through every existence whether human, animal, plant, the substance that your earth is made from or the substance of your universe. Spirit is energy. Energy is part of us all but we are also capable of generating energy. Energy flows between us. You say, 'spirit world' and 'earth world' but energy knows no barriers. We are one, we are together in this universal band of energy.

Those that lived many hundreds of years previous in your world were aware of energy, the force of energy, the creative force of energy. You have clouded, misted stories of what you call alchemists who used energy for their purpose. You have energy today that you cannot explain. Yes, there is spirit merging with earth life and in your seance rooms you see the results of this energy. Also it is not confined to seance rooms. You see the result of energy in your sky, your planets, your storms that rage, the wind that blows and your seas that man cannot control. You are becoming aware of the many vibrations that encircle your world. Your communications are fuelled on this energy but you cannot explain it. It is there to be used but you cannot explain from whence it comes. You are learning to control it but you have to be very careful because it is an energy that is not defined by man. It is utilised by man but it is not created by man. In the use of this energy you do not know what effect this energy is having.

You are all touched by this energy because you are all linked together as we are linked together. You are very particular in saying, 'our world', 'your world' and 'other parts of the universe' but you do not understand the thread that links all. You have to learn to blend and merge not encompass and overtake. You have to learn to share, to give but also learn how to receive. Be gracious in how you receive. Be humble in how you receive energy from others and energy from outside your normal sphere of existence. Value the energy that you have, use it wisely, diligently, accept it graciously but also return it out into the universe, out into the 'world of spirit', that you call us so that it can also be utilised for others.

You can feel energy. Look at your hands, put them together and feel the energy flow from one hand to the other hand. Feel the pull of magnetic force that is there. This is energy that you cannot explain but it is there. Is it human? Is it spirit? This is part of Creative Force. Spirit comes close and you see the mist of the vibrations rolling around you. Look within that mist and be conscious of what you can perceive of spirit energy and earth energy together. It is not 'your world' and 'our world' but together.

Can you feel the energy? Can you feel your fingers tingling? The palms of your hands are vibrating but can you explain why? Can you perceive colour between your hands? When you assist with healing you feel the warmth, you feel the energy flowing but can you explain why or from whence it comes? How is it created? You have a natural ability to know but do not try to define in formulas and logic with your human mind because it is beyond this and you, as spirit, are aware of energy without human thought. A mother instinctively knows how to tend to her infant. She knows the infant's reactions and the infant's needs. All this is energy. Try to define this and your world gets very complicated.

It does not need to be complicated. Go back in time to when this ability was a natural ability. When you instinctively knew how to utilise energy for good. Alas, there were those that knew how to use energy for purposes that were not good but we will not dwell on this because we are striving for peace and harmony as you know. Go back to that time. It is within you because you go back many generations in your blue print that makes you. Inside you have instinct from those that travelled the earth many aeons of times ago and used their instinctive ability. Go back and draw this from within you. Do not try to define, do not try to write, draw lines and mathematics because that is not necessary. By doing this you make complications because the human brain cannot balance the figures. You do not need this because this is instinct.

If you instinctively work for the good of others you unleash that energy from within you. If you wear a mask and appear to be one person but inside you are another you are locking the door to this energy. You can only utilise for the good of others if you genuinely desire from within, not to pretend but to desire from within. Then it will flow as a fountain but if you try to hide behind a charade your fountain will dry and you will only have a trickle flowing where there should be a stream.

Just a few word for you to think upon. Do not think too deeply because, as I have said, it is natural energy from natural source. Do not complicate. Blessings be with you. Take the energy with you. Energy can be destroyed by negative vibrations. Be wary".

Given 7 December 1999

A SPECIAL MESSAGE AT CHRISTMAS TIME

Golden Ray who comes to us on special occasions or to give a special message comes from the higher realms.

"You are approaching a time of celebration, a time of coming together, a time of sharing and joining together in thought with those you have shared your path with along your journey through your earth life. You send greeting to those, you wish them well and you send them thoughts of happiness and love. You send them wishes to carry them over the threshold into a new year and into a new millennium in your earth world.

Of course, there are many that do not celebrate at this time; many in your world who have nothing to celebrate and many who will be sad at this time. Much has occurred since your earth world has rolled round from previous celebrations of a year ago. Many changes and many occurrences leaving a trail of unhappiness for many. Send your love to those ones. Send them a ray of light that they may step forward bravely over the threshold into a new year with hope not despair. It is a time of sharing and coming together but spare a thought to those that are not so happy as others. Carry them forward in this glow of light, giving them strength and encouragement.

This is a time of new beginnings. It is a time of new energy. Grasp this energy and build on this energy in a positive way. Carry your love forward in a positive manner. Spread to those that are seeking the truth of spirit. The truth that, yes, their loved ones live on and that their loved ones are near to them. This is an important teaching but also share the knowledge of eternal progress open to every human soul. This does not just mean those that have gone home to spirit because you are aware that there are endless possibilities for progress in the spirit realms when you are not encompassed with the heavy conditions of earth but also you ones that are treading the earth path.

You also have opportunity for progress. Yes, you are surrounded by the gloom and despondency of earth but walk through this gloom and despondency. Follow the light of spirit and do not waste your time on earth lowering your vibration to that of the vibrations around you. Shed your light. Shed your knowledge of spirit to others. Show them that there is so much more to learn than the material world. You live within the material world, you exist in the material world and you have to abide by the circumstances of your material world to exist but you are spirit within that has brought with it a glow and a strength that can overcome the problems that beset you on this journey. Also, you can give strength to others who walk alongside you. You cannot walk their paths with them in their shoes but you can walk alongside giving them your love and your energy. They too are spirit within. They too have the spark of spirit burning within them and your spark can help to ignite theirs, giving them encouragement, persuading them to look for the good around them not for the despondency that is around them at this time.

Yes, we understand your earth world has many problems but also you all have many blessings but you are so beset by the problems you do not realise the blessings that are also around you. It is not until you do not have them that you realise the benefit that they have brought you. You do not realise the blessings of your health and strength until you have a period of illness, but you overcome that illness and you regain your vitality and your health. So soon you take it for granted again. You do not value friendship until a friend is taken from you, perhaps to journey on to another part of their existence in the spirit realms or perhaps, to move away to another part of your world. You do not appreciate the beauty that surrounds you from your earth world, the beauty of your scenery, of your plants, your trees and your flowers. When the spring comes and new flowers show themselves you are filled with hope. You absorb their beauty and you appreciate but as the seasons unfurl and the leaves become greener and the flowers become more bountiful you take them for granted. It is not until the leaves turn and fall that you realise the beauty of the summer that has gone.

You look at the winter skies. You look at the gloom and feel the energy waning but this is the rest period for your earth to prepare for rejuvenation of a new season. Again it is a blessing. Your earth needs rest so that it can bring forth again. As with yourselves, you are human in a human body. You have your cycle of your day and you need your rest period to revitalise your earth body. With your spiritual progress you also need times of rest, time to stand back, time to amass the knowledge you have received, the lessons you have learnt along your way before you step forward on another chapter of your progress.

Move forward through this time of celebration, whatever your faith, whatever your religion or whatever way you worship. Celebrate the coming together in love and thoughts of others: those on your earth and those that have taken a step further into the realms of spirit. Do not look back with sadness at times gone by but look forward to times ahead. Yes, you have had experiences of happy times, but you still have experiences to come. Do not all the time look over your shoulder at what has been. Acknowledge what has been. Be grateful for what experiences there have been but build on these for the future and step forward into this new energy of a new time on your earth. Take with you into this time your experiences, your knowledge and your wisdom from times gone by and carry this into your new millennium with a hope of brighter times to come - a time of rebuilding, a time of going forward linking with new friends of your earth and of spirit because as you gain in knowledge so do you attract to you different vibrations with different energy.

Look forward not in fear but in hope. Do not expect changes immediately because this does not occur. Change has to be gradual for progress because we all go forward at our own pace. We all experience at our own level but that does not mean that we isolate ourselves from others because we are all part of the whole. We are all part of Creative Energy, Creative Force. As you step forward, others are stepping forward at the same time because all are linked as one.

Blessings to you my brothers and sisters. Go forward in the knowledge that you are part of the family of spirit".
Given 5 December 1999

RESCUE WORK
AND HELPING THOSE THAT NEED ENLIGHTENMENT

There are some very advanced souls who work with trained mediums and knowledgeable ones in the earth dimension that undertake the work which is generally termed as Rescue Work. There are ones that have passed and not accepted that they are in the spirit dimension, others that are mischievous and cause concern. There are many examples of so called Ghost Stories. These, "ghostly happenings" may be a strange feeling, movement of material items, knockings and other noises, lights and with ones that are sensitive an apparition. Remembering that we are all sensitive to the spirit vibration to some degree and not necessarily a developed medium or even one accepting that they have a degree of sensitivity.

We are aware that our animals have a wider range of sensitivity and this is clearly demonstrated with the ability of a dog to hear noises outside the range of human hearing. Often animals will be aware of other levels of vibration and show signs of curiosity or perhaps distress, before a human.

The work of assisting those souls, who are unable or unwilling to progress is very specialised and requires a great deal of knowledge and protection to ensure success and to protect themselves from undesirable lower levels of energy. This is equally true of those in the spirit realms.

Over aeons of time the knowledge that souls who have passed to spirit in traumatic circumstances may have difficulty progressing has been lost or misconstrued. Take for example the Roman Catholic concept of, "purgatory", a state of being unaware and awaiting a signal to go forward.

During our experimental sittings we invite our spirit companions to bring visitors through who need experience of communication and per-

haps to learn they no longer suffer a disability. Also there are some that need assistance in their progression. In a protected condition these souls can experience returning to earth conditions through a medium and this can assist their progress. On one particular occasion we had a visitor who had some difficulty in communicating but was able to ask where we were and knew something of the area where we live. This visitor was also interested in which year we were living in and then related to a time in 1953 when she went to watch the coronation parade in London.

Mafra was asked about the benefits of doing this kind of work.

"We are trying to bring some realisation and some memory of being happy, being joyful and wanting to be part of others. This was helping to bring that one towards light".

When you bring those ones Mafra is there anything particular you wish us to do?

"They are all different. It is difficult because this one, when they first came, even the sound of your voice was a shock to them. Sometimes it is helpful to talk and to draw them in conversation but sometimes they are in a state of not knowing where they are. They cannot see you and they hear a voice. The voice is coming from nowhere and they don't know what is happening because they have been surrounded for a while with nothing as if in a fog. You know yourself that when there is fog in your physical world your senses are impaired. You do not hear. This is similar to the state these ones are in that we bring to you for help and as they come towards light we try to draw them closer to the light and you are able to help. Then when they hear your voice they may retreat because this is not expected.

I have given you an explanation of the conditions of your visitor on a particular date but this may not be the same experience with other visitors. Sometimes it helps to speak to draw them towards light. We cannot say what is best because each visitor will be different and you will receive perception of the best course of action. If you think of us and link with our thoughts and go by what you are receiving from us you will instinctively know what to do. You are communicating with us and we are communicating with you so be aware of vibrations we are giving you as to help each one separately.

They were asking questions and you were answering so that was good. They were confused as to where you were and in what time because they didn't know time. They wanted to get some idea of where they were. They knew they had left earth time behind but they were not aware of time on earth now. You mentioned where you lived and they had memory of that place and then we were able to bring in the colours to help. They mentioned the trees in your area and we brought in green which is soothing to help.

Also the memory of the hill they were looking up raising their vision - of course not physical vision but raising thought. We were working as you were speaking. We were bringing in conditions to help them and this was gradually coming through. You asked a date of their time on earth and they were confused, but the date that was most important in their mind was of a time when they were happy and it was a big occasion. It did not mean that was the date they were born or the time they went to spirit but it was a time in their lives that was momentous for them".

Can you please explain to me; if for arguments sake, there are 100 people similar to us sitting inviting these ones to come for experience that must be a very small number. Are there many, many that are still in this state?

"There are many. Spirit help, we help and there are those in spirit whose dedicated path of progress is to help these ones and they do. Sometimes it is easier than others. Sometimes they are able to draw them with the help of their loved ones and together they are able to link them with the ones that are waiting to greet them. Sometimes it is difficult, so it is useful for us to find someone of earth condition that can assist. As you know, these vibrations are similar. Eventually we would be able to help but it makes things run a little smoother. There is no time but it is progress and that one is not progressing for no particular reason. I am not saying that these ones are in darkness and have done many bad deeds being shut out of paradise! It is not as your orthodox churches teach. It is just a condition".

How are you guided to help these particular ones? Is it that they are stretching out knowing there is something there and they need help or is it something else?

"I have said to you that there are those ones in spirit whose dedicated task is to help these ones and it is those that link with us. They link with us on a compatible vibration and we are aware that we can help. It is not only myself and our group but also other groups. The one that is trying to help them and is not able to do as much as they wish finds a compatible energy that has a link with an earth condition and they link with that team. The team in spirit and the team on earth link and work together all part of the team. When we successfully draw that one we hand that one to the spirit that is helping and in turn that one will lead them gently onto their loved ones. It is teamwork not just one entity. We have explained how we merge and blend our energies and this is what happens. This is why, when I came to you just now, I did not come immediately but was gently taking my energy back slowly so that it would be a smooth movement. The one in spirit that was helping was drawing closer and I was stepping back. This is why I was talking to you slowly to make it as smooth as possible".

Can this type of work only be done through trance communication?

"It can be done in other ways but it is easier through trance communication because we are bringing that one to an earth body and they have some recognition of what an earth body was like. They then realise it is not their earth body and there is something different. You may recall this visitor said to you, 'It is different.' They acknowledged that it was different from their memory of an earth body. One moment they are in their body and the next they are in somebody else's body and they realised there must have been something else in-between. They were confused because of the difference.

You help with your prayers and thoughts. Sometimes they are able to bring these ones to an ordinary circle and encompass them with love and someone in that circle that is mediumistic can pick up the vibrations. This could also be done on the mental level but it would be slower because the one being helped would not understand what was happening.

This is something we can do to help. We teach but we do other tasks as well. It is very difficult for us to explain. You wonder why we do not adhere to our chosen path but we are flexible. This is all part of merging energy. Others need help and if we can give help we do. There are those that specialise but if we can assist them in their work we are happy to do so. It is the same as being teachers but if there is someone that can give us information who is not a teacher we welcome their energy. It is all about compatibility of vibrations. You may say 'thoughts' because you have a physical brain and you understand that you send thoughts but it is a wavelength, a frequency".

Given January 2000

LUCY A SUCCESS STORY

From time to time our spirit companions are asked to help with ones who have passed and for some reason their development is hampered and they need some enlightenment. Lucy when on earth was blind from birth and came to the conclusion that seeing was not for her and developed her other senses to compensate. She was happy not being able to see and when she passed at the young age of nine her development was not hampered by the lack of experiencing seeing. When her mother passed to spirit she was distressed at Lucy's inability to see and in particular to know what her mother really looked like.

When Lucy first came to talk to us some two months ago she talked to us about not wanting to see because she was afraid that her mother would not be as she had imagined. Over a relatively short time our helpers were able to gradually open up Lucy's ability to see and now she has seen her mother and many other things. She is happy and so is her mother.

Lucy told us the following on the night of Tuesday 4 April 2000, and we think there is a great deal for us all to learn.

'I want to say thank you because I am happier now. I was happy before but I can understand better.'

Can you see OK now?

'Yes, I can.'

Can you see your mummy?

'Yes, so that is good. You know it is still a lot easier for me to use other ways of sensing. You can do this but you don't. You said to me that I should see but I say to you that you should use your other senses because they are there but you just don't use them. Sometimes it is so much easier when you know how to because you can sense what people are really like not just what they look like. I don't mean by touching, I mean by other senses that you have but don't use. Somebody who you may think as being very ugly really is a very beautiful person and someone that you think is very beautiful may not be really beautiful at all. It is so much easier as well to talk to people because you are not looking at their expression but are feeling their vibration. Someone can look as if they are interested but perhaps they are not interested at all or someone may look as if they don't care but they really do care but are frightened of showing it. If you listen to the tone of voice you can find out a lot. You know when someone is tired, someone is worried or someone is not telling you the truth by the tone of their voice and the way they are saying things. If you are just looking at their face and not using that sense you don't know.

So I want to tell you to do that because you helped me by telling me and I want to help others. Don't just use your eyes but use other senses as well. Practise a little bit at a time just like I did and gradually a little bit more, not all the time but just for a short time. Look at somebody perhaps for five minutes and use your other senses. Then don't do it for a while. Then later try again. That way you will be able to think about it, remember what it was all about but if you did it all the time at first you would start to think of other things and you wouldn't always do it best. Do you know what I mean?

It is all learning. There are different ways of learning. There is no one to teach you, is there? You have to teach yourself. They don't teach you that in your schools, do they? If you learn you can teach other people. It is difficult because you can't say that you have to watch for this or watch for that because that would not mean that person was unhappy, sad or confused because everybody shows a different way. You will be linking with another sense and that will make it easier.

Someone is telling me what to tell you. They are saying why don't you have your television switched on and close your eyes for a few minutes and then not see the person but see what you think about the person. It is a little bit like listening to a gramophone record I should think but not the same because on a gramophone record they are doing it for you to hear not to see. On a television they would not be doing that but would be using their face and mannerisms to express themselves. So doing this would help you to sense what they are saying and what they are not saying. This was how I learnt because people would talk ordinarily for other people not just for me but I would learn about their voice and what they were saying.

If you talk to somebody who couldn't see you would just say words but if you didn't know they couldn't see you would be more relaxed and use other ways of expression. That is how I learnt and it was natural, as natural as you learn your way of living. Can I ask you to do that?'
Given 4 April 2000

THOUGHTS - YOUR FUTURE

Golden Ray is the name of a higher vibration. He / She explains how we create energy with our thoughts that can effect us when we return home to spirit. Also tells us about those in spirit who have chosen to serve others.

"I have come because I wanted to say thank you for the help you have given to me and to others. It is not easy for us to make this journey to talk to you. We have been in the realms of spirit for a while now and we have been accustomed to the conditions of spirit. Communication in spirit is so different. It is instant. We do not prepare what we are going to speak. In an earth body you need to think and find words before you speak but in spirit it is instant. This is why we have to be so careful as to which vibration we are using because when you on earth speak you sometimes bite your tongue and you rephrase what you are saying. Something happens on the spur of the moment. You are startled and perhaps your thoughts are not so high in calibre as they may be at another time. In spirit we do not have this time of preparation. You can imagine many that are struggling and it is so easy to become acquainted with vibrations that are not so good.

There are those in spirit who work instructing those ones that come home to spirit in how to become acquainted with vibrations and the raising of energy levels. You can perceive if someone comes over in a state of turmoil when perhaps their earth existence was not so kind to them. Perhaps, they had not the enlightenment on their earth path as others have and when they come to spirit they are still encased in these vibrations. There are many in spirit that are at this level and wish to stay at that level because they have not perceived there is anything higher, something brighter and more worth while.

There are those that during their earth life existence have surrounded themselves with thoughts to others of criticism, discontent, displeasure and not looking for the good in others but finding fault in others. There are some that are always complaining and always finding something not so good to say. As you know, what you send rebounds back to yourself. When they return home they are surrounded with these thoughts that they themselves have sent and it is very difficult for them to see their way through because they have created negative energy. They have surrounded themselves with negative energy and have drawn themselves into this vibration. When they go home to spirit that vibration is their level and it is difficult for them to find their way to a higher level because they have to work through the pain and problems that they have caused to others. They meant to harm others but they harmed themselves. This is why we say thought is so important because thought is an energy and if you send thoughts of negativity you are surrounding yourself with this energy. So my friends we are privileged that we know a little more and we are able to rise above this level.

It is through our own work and dedication. It is easy to stay on a level on your earth plane and go with the flow, go with those that are despondent and go with those that criticise. It is the easy option. It is more difficult to rise above and look for the bright light, a more positive light. My friends, as I have said to you, when you go home you surround yourself with energy of your own creation and there are many that have come home who are unable to see through this negativity. It is to those that the enlightened ones shed a light to try and draw them forward. They have to work through the negativity they have created on earth because that cannot be wiped away as it is natural law - what you sow you reap. They have to work through that but the ones in spirit on the higher levels work to try to stop the negativity so that as they work through their despondency they do not add to this despondency but become aware that their thoughts are creating an effect.

You say sometimes to those that come to speak to you from spirit, 'What is your work in spirit and what do you do?' Some say they heal. Some say they teach. Some say that they help those that have come home to spirit. There are so many different ways of helping those that come home to spirit because they all find themselves in different situations. Some, as I have just spoken of, have come to a situation they have created for themselves and natural law predicts that they have to work through that and it cannot be wiped away. There are those in spirit that try to help to stop them creating more negativity so they can eventually break through when they have worked through the problems they have created for themselves.

There are others that assist those that come to spirit in so many different ways.

Some enlightened ones come but need a time of rest and adjustment because their physical bodies have taken a toll and they need healing and upliftment before they can continue their existence in the sphere of light they have earned.

There are those that come suddenly to spirit and need a time of adjustment. Again, there are others that work in this situation.

There are those ones that came home as young children. You realise that they do not always stay as young children because they may be an evolved soul. However, there is a link with the earthly parents and that one sometimes needs to stay in a child's condition so that there can be a link with the earthly parents. The earthly parents may or may not be aware but it is a natural adjustment. A gentle severing of links and not an abrupt one. There is healing needed for the ones that are on earth as well as the one that has come home to spirit.

There are those that have come into a situation of uncertainty, not because of their thoughts of negativity but because of their belief on earth. They were not enlightened because they were told they would sleep and that is what they are doing. They are happy in this situation.

I have spoken of just a few examples of when one comes home to spirit and the different help that is needed. When someone from spirit says to you, 'I help those that have come home' there are many ways they can help and each is specialised. This help does not stop because as they progress help is still needed at each level of development. There has to be someone that is there to give them love and guidance.

You say that there must be so many in spirit over the centuries of earth time. In thousands of years of earth time so many have come home to spirit. What are they doing and where are they? I cannot answer. Some have chosen to return to earth for a dedicated purpose to assist those that walk earth's path. Some have chosen to return to experience a condition for whatever reason. Others have chosen to progress on other levels. Others have chosen the path of service to others and it is these dedicated ones that bring so much light and energy to assist those that are travelling with them.

You say to me, 'Why is it in all circles, in all groups, in all churches we get so many that have taken holy orders?' They came to earth from spirit. They chose a path of service to others. This was their choice and this is the work they are still continuing, giving unselfish love for others. You get others of course. You get teachers, those that work for your medical profession, those that spoke and gave words of wisdom from whatever religion they followed - all dedicated to the service of others. You get those who, you say, are more humble because their station in life was humble and they served those that were better endowed than themselves. That again was a path of service. They may have led a humble existence but the spirit inside may have been a lot brighter than those they served. So many, in their everyday existence to earn their money to eat and exist, serve others on your earth now and in years that have gone. Those that protected your land in times of problems, those that wore uniform, those that held high office in governments. Those that served those that held high office in governments. Those that supported others that served. All in service to others. I have spoken of your professions, those that were educated and trained whether it was medical, teaching, whatever, but behind those ones that had letters after their name there were those that served them. They may not have been so educated but still served. Can you perceive how many that have come home to spirit have been involved in service to others? Why should they not continue their service to others?

Of course, there are others that wish to take a completely different path. They wish to explore avenues for themselves. Perhaps your scientists are a good example. When they come home they wish to explore so much more than was comprehensible to their human brain. They were striving to find explanations but they were limited in their scope, but without that limitation there is so much more to explore. They again, in turn, may wish to assist those ones that follow that dedicated path on earth, so service still continues.

We have our cycles of service and we have our cycles of learning. To be of service we need to be aware and the more wisdom we can gain from those ones that teach us, the more we can pass this on to those we serve. Also, we need time to assist those ones but we also need time to rebuild our energy because, as you serve and you drain your energy, so do those in spirit that work with the negative energy. They put up a field of protection of course but they are dealing with a negative force and this can cause depletion of energy. They too need time away in another level of vibration to learn and recharge their energy.

'Yes' you say, 'but we have those that come to talk to us. They come often to talk to us. Our door keepers come to talk to us and we know they are always there. We cannot operate without them because they are our protection so when do they have opportunity to recharge their energy and learn?' It is simultaneous. You are thinking in a human mind where you have to live in compartments. Your human world is in 'boxes'. You have time when you work, time when you rest, time when you learn, time when you socialise with others. You see, my friends, in spirit we do not have these confines and limitations. I cannot explain but while these ones come to you they are still able to link with a higher energy to recharge and become more enlightened themselves. If you are mediums linking one vibration with another, because this is what you are doing, you are linking a human vibration with a spirit vibration. So my friends are your helpers. They are linking various levels of vibrations and are transposing these vibrations for enlightenment.

I hope these words give you some thoughts. It is nothing new. It is nothing you did not know before but I was trying to explain a little deeper. It is so easy to say, 'Oh yes, well when I go home to spirit I will learn to help this and I will learn to help that' but you do not realise how delicate the vibrations are and how much work is done in so many different fields just assisting others. Also, I wanted you to be aware of the energy fields that we are always striving to rise above to the highest one you can achieve. You will return home to spirit, as we all have, and you will experience the vibrations you have created. No one returns home and goes to the celestial heights because you have walked earth path and you have experienced human frustrations and being a human you have negative thoughts and you have thoughts of fear and doubt. This is why we have said to you so many times do not return fear with fear but send enlightenment and hope for those that are fearful and you are rising yourself in your vibration with the vibrations you are sending.

Thank you for reading these words and thank you for your love you send out to others".
Given 2 February 2000

COLOUR ENERGY

Kimyano is a lady from the spirit realms who lived in Japan and brings us knowledge about colours and how they can be of great assistance to helping people. Firstly she tells us about colour and healing.

"Colours are vibrations and of an infinite range of tones. Spirit colours are more vibrant than that perceived by the human eye. Although we may say that projecting the colour blue while sending out healing thoughts, that actual tone of the blue colour needs to be compatible between the healer and the patient. In some cases one healer may not be able to project the exact frequency of the colour vibration or the patient may not be susceptible to accepting the healer's thought waves. By trial and error if the patient is not responding to the particular healer's work then another healer should take on the patient. This does not mean that the first healer is no good but it's a simple "fact of life", that some people are not compatible with others. We all need colours to give us vibrant energy. Dull or negative colours will depress our human spirit.

Colours are also important in giving the right conditions for communication. The colours need to provide a peaceful environment. Pastel shades therefore put you in the right frame of mind to feel relaxed and not threatened . Therefore the environment is more conducive to good communication.

There are many colours in the places where you have a peaceful environment, like your churches and other places where you go to link with your friends in joy and happiness, many colours like paintings of spirit with their vibrations. They have painted your room with colour, red, blues, pinks, mauves, gold, yellow, green, clear sparkling white. Very pretty. Lots of energy, lots of energy around all of you come from all of you to us like rainbow, very pretty. Our colours are so different to yours. Our colours are alive. You touch our colour. You feel our colour. It is alive. It is moving. It is all around you. Your colours in comparison are flat. It is like looking at a painting and looking at a 3D. Our colours stand out, more energy We transmit on colour. You see our vibration. We are colour. We link with colour, send out our love on colour to others. It is living to us colour. Our colour is like your breath, your air, your oxygen. We live with colour. We need colour to exist as you need air to exist".

Kimyano was asked where do our spirit friends draw their colour from ?

"We do not draw. It is there. It just grows. If we need a colour, say for healing, the energy is absorbed into the colour we need and that colour becomes more vibrant. If it is needed for a nervous condition the colour will be more green than blue because you just have colour but we have colour with so many shades. You know a little of what I say because you have a paint box with say five or six blues or five or six greens but our colours are more different, many, many more colours of blue or green or yellow than you will ever imagine. Every colour has its own energy although energy different. We are all different, as you here on your earth are all different so we in spirit are all different and we each have our own colour slightly different. You think if you were spirit what colour would you like to be? and why would you like to be that colour?"

Kimyano then tells us our auras or the colours that are all around us

" As one of your spirit friends I can sense you aura. An aura as you can understand is not as we understand it is only something that you can perceive when you are in body. Others who are gifted to see what you call aura have this ability. Although it is a spiritual ability it is still linked to your physical sense so it is, I say, flat. It is a surrounding of colour but what we perceive is movement, vibration, colours not one on top of the other, mixing and blending and all the time swirling around of you, not something that stays the same. Changing all the time as your thoughts change so your colour change. When they say you have break in aura this is not so. You have movement in aura. Your aura is moving all the time. It cannot break because it is part of you. It just is always changing. It changes with your thought. It changes with your bodily health condition. It changes if you are asleep or whether you are busy, with what your physical mind is doing and your spiritual mind. So many things.

    I like colours, bright colours. It would be good if you understood colour. Colour opens the door for you because colour is vibration. We are a vibration so we link with colour. It is just a step for us. Once you understand colour vibration you will find it a lot easier to open door to link with spirit. In your meditation you travel to your garden or perhaps another location. Think of the colour in that place. If you sit on the grass or on the beach, look at the sunshine. The sun is gold. The sky is blue. The ground is green or yellow, depending on where you sit. The rocks, stones or pebbles are different colours. Different coloured birds, butterflies, animals absorb the colour and vibration.

    Colour is very important because it is us. We are vibration but you are colour also. You are colour in your energy, in your thoughts. You send thoughts. Thoughts are energy. Thoughts are vibration which turn to colour as they leave you and go off wherever. You must think of sending out good colour not dull colour. More love sent more vibrant your colour, the more positive your thought the brighter the colour. You send healing with love. That is good. You send **knowing** that healing is going so that is good. That makes colour brighter. It is **knowing** that makes it easier for us to help. If you visualise the one you are sending healing to, visualise their face and surround their face with colour. That helps. If you want to go to the part of the body where healing is needed, visualise that part of body and put colour around there and send it. It is like key. It opens door. We do not like dark colours. It is good to have a dark colour but you must have a bright colour with it. That is good. All colour has energy, even greys, but if you put bright colour with the dark colour you have more energy because you have contrast. It takes one vibration from the other and makes stronger energy. The bright colour bounces off the dark colour so the energy becomes more vibrant. In your fashions you see patterns, perhaps if you had curtain and your curtain was all one colour. Perhaps it is red, very good red very bright, but if you put red on a black background it would become brighter because it would bounce off of the dark colour. Black is no good on its own but helps to assist other colour to reflect energy.

It is good when you consider the soft tones and you merge them together, not what you call your primary colours, your more pastels colours which are merged from other colours. Similar colours, perhaps you have pink, mauve and blue and they merge together because they are compatible because they have the same colours in them. This is like people. Like attracts like. People who have the same interests, the same beliefs, the same energy within them merge together and are compatible as your colours which have the same energy within them. One assists the other. It is the same with your animals. You have your animals in the wild and you have your pets. In other countries you have animals which live in same area sharing the same colour. Those which share same colour are safe but if you have one which contrasts there is a problem because it stands out and others can see".

COLOURS IN HEALING

"You have colour all around you but energy is different from something that is living. Perhaps you have picture of a field with green grass. If you put your hand on that picture to feel energy you will feel a little energy but if you put your hand on grass it will be much more vibrant. We say to you that when you walk in your garden and you see your flowers blooming, don't just look and say, 'that is a nice colour' but look at colour, feel colour, absorb energy of colour then you will really know colour. If you have petal or leaf hold it in your hand and learn the energy from that colour. When you use your paints to colour it is still energy but it is not so strong. When you see colour of spirit around you can feel energy of colour.

You do not realise how much energy is around you by absorbing colours in your homes, in your countryside, in your gardens in your market places where you buy there is colour. You do not realise how this colour affects you because you are so busy existing and living. You do not always realise when you walk into a building how colour meets you and how you feel about that building is not only what you see but what energy you feel.

Children will tell you about colours in their lives and how they use colour because children are much more aware. As you grow a little more senior in years you take things for granted. You think that it is always there and will always be there, but when you are young it is an adventure and everything is new. The children are eager to learn, wanting to discover. Life lies before them with so much they want to do and so much they dream about. This is a good energy.

Kimyano I have been noticing some extremely beautiful sunsets recently but I do not take these for granted.

Of course not but some people go around as if they have a mask over their face and they do not see what is around them. They look just at what they want to look at but do not look at either side of them. They do not look up to the heavens above and see the sky above their head but just look ahead, at their feet or what is in front of their nose. You absorb colour, my friend, and that is good. You not only see the colour but you feel the energy from colour. You may not be aware of this but by opening your physical vision and absorbing the beauty you are opening your wider senses to open up and absorb. It is as I was saying, looking at a picture and looking at something that is alive the energy is so different.

We understand that your world is busy, you are rushing here and there and you do not always have time but make a small part of your day for yourself to absorb. I am not saying you should take your attention away from something that is important because I know you have a busy life and you drive your vehicles and cannot take your attention away from what you are doing but make time when you can to take your attention away from something. Make time when you can walk around and absorb energy.

I am not criticising but this is the way of earthly life. You come to earth into a child's existence and it is an adventure. When you take on more responsibilities and more duties you do not have time to be so free to absorb because you have other things that take your time. I am not criticising but just making you aware. Sometimes when you are away from your usual routine you then have time to be a child again and to absorb what is around you. If you went on a trip to a garden or even another street or building you would take time to look and observe the new vista in front of you. Why don't you sometimes pretend that you are on a trip when you are at home and look at things as if you are a visitor and absorb things as if they were not there every day? Imagine that you are seeing things around you for the first time. How much more you would observe than your normal observation everyday. Sometimes be a visitor in your own garden, in your own street or in your own home and see things as if you are seeing them for the first time. You will absorb so much. Perhaps you may have a visitor and they will say to you, 'Look at this' or 'Look at that' and it may be something you have taken for granted.

Do not stop exploring. Do not lose the energy and your inquisitiveness of discovering because this is all part of growing and learning. All your existence is learning. We are still learning. The more you do something the more you shut yourself into a shell. Do things as if they are fresh every time.

Every sunset is different, my friend, is it not? The sun rises and the sun sets every day but the colour is different because the clouds are different. Your winds are different and blow across your sky. Shadow is different, the length of the rays of the sun are different as your year advances and wanes. Therefore, every day is different. So many people say, 'Yes, that is a sunset I saw that yesterday so I do not need to look at it today' but you, my friend, absorb each day as it comes. As you open up to this energy you are also opening up to the energy of spirit and this helps you on your own path of progress because you are opening your senses both physical and spiritual to energy. What is communication with spirit but energy. In your healing you are aware of absorbing energy and passing on energy to those that you serve. The more you help yourself the more you are helping others and by helping others you are growing yourself.

Take these colours, absorb these colours, warp them around you and pass them on to others. When you think of others to whom you send healing, send them colours. If they need energy send them the glow of the sunset. If they need soothing send them the blue of the sky or the green of the trees. Send them a little energy not just the colour, a living energy. Send them the sparkling blue of the sea as it glows in the sun. Send the fresh blue of your bluebells, the yellow of your daffodils or the pink of your blossom. Wrap them in energy. Live with colour and absorb colour. As you listen to music close your eyes and absorb the music but also absorb the colour because colour and music blend together. Nothing is separate in your world or our world. Everything blends with each other in harmony. This is existence that is eternal, energy that is forever blending, growing and merging, continuous energy. Feel this and absorb it. Think of your birds flying across the sky. In your part of the world perhaps your birds do not have so much colour but in other lands you have brightly coloured birds flying across the sky. Send these colours on a wing as if they are a bird to those that you wish to serve.

Blessings be with you my friends".
Given 13 February 2000

QUESTIONING MAKES PROGRESS

John Lyon telling us that he heard his name mentioned at a public meeting we had presented two days previous on the 17 September 2000 and his "ears pricked up", and gave the following thoughts.

"We work as a team as you know and we are linking with many others, from other groups. Some you know of. Some you do not know of. We are part of a group of those that serve and as such we serve wherever service is needed. We come to teach of course, as you are aware because that is the chosen path of many of this group. We are striving to enlighten and bring awareness of spirit to others in your earth world, who are seeking answers to their questions. Questions they have perhaps been asking for a long while. Answers they have received either through their reading or listening to others from perhaps your religion or other religions have not satisfied them. The knowledge they have is sufficient for a time and then they realise that there is more. There are still questions that are unanswered. As we have said to you, this is an event that is continuing. More and more are becoming aware that there is more to existence than just your earthly turmoil. What you are experiencing in your earth world stretches much further than the few short years of your earth life.

There are many, many questions and this why we say to you we are training teachers. There are many enlightened ones at this moment in your earth world, in earth bodies, who have come to bring wisdom and knowledge and many more still to come. There are also many in spirit who want to assist in this service to return the knowledge to your earth world that has been hidden for so long.

Fear has ruled in many countries. Fear has ruled many religions and people born to the earth world have been misguided and have been living in fear and despondency when they could have been living in enlightenment. If you think that your earth life is all that there is to existing, you would become despondent. You would become resentful of others. You see others that you consider who live their life perhaps not to the service of others and they have blessings, you consider, bestowed upon them and why this is happening? However, you are only looking at the few short years you have on your earth life. You can not understand, in the religions that have taught men and ladies of the earth world, how these events can occur. You look and you say well if there is a God, why do these things happen? This is because you have been encased in religions of fear not of love and there is so much more to existence than the few years. I say a few years; if you live to be one hundred it is a few years in comparison to the existence of eternity which is yours.

You are part of creation. You are part of the energy force that knows no bounds. Progress is there for all those that wish to progress, all that have the desire to progress. If you do not have the desire that is your choice. No one enforces progress on you. Yes, your loved ones and your guides, helpers, companions, whatever name you call them, would dearly love to help you on your path and to lead you forward. However, if you do not desire this, that is your choice. Free will is yours. So many chose to ignore the love that spirit send to them but there comes a time in each existence when they look upwards towards the light and accept there is more. For some it takes longer than others and those in the realms of light are forever helping to draw forth those who are clouded in mist of doubt and despondency to try to bring them through into the light. This is a continual path of service and those from the realms of light are very patient in this work.

Please continue your work to shed knowledge and light to others. To give them something to think about so that they can stretch their thoughts outwards from the conditions of earth knowing there is more. Knowing that the problems of your earth world are something to be endured at this phase in their existence but they can help themselves and help others to strive towards the light".

Given 19 September 2000

GOING FORWARD WITH A VANGUARD OF TRUTH

"Good to speak with you. So our work continues. It is a continuous effort, an effort to assist. The words you use on earth have a different meaning to us. We would say a control but a control on earth means something different. We try to control the energy but energy is uncontrollable because all the time it is changing by factors that are beyond the control of an individual or even a team such as ours. Occurrences occur, events occur and these events cause thoughts, actions to come into being. These in themselves instigate further reaction and so all the time there is change.

Yes, there is a path of destiny for all. There is a path of destiny for individuals, for groups, for existence within an earth life or existence within a wider scope than earth. All the time there is free will and there are human emotions of fear, of anger, of indifference, determination. All have an effect. So many unsure, so many without a purpose, so many waiting for a sign or a direction in which to focus their intent. There are times that bring people together, times of crisis, times of celebration when you feel a unity between you, whether in happiness or sadness. At times like these you look for guidance, sometimes from someone from your earthly world but sometimes from a higher existence. When these times have run their course and your world returns to its ordinary existence, whatever that is! There is no such thing as ordinary. When you are experiencing a time of mundane occurrences another part of your world is experiencing turmoil or celebration. When you return to this existence that you say is mundane the link that binds you becomes looser. The determination to pull together is not so great. The endeavour to share experiences wanes and like sheep that are lost from their shepherd man wanders and strays without a purpose each trying to find their own way to the green pasture of their endeavours and the flock goes in many directions. So it is with your earth world, many aiming but losing their intent. Many with desires but when they achieve their desires there is still a void, still a wanting, still a hesitation. There is not the fulfilment they aspired to. If only men could focus their thoughts together and aim together they could achieve so much more than stretching as individuals in their various directions.

You do not want times of trouble, turmoil, unhappiness but if only there could be a coming together by some other means. A means more harmonious, a means of enlightenment. Keep striving for this. Keep striving for the light of enlightenment. Carry your beacon as we have taught you and lead forward through the indifference to shed a light that others can follow. To shed a light that gives some guidance to those that are unsure of their direction, unsure of their desire. They know there is something more. They know there is a higher energy power that governs all but there have been so many that have come to your earth to guide, to lead, all with good intent, all with a purpose but now so many follow so many directions. There is no unity of purpose.

So send, as always the light of hope, of peace and unity to feed not only the earthly body. Yes there are those on your earth that suffer from physical malnutrition and are physically wanting. Yes, this is a problem that your world needs to overcome because there is food for plenty but this is not what I was referring to. I was referring to the food for the spirit, the light that encompasses all, that can help you to grow within your earthly existence so that when you return home to your natural abode, as we all do, not only have you become wiser in your worldly matters but you have gained wisdom for your spirit to also grow.

Send your prayers as always for peace, for harmony. Do not doubt, do not doubt that we are working with you and we are all advancing in our progress. Yes, you hear of problems in your world and you will hear of problems in your world but what you do not hear of is the progress that is being made. It is a fragile progress and there are those forces that would wish to destruct the progress. Progress is being made quietly at levels you do not understand but you will see in days, in years to come as you look back at this time in the history of the world it was a turning point towards enlightenment. The awakening of endeavours to learn more and to live in harmony. Those who publish newspapers are men who make their material living by bringing news to you from all directions. They need to supply you with sensation so that they can further their own financial gains. So, of course, the news you hear is true, my friend, no doubt, but there is much other news that you do not hear about.

Walk forward with peace in your hearts. Do not become despondent when others paint pictures of gloom. Do not be unsympathetic and turn your back on those in need. This is not what I am saying but rise above. Accept there are problems but also accept there is enlightenment. Blessings

be with you in your search and endeavours. Go forward, I say, go forward knowing we are all working together as a team. A team that is not of one nation. A team that is not of one dimension. A team that is inexplicable by the comprehension of a human mind".
Given by "Mr Go Forward" 29 August 2000

ENERGY RECOGNITION

These words were developed from a conversation with E-OB-BA in September 2000 regarding the recognition of different facets of spirit energy.

Our human brain has knowledge that has been built up from our experiences, including what we read, view on the television, hear described in graphic detail, touch and the aromas we link with experiences. We have this knowledge lodged in our memory but of course there are many experiences we have not encountered.

It is a known fact that our eyes only see 20% of what our brain tells us all in a matter of "no" time. It is therefore not surprising that on occasions we make assumptions and only see what we want to see or recognise in our brain. On this basis it is not surprising that not everyone perceives the same message.

There is a general perception that the spirit energy we decode or have described to us by a clairvoyant is in a human form. The spirit communicator is passing on memories to the medium of their stature, colour and style of hair, type of dress, even the last memory of their physical condition. This mixture of information is decoded and a picture is perceived in the sensitive's mind. To convey this picture is a skill in itself and of course the ability of the recipient of the message to build a picture in their minds from the information is another matter. Sometimes it is just a trigger of information that gives recognition and once the link is established more information flows.

We are told that all existence has a spark of the Divine Energy within it to exist in whatever form. We are aware that the animal kingdom is part of a group soul and when animals die their spark of divine energy returns to their group soul.

What we do not always consider is the spirit energy associated with every other vibration on our earth - the plants, trees, any living thing. The spirit energy that looks to these forms of life, we are told, is something different and not the same as the spirit energy that experiences an earthly existence. On occasions sensitive ones, not necessarily developed mediums, sense an energy form while in places such as gardens and forests, especially where there is the energy form water in close proximity. This energy form is decoded as something within the brain memory. A bright moving energy, is it a bird? A butterfly or other flying insect? Or something else? It may be that the person sensing this energy and the most logical explanation could be decoded as a fairy, elf or other memory from a picture within the brain. This could be especially logical to a young child. Explaining what has been perceived is therefore limited by the memory and ability to decode.

There is a well known writing by a Lizzie Doten relating to, "God of the granite and the rose, soul of the sparrow and the bee the mighty tide of being flows through countless channels Lord from thee". Although the words are poetical the meaning is that the Divine Energy is within everything.

COLOURS IN EVERYDAY LANGUAGE

"I wanted to come to talk about colour.

Colour is energy, colour is a vibration but it is not on its own. It is also part of other vibrations. You know of music, you know of healing, you know of the vibrations of earth. You use colour in expression on earth. You say, 'everything is **rosy**' or 'you are feeling **blue**', or 'you are **green** with envy'. Have you thought why you use colour in your language? Not only your language but if you lived in another country you would use colour but, of course, it would be a different word. This is something that has been used over many years and is not something you are using now. Why over all these hundreds of years have you been using words about colour? Do they mean anything or is it just an expression?

Sometimes, you know my friends, something happens with a colour and that can cause you to think about a colour in a particular way. Sometimes this makes vibrations that were not there before. I am having problems trying to explain so I will give you an example. Some people they say the colour green is unlucky for them but it is not the colour green that is unlucky but it is the thoughts that have surrounded that colour. Green is a vibrant colour. It is also a healing colour. It is the colour of rebirth and rejuvenation, so how can you say it is unlucky? Over years people have taken on the assumption that green is unlucky so you have built this vibration around. It is not the colour that is unlucky but it is the thoughts that have surrounded the colour which have made the vibration. This is why we say to you to be careful with your thoughts. You can give green to people for healing. You can give green to people for energy when they are feeling tired but if you gave somebody something that is green they might not absorb the positive energy because of the intent that has gone before. Try to rise above these conditions of earth and look deeper into the colour and the energy.

You see a colour and you look at colour and feel something with the colour. One person may like one colour but another may not like that colour but prefer another colour because you are all different. What appeals to you may not appeal to another. It is an energy that is compatible with your energy that makes you feel better, more lively or happier. It may have a different effect on another person and they may get that effect from another colour. Do not take notice of superstitions that have grown around colours. Look for what you sense from a colour yourself. You see a page in a book with colour and you feel something, but it is only a faint feeling. If you see the colour in something that is alive; as a flower, a petal, a leaf, the blade of grass, a bird with coloured feathers, an animal of that colour or fruits that are growing, you will absorb the colour so much more because it is alive and vibrant. It is not just a copy of the colour but it is real and has energy. You may walk through a pretty garden with many flowers and I know you are attracted to flowers because of their perfume, but for this minute do not think of perfume. Just go to the flower that attracts you for its colour. You may go to a bright sunflower but another person may go to a red poppy and another person may go to a pink rose and for that person it has a special energy.

Go to that garden the next day with all the same flowers, but you may be attracted to a different flower than the day before. Why is this? It is because your energy is different from the day before and you need something different. Perhaps you need a little more brightness, a little more calmness or a little more balance so you go to a different flower. You do not turn your back on the other flower but because you are a healer of yourself, instinct is within you as to self healing and you are attracted to the vibrations that help your condition. If you are anxious you may be drawn to a colour that gives you calmness. If you are tired you may go to a flower that gives you energy with its colour.

Now I will bring in the perfume because all flowers have different perfume. The more the flowers are interbred one with the other the more they lose their perfume because they are sharing the vibration essence of their creation. The more you go for flowers or plants that are in their natural abode growing wild, the more you see the energy of the colour and the more you feel the fragrance. It may not be a perfume as your rose. It may be a dandelion that is growing in the field but it still has its own smell. You would not call it a perfume but it has its own particular smell. Your animals are aware of the difference in smells because this is how they live by their instincts. You do this as well but your instinct is more blurred than the creatures that live by this means. You can still absorb that smell without realising it. You may not be conscious of the smell but it is a vibration and you decode vibrations.

I have spoken about the flowers but do not forget the butterflies, bees and other things in your garden, the ladybirds, the little creatures that fly but have no particular beauty for you but if you looked at them under a microscope, you will see the beauty in their wings and features. I am not telling you anything you do not already know but am just reminding you.

Soon now you will have many colours around you in your part of the world. Your leaves will change their colours before they fall to the ground and then you will have carpets of colours around you. This is something that has to occur. Sometimes it is not so good because you think of the trees being bare and then the time of sleep for your trees and earth life. But this has to be so that you can have the beauty of the blossom in a few months time. It is nature's way of giving you the beauty so that you can absorb this energy from the colours before the quiet spell of your winter. Do not look at your autumn as something that is unhappy because it is the end of summer but look at it as a blessing because of the colours that are there for you to absorb. The rich colours of autumn. Take these into you and store them in your store cupboard of energy so that when you look at the trees silhouetted against the winter sky you can close the eyes and bring back the colours of the season you are now approaching. Then look forward to the beauty of the new rebirth of spring with all the colours and all the glow and hope of a new season. Even in the darkness that you call winter there is still beauty. There is still colour if you find time to look. I know my friends that you look at the sky and see the colours there. When you look at the frosty skies of winter you will see many colours. Yes, there will be grey skies but there will also be contrast. Absorb all the energy. Take in the energy. Do not just look but absorb".
Given 10 September 2000

HEALING NEEDS TIME TO BE EFFECTIVE

The communicator is Mafra who while on earth had a port wine business in Oporto, Portugal. Mafra is the leader of our group of communicators and these few words illustrate the diverse topics the group cover and draw on each others specialities to convey information to us.

"No doubt you have heard before that when healing takes place so often you are so impatient and you expect to see something happen immediately or soon after. However, it takes a while because healing is involving your whole body, the whole of your energy centres. To go to one part of the body where there is a problem is good to concentrate or focus on the problem. However, if you do not generate the healing to go throughout the body from one energy centre to the other, to calm, to level, to balance and then to rejuvenate the healing does not have a lasting effect because the energy is focused in one area and this causes an imbalance in a body that is already imbalanced. As you know when there is illness it results in imbalance, that is often caused by another imbalance but because of the stress of the problem wherever it is in the body, other parts of the body are taking the strain. Whether it is a fever, a disease of an organ a rheumatic concern or an illness that causes a problem or as a virus that attacks the immune system. Whatever the problem, however minor, however severe, the whole body needs to be readjusted and your healers work on the entire system.

This is why we say to you it takes a while to see results of the healing with the effect on the whole body becoming balanced and working in harmony again takes a while. So often you do not assist yourselves because healing is given with your acceptance but you return to your busy lives and you are working against the calming effect that the healing is trying to have on your system. This is why we say to you healers when you administer healing to tell patients to accept the healing, give thanks for healing, but do be careful to relax and give the healing time to rejuvenate the whole of your system. Sometimes the effect is seen gradually over days or weeks but it is more successful than healing that can come instantly because if there is an instant response you, as humans, return to your busy lives returning to the problems and the stress that perhaps caused your problem initially and you will return to your healers and say, "well this does not last!". Gradually, as the healing works through your system and you work with the healers to allow this to occur you will see a lasting benefit. We are not saying that you should take yourself away from your world and do not have desires to recover. This is not what we are saying because however much a healer is successful with their healing, if there is not the desire to recover, the healing will not be so successful as would have been wished.

You may have experienced patients returning with another symptom, another problem within a few days or a week even a year later following healing sessions because there is a problem within the mindset that that one has got to come to terms with. We are saying you do know that healing works. Accept it is working. Do not become despondent because there are not instant signs of recovery but accept it is working. Be positive that it is working. In this way you are helping, but in your desire to become well again do not stress your body. Allow time for the healing to take effect".
Given September 2000

MIND IS MORE THAN BRAIN

"I have come to share a few moments of your time together. So my friends you have walking a little further along the path all the time.

You perhaps think that nothing much has happened. You have not gained much knowledge. You have not learned much. You have not been able to share your knowledge, but you do not understand because it is inconceivable in a human body to know how you have grown. You are amassing information and sometimes you think to yourself, 'I am not remembering this information. I listen at the time to what is spoken to you and it makes me think at the time but alas, my everyday chores take me away from this thought matter and I have to live my earthly existence. When I have time to come again, I allocate time to join with spirit. I have a job remembering what happened on the previous occasion I was joining with spirit.' Do not worry, do not be concerned about this because you are in an earthly body and you are here to live an earthly existence. You cannot give your attention to spirit dimension for more than the allocated time that you dedicate because what would be the purpose of you being on earth? You are here to exist on earth.

However, within the human body you are spirit and that spirit has all the knowledge that you have brought with you on your journey but it is there for when it is needed. If all the knowledge that you have brought with you was available to you as you walk your earth path, my friends, you would sit back and not walk your earth path because what would be the purpose? You would know your destiny. You would know your path. You would not be concerned when obstacles came in front of you because you would know the outcome so you would not be learning. You would not be stretching yourself to overcome and by overcoming and coming through a situation you come out, hopefully, the other side a little wiser.

My friends, do not be concerned that the precious time you spend together with spirit is to your conscious reasoning put to one side because if that knowledge is needed at any time it will come to the fore. You are in a human body with a physical brain but beyond your physical brain you have mind and your mind is more than your physical body. Your mind is a vibration, an energy force that is not confined to your human existence. It links with your human existence, of course, because with your human brain is an organ within your human body that is the command centre of your human body. Your human body could not function without your brain but when your brain is no more and your earthly existence is over, the emotions, the sensations, the memories will go with you as your spirit is released from your human body. This is all part of mind. Mind is part of your human body but also part of the over all vibration that is you. It lives. It cannot die as your human body will die. It has to exist, it has to continue. Your brain thinks for your human body but beyond the thought process there are other sensations that your human body experiences which are emotive. You feel for others, you feel sadness, you feel happiness, you feel responsibility, your knowledge of right from wrong, your sense of duty, your sense of knowing instinctively if something is right or wrong. You may say that it is inborn. It is something that is handed down to you, taught to you from a young child but it is more than that. It is deeper than that.

The word 'conscious' has been used, 'are you conscious of something?' but also 'are you conscientious?' This is slightly different. You may be conscious, you may be aware but are you conscientious? There is a difference. You may have a responsibility to perform a certain action and you can either do it flippantly or you can do it with consideration for others and thought for others. This is the difference. You human brain will tell you how to function, how to go through the process of performing whatever, but the way in which you perform it, whether it effects others, whether it brings happiness or sadness to others, this is more than your human brain. This is something deeper, something that is a higher level of reasoning and this is the level of reasoning which you link with when you link with spirit because you are part of spirit and you are part of Creative Force.

Whatever action you take, whatever thought you send out effects others that are also part of Creative Force because you are all linked. No one is an island. This is an expression that you use and it is so true. You have what you term as cause and effect. Others have karma, yin and yang. There are so many ways of explaining but you have a balance and you have a pattern. What happens to you will effect others. In turn, how you effect others will effect you because you are all part of Creative Force. You cannot escape this whether at this time you are in a human body or you are a free spirit. Our thoughts, our vibrations effect others, as do yours. You are just pulsating on a slower vibration at this time in a slower energy field that is confined to your earth world and the circumstances of your earth world. This does not mean you are not part of a higher energy level, a higher source of energy that is free of the earth world. You are part of spirit, you are part of the universe, you are part of existence.

It is all very well to say, 'I am human, what happens outside my human existence is no matter to me because I am here. I am protected and I have excuses for behaving as I do because I am a human.' You have greater responsibility being a human because you are linking with so many more people, so many more circumstances than you would have the opportunity to if you were spirit. This puzzles you because you think that in spirit we are free to do whatever we wish and go wherever we wish. Yes, my friends, this is true to a certain extent but we are limited to our vibration field. We work with those that we are compatible with. If we choose to help others who are of a different energy field, we do this with a team of others that work at that particular task. During your existence in the earth world you have the opportunity to meet so many different vibrations, so many spirit who are in a human body at different stages of their spiritual evolution. Sometimes you meet those that inspire you. You realise that although they are human there is something more to them. They are truly inspired souls and you enjoy their company. You enjoy their vibration. There are others that you meet who are at an earlier stage of their evolution and you cannot quite understand why they act as they do, why they do not take the responsibilities that you would yourself. You have the opportunity of trying to understand and learn a little about them by talking to them and being with them, absorbing their energy. At sometime in the future, perhaps, when you return to your home in spirit, you desire to work in a different field of energy. You can recall that experience that you had on earth and that will help you in the work you choose to do if you should do so. I am not putting thoughts into your mind but just giving an example.

Do not be concerned that you do not remember everything because we share our time with you and we enjoy our time sharing with you. You have to walk your earth path and we understand that. No knowledge is lost but is there for you when you need it".

The communicator is John Lyon on the 17 June 2000. John Lyon lived to the west of London and passed to spirit in 1592. He was an educationalist and founded The Harrow School for Boys.

THE IMPORTANCE OF THE NUMBER 7

Seven stars shine above, seven seas, seven continents. The word 'seven' is important. Seven prophets, seven suns, seven stars. Watch for the number seven. It comes in stages, seven stages, stages of progress, stages of understanding, seven spheres of love, seven blessed ones.

I try to talk but it is not easy but I want to give you wisdom. I have had difficulty speaking but I have passed this information to you another way. So take the love of these seven wise ones that come to you.

Is there a name we can call you by?

'Seventh Star'.

You are one of seven.

Mafra then followed with an explanation and further information regarding '7'.

That one came to bring you some wisdom but found it very difficult to do this because they are so far removed from the earth world and there was frustration in not being able to communicate. The last memory was there but it was a very distant memory. This caused frustration because it was so different to the vibration they are now. To permeate through the levels of awareness to be able to come here to speak to you was quite a journey for them. They tried to communicate on a higher level but realised you needed some other form of communication. They tried to talk but this caused frustration, frustration of being in a condition that they were not used to. The only way of communicating was through memory because there was not recognition with this medium's brain because the words were coming straight from them, no thoughts. There was no linking and the tongue would not move and the mouth would not form the necessary function that they wanted. It was as if there was no use in the mouth. They wanted to talk without thought. I am speaking but my energy is decoding something within the memory and making word. There is no thought as to what word to find but there is an awareness, but there was none of that with this one. It was just completely straight communication.

What was told you will not understand at this time but it is something for you to watch for as you progress. There are some things that you do understand but as with all things you do not understand everything, so we come to the same stumbling block. Your higher brain is being educated, shall we say?

We have tried to tell you of a sequence. You work with numbers. To a certain extent you are a mathematician, not perhaps to the same degree as a scientific mathematician but you understand numbers. Perhaps you understand there is a sequence of events where often a number will recur. For no particular reason there is a repetition. This is not at random. There is a system within your laws of physics, within your laws of matter, but beyond the law of matter there is structure. When you are working with large figures quite often you will see the same figures recurring. There a sequence and everything works within a sequence".
Given 17 May 2000

Numbers Worth a Thought carries on this theme

NUMBERS WORTH A THOUGHT ?

We probably all think of seven as a lucky or special number. Have you considered if there is more to seven than meets the eye? We had some interesting discussions with our spirit mentors. This started with a new communicator from the higher realms who firstly started talking in a foreign tongue, probably Ancient Persian, but eventually our tongue. The communicator gave the identification of Seventh Star and spoke of watching for the number seven. Seven stars shine above seven seas and seven continents. That seven comes in stages, seven stages of progression and progress, stages of understanding, seven spheres of love, seven blessed ones. We then had Eileen's protector Mafra talking of seven and multiples of seven in sequences and then another new friend Erik. When on earth Erik was a mathematician from Copenhagen who taught the subject, and he told of the use of all sorts of sequences of numbers that relate to seven.

All this started us thinking of the seven links with spiritual awareness of various beliefs and clearly there is more to the number seven than we really understand. Just a few examples, you can probably add many more :-

The Principles of Spiritualism.

The Body Chakras - root - sacral - solar plexus - heart - throat - third eye - crown. As used by many healers in their particular understanding of concentrating energies.

The Earth Chakras -Mount Shasta (U.S.A.) - Lake Titicaca (South America) - Ulura (Australia) - Glastonbury - Great Pyramid of Egypt - one that shifts with each new age - Mount Kailas (Tibet). Considered by many as energy centres and places where they are closest to spirit.

Wonders of the Ancient World.- Pyramids of Egypt - Hanging Gardens of Babylon - Phidias' Statue of Zenus at Olympia - Temple of Artemis at Ephesus - Mausoleum of Halicarnassus - Colossus of Rhodes - Pharos (lighthouse) of Alexandra.

Colours of the rainbow.

From the Chinese - Texts some dating back to 1000 BC talk of the importance of the number seven and seventy.

From the American Indians - Wakin Tanka, the Great Spirit, arranged the six directions, east, west, north, south, above and below, with the seventh direction the most powerful of all, the one containing the greatest wisdom and strength being within.

The ages of man and the seven year itch.

The seven year cycles of our body is well known as of course is the bodies 28 day cycle of natural functions.

It is interesting to look at numbers and see how seven and the multiples of seven recur so often. The visitor Erik told us of the strength of numbers and as a number that can not be divided that it has more energy than other numbers that can not be divided by another number three and eleven. It would seem that there is much more to seven and its link to natural law than we can possibly comprehend at this time. Erik brought us a deeper understanding at a later date and we aim to share this information later in this article.

So something a little different and when a spirit friend comes to talk about higher mathematics, calculus and the like, it gives an insight as to how our friends are able to continue and develop their knowledge from their earth existence.

The following information is part of the discussion with Mafra on the 17 May 2000.

"As those that understand codes and ciphers know: however many numbers, however many shapes, signs, symbols, if you know the key these can be decoded. As it is with the universe and the creative force, there is a sequence, a unison but this is something beyond human understanding. Your scientists and mathematicians understand this to a point when they delve and discover your atomic structure, your subatomic structures.

The systems within your body: your body is made up of chromosomes, how your body is made up of your DNA, how your nervous system works, how your subconscious works. It is very, very complicated but there is a sequence of events.

The one that came was telling you the importance of the number seven in these sequences of events. I do not mean 7 minutes, 7 hours, 7 days. It is beyond that. You cannot divide seven and you cannot divide five but seven is a number that is very important. You can go to your next number. That is not an even number, nine, but that is divisible, seven is not. You go to eleven and again that is not divisible but seven is in-between. As your formulae are formulated seven is very important. You may have read or listened to words that have been said about different levels of awareness and seven spheres of learning, seven this and seven that. This is a way of explaining to you but it has been phrased in a way that can be understood in your earth world. Of course, you are aware there are more than seven levels of learning but this is how it has been decoded. Those that have brought wisdom have tried to impart wisdom and seven has been decoded as a magic number, but you cannot understand with your human brain the importance so it has been decoded in this way.

Suffice to say, just watch and listen whenever you see or hear the number seven and see whether you can observe a pattern. Do not worry as what the pattern is, but just take note whenever you see a number 7 and what connects with that particular No. 7. See whether one links with another. See whether it might be a 7 on a number of a house. It may be a 7 in a conversation. It may be a 7 in whatever. Of course, they do not all link together because there has to be random within sequence as well, but watch 7 and see whether you notice any links. Do not look at every house that has 7 on it and expect them to look identical. This is not what I am saying. At your leisure, as a matter of interest, take note. Make a note to remind yourself or remember within your brain. Take note particularly of any numbers that have a 7 in them in your awareness. Also, my friend, you get multiples of seven. You may have a number that does not have a seven, but so many times seven will make that number or seven may be divisible within that number, or two numbers added together may make seven. Just watch for the importance of seven and you will be surprised how often seven appears. By multiplying together, by adding numbers together and then you will wonder why. It is important how everything within creative force is linked so your number seven is also linked with many.

We have said to you before about stories that have been handed down and how they have become legend and how they have changed and altered, but if you look way back you will see a truth in them. If you look at some of the old stories of times long ago, particularly linked with perhaps the eastern continents, you will see seven. Do not worry too much, but it will be just interesting for you to take note that seven is very important if you could understand formulae, structures and energy forces and how seven is involved with a certain kind of energy.

I am just relaying to you some of the vibrations this one has left with you and I (Mafra) speak for him/her.

I also have to tell you something else. The doctor that we have working with us want me to tell you that there is a change in the human body every seven years. In the structure of your body, in your cells, in your organs, there is a change, also in your glands. As you know your glands are linked with your energy centres. Some will say, 'chakras' and some will say, 'energy centres'. This again is a way of understanding the importance of seven and the structure beyond your human body and how you are linked to forces outside the human body. You have to be because you are spirit within that human body so that spirit has to have links with beyond earth matter. Something else for you to ponder upon, how one inter-links with the other".

The following answers were given by Erik on the 20 June 2000 to questions sent from our good friends in Portugal with whom we have special links.

Are all Prime Numbers PROGRESSIVE but diminishing in power as they demonstrate greater volume?

"As they become greater in volume they take on the property of other numbers. I told you before that each number has its own vibration. When a number becomes greater, it the takes on property of the other number so the original value is diminished. I will try to explain; if you think of people 1, people 2, people 3, people 4, each one has their own vibration. On their own you feel the vibration of that person so you can also feel the vibration of each number. But when you add one person with another person, and then another person, those multiply with more people greater in number, but the vibration of each is changed because the vibration of one number may be more dominant than the vibration of another number. That will subtract energy from the less dominant number. Perhaps I confuse by trying to tell of people but I thought that may be easier to explain. Think of numbers. Each number has its own vibration and when you understand numbers you can understand the vibration of a number. But when you multiply with another number, the other number might be more dominant than the original number you started with, even though it is a prime number. Prime numbers each have a different value so one prime number may be a more dominant vibration than another prime number. When multiplied together a more dominant vibration subtracts from a less dominant vibration. Some prime numbers or multiple of prime numbers will be different value to original prime numbers because one vibration working with another vibration makes a slight imbalance. Hope you understand".

Is the energy value of a big number
A. *A combination or total of the energies represented by the individual numbers contained in the big number ? or*
B. *A blend of the energies represented by the numbers contained in the big number ? or*
C. *A specific energy represented by that number and therefore unique to that number?*

"It is a blend but a blend makes it different so it has to be unique. Let me explain. I will not give a very large number. I give a small number. I give number 10. 10 can be made up of 6 + 4. It can be made up of 7 + 3. One is even and one is odd number. Odd numbers have different values to even numbers. Understand prime numbers. 10 cannot be the same value as 3 & 7 because they are a different value to 6 & 4 so 10 has to have its own value. Of course, when you speak of much bigger numbers there are more multiples involved, so it cannot be made up of vibration because it is too various. Each number has its own value, its own vibration assisted by other vibration but it takes on its own vibration. I have already told of dominant and not so dominant (recessive)"

Does it follow that everything in the Universe can be expressed as a mathematical formulae?

"Interesting. If universe harmonious, yes but universe not always in balance. Always changing. You calculate a formulae of a structure on earth in construction and you build on that formulae. Then when you build, you find not always works to formulae, something different has been added so there is an imbalance. You build to formulae and good but then you wish to add another building, add another structure. Then you have to alter. So can you imagine universe all the time changing? It is alive, it is existing, vibration, yes, but all the time changing. One vibration effects another vibration. If universe was static life would not continue because you need to always change and alter. So, yes, each alteration can be defined by new formulae. There is a change. There has to be change but if you analyse change you would see variations of original formulae, not complete breakdown but variation. Sometimes you have been told that everything goes in cycles. So if you understand energy you understand that energies have vibration and there has to be a returning of vibration from one to other. So if you think of events, good example, something occurs in the world. I not talk of universe I talk of planet Earth. Something occurs, 10, 20, 40, 100 years similar event occurs, not identical but similar, similar upheaval, similar consequence. This is because the vibration, the original formulae has come around again, changed, altered many times but original come back again in a cycle but different because it is occurring at different times in earth world with different circumstance all with own vibration that formulae is reacting differently but same consequence. Yes, everything has formulae but formulae has changed. You cannot say that that tree is constructed with energy and it is that formulae because tomorrow that tree has got a new leaf, new branch so different formulae. It is difficult for me. I want blackboard and chalk!"

Is the POWER OF ONE the basis of our Creator?

"Who am I to know the basis of our Creator? I would be Creator if I knew. Creator is part of all so if you add vibration of many, many must start with 1 but much added. You think of 1 as number that is in every other number but even numbers have different vibration to uneven numbers. Interesting there is part of earth world where certain numbers are considered lucky and some considered unlucky. In other part of the world it is reverse. So why? I ask you question now! There is different values and different energy on all numbers but, as I said on previous visit, different people look at different numbers differently. You are attracted to a certain number. Your friend may be attracted to another number because each has their own energy and you are attracted to energy of number. Creator runs through all of you regardless of your energy you are all part of Creative Force. So whether you favour even or odd number you are all part of creation. Great Creator of all is part of all, even those numbers that some people in your world would consider unholy. How can this be so if they are all part of Creative Force? Again, you say some numbers are unlucky but some lands on earth consider then lucky but your part of the world may not. Thread runs through you all. Another thing to tell you; if you think of what I have just said. You consider some numbers lucky. Other parts consider them unlucky so this shows your energy and perception is different because of your background, the way you perceive.

In your world now there are so many living together in the same area. This is why you have conflict and imbalance. It is not that you do not wish to live side by side but your energy is different and you have to learn to live together. Energies are coming together and changing because you cannot have conflict because you have to have the formula to live together".

Would you please clarify your comments when you said the formula of SIGN over STRENGTH OF NUMBER equals ENERGY VARIATION.

"When I speak of sine I do not mean sign, plus, multiply or divide but mean sine that we use in geometry, trigonometry, shapes. That is the sine I mean. So sine over strength of number equals energy variation. When you have sine over strength of number (this is something I said earlier), you have a structure that needs to bend, needs to move. It cannot be rigid. It looks rigid, yes, but you know everything in world is part of atomic force so it is not solid. Even a tall building looks solid but it is not. It has to be part of flow of air, wind, earth movement so it appears solid but is not solid. This why I say variance because you have to allow for variance. This is the same with people. You may be a big strong man to outside world but this is what you show world but you have to be flexible. You have to be variant. You have to have ability to alter but still seem the same.

We go back to number. Numbers are all different vibrations and when you have numbers that are compound, one on another, these have to have variance to work together because each has own energy. If each was dominate to its own energy they would not merge together in total. There would be a disruptive influence and this would cause imbalance and may cause shattering, breaking. That is not a good word but I cannot find a better word to explain. This is why I say sine over strength of number has to be variance because each number is vibration and if each vibration came together without ability to vary it would be disruptive not harmonious. This, of course, can happen and has happened with events and disruptive elements. This is why I say sine over strength has to be variant.

Think of numbers as alive not just figures on sheet of paper. As you live life on earth, numbers come into your life so many times and you dismiss them as being squiggles on paper, but you think before they are squiggles on paper they are an energy force. Squiggle on paper is your last action. Before that they are a vibration. They are an energy because they are alive. They are not just squiggles. They are a vibration. Do not look at all printed words and figures but look before that because they were in someone's mind being created. They were thinking of energy. They may not realise this but they are using energy. Energy is so much around you everywhere. Be open to energy and use energy wisely.

Thank you. Bless you my friends. Ask people in another country what they think of numbers. Ask them to write on a piece of paper a sequence of numbers but do not write these numbers in a straight line. Ask people what number they are attracted to and see whether there is a pattern. Then ask them to choose a colour and see how many that choose a certain number choose similar colours to each other. Don't let others know what each one has said because they may copy. I like experiment because it is live. It is using energy, make energy work for you and don't just read squiggle on paper. Then get clever and you can ask for note of music and do the same experiment. You may think of other ways to experiment also"

THE ENERGY OF A SINGLE CANDLE FOR CONCENTRATION

We find it helpful to use a single candle as a focus when sitting in meditation for contemplation or in preparation for communication. If you use a candle take note of the increase in size of the flame as the energies build up. On this occasion we were not sitting particularly for trance communication and quite unexpectedly Running Bear took control of Eileen and gave an insight into the use of fire when he was on earth living in the area we now call New England. This is followed by Running Bear communicating another companion's words.

"Greetings, I am here. Light gives energy, it gives you focus for thought, gives you vision of energy. Flame goes straight, goes round and changes direction. As your thoughts vary with thoughts going in different directions so energy goes in different directions. Symbol of light in darkness showing forth energy.

You in your world today you do not have focus for thoughts, you do not have focus to dream and your thoughts to fly in different directions. We had fire, we would look into fire and see many signs, many dreams, visions. This was a way of training young ones to concentrate, you may say to use imagination but we say releasing thoughts of mundane matters, releasing your true self and your true spirit to come forward and interpret visions within fire itself. Also in smoke that leaves fire and goes upwards in spiral or different directions. We would sit in meditation around fire with our group. This was way of helping others to link with ancestors and to link with inner self, true self. Self not of material world but self that has come from generations before.

From your little candle you have inspiration. Also cleansing and sanctifying because fire is cleanser but, of course, we understand you have to control because fire is powerful master if it is out of control. As with all elements you have to treat with respect. You treat your world today and abuse your world today. You do not respect. You do not speak to Mother Earth, do not commune with Mother Earth. You take from Mother Earth without asking, without returning thanks for what Mother Earth gives you.

It is the same in other directions also. Brothers and sisters of your world whether blood brothers and sisters or no connections, they still do not treat each other with respect.

We understand it is difficult in your world so many people in so small areas, your space is invaded one to other. You do not have room for your thoughts because others are encroaching on your mind space but we advised you to be strong? Have you understood the importance to put up shield of protection around yourself so that your thoughts are yours? To share with others, yes, but you are also protected from thoughts that are not so good that are directed at you. At times of weakness, in times of low vitality, you are open to these intrusions which can cause you problems. Rise above, take time to meditate each day. You say that you are too busy but take time. You only need a small time, we are not asking you for a whole day just a few minutes of your day to shut yourself away from material world and then recharge your energy with spirit energy. Then you will be strong against elements that are thrown at you from all direction of material world.

We know you have problems, we know you have hurdles to overcome but we walk with you and give you our love. We just ask you to dedicate a small moment of time to recharge your own energy because this is very important. We are happy with progress being made but no rush. You have many words that have been spoken during our meetings together. These can be used now".

As you were coming there was another gentleman there who put his hand up to Eileen's collar of her shirt. Can you tell me who that was please?

"That was big man who comes to talk to you (Mr Go Forward). He was coming but there was not enough energy at this time but wants you to know he is here. He says to me,' Go forward into new time on your earth because it is new time on your earth which he has spoken of many times with you. The light of spirit is ever stronger, forceful, steering course for you that walk on earth path. He wants you to continue sending your thoughts of love to many areas in world where there are problems. He has told you that there will not be peace because it is a material world and one problem solved, then a spark ignites another problem. This has happened through many hundreds of earth years so you cannot expect peace because all those thoughts, all that energy that has been hostile to one another has to have a repercussion. You are aware of energy centres and problems where there is incompatibility of energies in these energy centres. You have different beliefs, different creeds, different ways of thinking, instead of putting aside your thoughts of disharmony and coming together. It is not possible to wipe slate clean. There are marks still on slate from previous times and these have to be worked through. They can be obliterated for a while but as you realise every thought is energy and this has to have outlet.

Please still send your thoughts of love to many areas in world, some you do not know of at this time but you will hear of in time to come. Still need love. Your planet still needs love. Those that live on planet still need love because it is not just confined to your planet you understand. We live alongside you, exist alongside you. Those that go from your world to our world bring their thoughts with them and this can cause disharmony in different dimensions that you are unaware of. This is deeper thoughts for another time. He just wants you to know that he is grateful for work that has been done and is continuing to be done. He emphasises but sends love and gratitude from all of his team because he say that he is part of team. His team sends gratitude for your love and love from others. Bathe the world in golden light, send healing on this beam of light, send a rainbow encircling your earth. Visualise your earth spinning as it does in space just a small ball in the infinite universe but imagine this globe that you call earth spinning and encircle this globe with a rainbow of vibrant colours. Colours that are full of energy, not just a paint box of colours but live colours glowing, mingling one to other encircling your globe as it spins on its course into its destiny. Obliterate the dark clouds. You are aware of dark clouds in your earth condition but you know above those dark clouds there is blue firmament and a sun that shines. So it is with your earth world with all its gloom and despondency of earth problems all its hatred one to other. If you can go above this you can encircle with these colours and they will permeate through the darkness and gloom to those who are striving to bring light and encouragement to others helping them with their task. These are words from man to you, not from me but from him.

Blessings be with you".
Given 4 January 2001

GOD OF THE GRANITE AND THE ROSE

Brother Wilfred is one of a group of friars who came from Whitefriars at Gloucester around the time of Henry the Eighth. He is one that only speaks on rare occasions and we thought you might like to share his message.

"I know that I have not spoken to you for a while but we choose our time, we choose our word and do not use words to the excess as perhaps some people in your world would at this moment. I am here to say to you that there is work for you all to do but do not be impatient. You, may be similar to myself and have chosen a path of service to others. This cannot be hurried or rushed. To serve others you have to understand yourself. You have to understand your inner thoughts.

You have to be able to attune to your God, your mentor, your leader, your guiding angel, whoever you raise your thoughts to because there is no name for this Supreme Energy that feeds all. In our earth life we choose to worship at a particular shrine, we choose to link our thoughts with a Divine Energy. It is difficult to visualise an energy that is running through every aspect of existence. Yes, you can perhaps visualise a God sitting above all others surrounded by light, surrounded by heavenly choirs, peace, contentment. Can you imagine a Supreme Energy that runs through all not just the ones that are inspired and use their time to good effect but to all whatever their level of progress, whatever their station in life how ever humble, how ever they mingle with vibrations of all.

You look at your animal kingdom and you see animals that you are attracted to because of their looks, because of their character, but you also see animals that you turn away from, the insect kingdom, the lower stages of evolution, your rodents, your creatures such as snakes and amphibians. The Supreme Energy runs through all of these. You are all part of each other. You may wish to turn your back on some of them because you do not feel a link with them but the Supreme Energy runs through all things, all creatures, all humanity, all life that exists, your plants and foliage. It runs through everything, your rocks, your mountains, your gravel, shingle, water. To gaze on a field of golden corn is a beauty, to gaze on a pool of muddy water perhaps is not so beautiful but it is all part of creation. All are linked together, all there for its purpose and its service to each other. As you are serving others so every part of creation serves each other perhaps not through desire but through existence.

All are linked together, all have their part to play in a great cycle of existence because it is a cycle, a cycle of regeneration. Nothing is extinct forever. Yes, you say that there are creatures that were on earth but are on our earth no more, there are plants that we see no more but they are an energy and that energy lives on in another form as you will live on in another form when your time on earth has finished. There is a continual cycle of rebirth and regeneration.

As you go forward and seek new avenues, new thoughts, new quests remember you are part of a vast creative energy and you can draw from this creative energy that links all. As you share with others so others share with you. You cannot keep to yourself any knowledge. Yes, you can hide your treasures under a rock but that rock is part of living creation. Your thoughts exist, your thoughts cannot be confined within a cupboard, within a book or in a vault. Your thoughts are part of existence and can link with many others who are thinking similar thoughts on similar vibrations. You share with each other perhaps not consciously but you are all part of the Universal Mind. All thoughts are there for each other. Therefore be wary, my friends, of your thoughts. None who walk the earth path are so evolved that they are on a level of existence where their thoughts are always pure and light. We do not expect this because this is all part of progress. We are all learning, we are all progressing but we, as you, are privileged to be aware so be mindful and raise your thoughts and energy above the destructive energy that, alas, is, always has been around and will continue to be around all that exists. Rise above. You have this ability. Do not let the thoughts, the vibrations of those that despise, those that are fearful and would drain your energy. Send them love, do not turn your back on them but send them the light of hope and inspiration and the knowledge that there is much more to existence than despondency.

Take your time. Live each minute, each hour, each day to the full but do not tire your energy so that you are only half existing. Exist to the full and enjoy your existence, enjoy those that share your existence with you and those that give you their thoughts and energy from the world of spirit. Peace be with you my brothers and sisters. Go forward with love but be aware of all of us in our team who walk alongside you. As I started I said to you we use words for a reason. We do not speak to you every time you sit and link with spirit but when we do we give you words that you can think upon and hopefully will give you inspiration so in time you can inspire others and fill others with the energy of wanting to learn, wanting to grasp, wanting to share in love.

Blessing to you".
Given 8 August 2000.

FINGERPRINTS MORE THAN JUST A HUMAN FEATURE

Mafra answering a further inquiry regarding fingerprints, why they are unique for each person.

"I will try and explain further. I explained before in detail about the genetic effect of inheritance so I will not recap. Yes, each one has their own particular individual identity and no two spirits are the same. Spirit comes to a material body and puts their own identity on that human body.

I will recap briefly concerning when the spirit actually connects with the developing human body. At conception the sperm and the egg join together to become one and this forms a nucleus. When this separates for the first time and divides to become two cells at the point of creation this is when spirit enters the human form that is to be. At that point there is the division into two cells from those two cells many, many more are to follow and the embryo gradually takes the form of a foetus. This is just to explain the entry of spirit into the creating human form. In that human form there is the genetics to create the child, the blueprint of what that child will carry for the rest of its earthly life. This developing form has the features, intelligence, organs, everything that is encased in that miraculous cell that divides into two carrying the genetic blueprint.

We are talking of your human body and without the human body you would not be able to exist and live your life on earth. Into that human body comes spirit that has come from the spirit dimension. It brings with it knowledge, intelligence and memories. Some of these will not be to the fore therefore you will not be able to recall why you are in your earthly body. This is part of the plan that you only carry with you what you need for your earthly experience. You are here to live and experience life on earth and what comes with you are your tools and bare essentials for that existence for you to build on.

In this human form that is developing you have a blueprint. I will come a little further along the path to the birth and the human child so that it is something you can visualise. You have the new child that is born, you look at this child and hopefully this child is perfect. You will look at its features, body, hair and its eyes that are opening. You will look at its feet with its tiny toes and toenails. You will look at its hands and its tiny fingernails and thumbnails. You will open the hand and you will see in that hand the basis of what will be that child's main tool for its life, its hands. Whatever path that child travels hands will play an essential part in that child's life also in adulthood. Perhaps these days in your world you do not have so much in the way of crafts where you use hands as much is done by machinery. Just consider your hands, how you use them, how from a small child first you grasp, stretch out to grasp items that are near you, you grasp your parents hair, you use your hands to touch the feature on their face. Gradually before you even are able to visualise and focus your hands are essential to you because you are exploring with your hands, you are gripping with your hands. You can see how important your hands are.

As you open that hand and look at that hand you will see lines on that hand. You will see what will be fingerprints, very, very faint tiny little fingerprints. If you put them under a microscope you may see more details but when the baby is so tiny they are very difficult to define. You will see lines also on other parts of the hand, on the palm of the hand. These are very, very tiny again but you will see the traces of what will be there. You will see the folds in the skin that will develop into more lines as the child matures. Each child is individual and each child is different. There are those that are talented in looking at hands. Much can be defined from a hand.

Your learned medical men can tell a lot by looking at their patient's hands. There are different signs of illness that can be denoted by signs that are on the hands, nails, skin, the texture, etc. There are also those who say they read hands because of the markings on the hands. I know I am not talking of fingerprints at this moment but bear with me a little longer. Hopefully, you all have two hands. In one hand you have your destiny shown in the marks of your path on earth. These cannot be depicted as a child but gradually these signs come as you get older and the older you become the more detailed these lines on your hands become. The other hand is what you make of your destiny. If you look at both your hands you will see lines that are similar but your hands are not identical. You are given your life on earth, you are given the blueprint for your life on earth but it is your responsibility what you make of that blueprint. As you develop through life so your hands change and the lines on your hands alter to depict the route you are taking. This is sufficient on lines on hands as it is just a background picture.

We will come back to fingerprints. As the spirit enters the developing foetus it brings with it a vitality, a liveliness, an energy, a vibration into that body that is developing. As that body joins the human world and becomes an independent living person you can look at that body and see signs of its individuality. You can see signs that there is something deeper than just a body that is functioning. It is easy for me to say to you look at the eyes because many of your people have similar eyes, blue, brown, green, the shapes are varied, the sockets, eyelashes, eyebrows. They are different but if you look at eyes each eye is different because behind that eye you have spirit. You can look into the spirit through looking through someone's eyes. It is very difficult to hide yourself through your eyes. When someone is looking you in the face and they are speaking to you if you have eye to eye contact your communication is much stronger. I am just telling you about eyes because I am trying to explain to you how the spirit demonstrates itself through the body and the eyes are an obvious sign. There are many other ways also and fingerprints are one of them. They are all individual and the spirit is making its mark on the body in various ways, one I have said is the eyes but another is the fingerprints. You do not go around looking at people's fingerprints and try to see spirit through a fingerprint. This is something that is not done. You go into a room and shake someone's hand but you do not turn it over and say. 'Just a moment I will have a look at your fingerprints.' It is something you do not do but you look at eyes.

There are other parts of your body also that if you look they are individual because this is the spiritual fingerprints showing themselves through and identity. You can also define spirit through the personality of a person but there again, a personality is a little different because it is not something you can pin down and examine, it is something that is not seen but can only be demonstrated. You know of auras and how auras are around people that denote spirit. Your aura is part of you, the way you present yourself, your looks, your expressions. You can tell by looking at someone whether they are happy or sad. You may have identical twins who look the same but if you look into their eyes you may see something different. If you watch their expressions you may see something different. Their facial expressions, their mouth, perhaps one is a happy soul and the other not so happy. One may frown a lot more than the other. These are all signs you can look for which show the spirit identity.

You all go through times when you are happy and sad but you handle yourselves differently according to the spirit that is within you, the experience that spirit has had and the light that spirit brings with it. Of course it is blended with your human traits that you have inherited but your spirit is there and it is shining through.

I come back to fingerprints. They are all individual. It is a manifestation of a spiritual fingerprint, a spiritual identity that is demonstrating itself in the human body.

There are other signs in the human body but I do not want to go into these at this moment in your progression but I hope I have answered the question. I hope this gives some insight for you. It is an identity and every soul is different. It is a spiritual fingerprint that is manifesting itself and you will not get a repetition. It is difficult to understand why you cannot get a repetition because you think the laws of average must run out of patterns and eventually you must go round again but you can only take my word that this is not so and there is always a new pattern to unfold. These fingerprints develop they are not there from birth as such. They are there in a basic form. You look at a new child's hand and you will see a fingerprint forming, the outline but as that one grows and more of its identity and personality shows itself so these fingerprints develop, as the lines on your hands develop. Once they are developed when you become to your teenage years, fifteen to sixteen years old, they stay with you forever and do not alter".

Given 18 August 1998

LOOKING AT THE ENERGY BEHIND THE WRITTEN WORD

"Greetings from the realms of light. We have come again to greet you and share a short while of your earth time with you. You are a few together but we are able to link closer this way. We come to share with you your joys, your sorrows, your fear, your progress, your learning. We too are progressing but, of course, with a different energy and different purpose. You are learning to exist in your earth world. You are learning to share your experiences with others that travel with you. We, who are treading a little more enlightened path are also learning, also sharing but sharing a different energy. We are linking with those from the realms of light, those that are not pulled down with the fears and terrors of your earth world. Those that have learned to put these behind them and to bravely strive forward towards the light.

It is not easy for you treading the enlightened path when you are surrounded with so many distractions and so many doubts and fears. How easy it would be for you to follow the path that others follow putting your faith and trust in another who wears a cloak of office to tell you which way to tread and what path to follow, not to think for yourself but to follow their words and have faith in what they tell you. How easy it would be for you but, my friends, you are treading a different path. You are searching for answers yourself. You are not content to accept what others throw at you as seeds of wisdom. You wish to nurture your own seeds. You wish to sow your own seeds. You wish to see them grow and flourish. Of course, not all will grow, some will fall along the wayside as the parable tells you some fall on stony ground. However, my friends, you have your earth world, look at the seeds that are sown by your farmers and those that till the soil. Yes, some seeds grow and flourish, some do not because they are not nurtured or have fallen on ground that is not fertile but as you look along the wayside you see other seeds that have been planted many years previous but they have struggled and found their way through towards the light of your physical world's sun. So, my friends, the seeds that you sow and have fallen on infertile soil will not grow at this phase in existence but they will lay dormant until there is light and they can struggle towards it. No seed is wasted.

Some will despise you for your thoughts, for your words. Do not let these destroy your intent. Walk forward in the knowledge that you are walking in the path of enlightenment. Perhaps others are not quite ready at this stage. Send them your love and send them brightness for their path.

I do not say walk blindly forward. Of course, seek, search and enquire for yourself. Do not take every word that we give and accept. Think on these words, question them within yourself, question, question, question.... My friends, the explanation that you first perceive may not be the explanation you will perceive in one year, two years, three years time because as more knowledge is added and the more experience is gleaned by yourself through your existence the more you will be able to read into those words. So often you hear words spoken by those that preach or you read words in good books that have been inspired for your earth world and you say, 'Yes, I have read that, I understand those words, why do you tell me again and again?' This is because, my friends, each time you hear those words or read those words they will go a little deeper into your reasoning and you will be able to glean more from these words than you first appreciated.

We do not bother with words, we work with vibrations and we understand that vibrations are always changing, always fluctuating, always varying because they are alive, they are existing. So, my friends, it is the same with yourselves, words are written on paper. They are written on a flat surface with a flat substance and they cannot change but the vibration that formed that word can change. So beyond the printed word there is vibration, a live energy, a live force and that is what you link with not the word on paper but the thought and vibration that preceded that printed word. This is why in times gone by when wisdom was given by voice or by thought without those that had the knowledge to read or write these lesson, these thoughts, these inspirations were accepted with an energy force and more thought was involved in accepting these words than when you sit and read a flat piece of paper.

So, my friends, when you sit and read, look at the paper, read the words of course but do not turn the page and continue to the next. Spend a moment looking at that page trying to absorb the energy behind those words. The energy of those that gave those words whether it be someone that walks your earth path at this moment in time or someone that walked many centuries previous because the energy is still there and has been passed on from one generation to another. Like a flower that blooms and when that flower fades and dies another grows from that stem and the stem grows, the bush grows and more flowers are abundant. So it is with a thought, with a vibration, it produces one word but that word can grow and spread. However, one word of caution as this word spreads and grows it is tainted by your conscious reasoning and also the conscious reasoning of others who absorb this energy. As the words are spread so their meanings change and alter so you must look deep within for the true essence that was the starting spark of energy that came from an inspired source.

Of course, you have to alter your words, you have to change the way of expression for each generation of your earth world because your world is a living energy and your world is changing and so do those that live on your world and exist in your world. The books you read when you were at school, some were truly inspired, some were of that period and are read no more and your children of today would not wish to read those books. The books that are inspired live for many generations so you can see a little of what I am saying. The inspired word lives and exists for durations whereas the feeble uninspired word lives to serve its purpose and is then discarded. It comes from a different energy source, a different vibration.

So, my friends, think on these words. Read well but also give yourself some time to absorb the energy behind the words. Thank you for your kindness and your love. Golden Ray has spoken".
Given 9 April 2000

Ectoplasm

Some time ago a member of the group spoke about ectoplasm. Ectoplasm used to exude from the medium's mouth to enable spirit forms to be built up. You were telling us that there were developments of creating what we call ectoplasm from other sources. I was wondering whether anything is happening and how the development is going?

"Of course everything progresses. You imagine ectoplasm to stay the same, perhaps not from the same source but you wish to absorb and visualise the same phenomena but you must appreciate that it will not be the same. It cannot be the same if it comes from another source.

The young lady that came earlier (Katie) was speaking to you of a different vibration. She was saying to you that you are much slower, 'much more sleepy' were her words because we work on a much quicker, brighter vibration. Your energy is of the earth world and the earth world is much slower. You witness this in the formation of articles around you, of yourself, everything vibrating at a very slow pace. Whereas we vibrate much quicker and we are not pulled down with solid matter as you are pulled down with solid matter. Yes, there is matter in the universe but it is not controlled by the gravity of earth and the pull of earth makes that matter even denser. When we come to you as a spirit we slow our energy down to come within a human body, We slow our energy down if we wish to communicate via a medium in a mental capacity so that she can absorb our energy, transpose and decode it to the one she is speaking to on earth.

We have said to you there is matter in the universe and this matter is not effected by the pull of gravity. If this matter was effected by the pull of gravity it would be pulled into some kind of form or shape. This is not what you call ectoplasm which comes from a human body but it is matter from another source. You may well call it ectoplasm because ectoplasm is a word you have associated with a build up of energy which is used to build a form of spirit entity. Whatever word you use it is a label of your language that you have formed. Spirit are working on this matter. Your scientists are aware of matter. If you read your scientific journals you will know that scientists are working on matter. This is a little way to explain to you how spirit are trying to identify themselves through another source, controlling matter and bringing it within the pull of gravity so that it can be pulled into a shape and format that you can recognise. When it is finished it will be released from the pull of gravity and take its place again within the universe.

Your scientists have realised that space between you as individuals on your earth, space as you see it, is a void. You look at the horizon and you see trees, you see mountains, you see sea but between those there is a nothingness but that your scientists are discovering is filled with matter which they are having difficulty defining at this time. This is some way along the path of matter that we are working with. It is an energy, part of creative force, as we all are but difficult to comprehend with a human brain. Your scientists understand matter but not so much information has been passed on to the ordinary people within your world because, can you imagine, if this information was used for purposes that were not so good how this would disturb the balance of the universe. It has to be handled with discretion. As with all discoveries there will be mistakes. There will be experiments but this is part of the learning process. Only so far along the path can they play and they will be brought back to balance. As your children have to learn by play so do the older ones within your world. It is learning but with bigger toys!

Do not be fearful because beyond these ones there is an overall energy that controls and if fingers are burnt, figuratively speaking, there will be a pulling together of vibrations to ensure the balance of the universe it is perpetual. Be not fearful, everything is working to a purpose.

I hope this give you a little insight into the work we do together".

CAUSE and EFFECT

"Good evening it is I, John Lyon. So my friends your world is rolling forward. There was so much trepidation that the new century was coming and so much was going to happen. So much was going to change, so much fear, so much anxiety but, my friends, you have now entered the year 2000 many weeks have passed by and your world is still existing. Yes, you have stepped forward into this new energy. There are still problems in your world, there are still those that are enduring trauma and hardship and you wonder where is this new energy.

We did not promise you a golden age. We told of new energy. So many thought have gone out into the ether, so many thoughts searching, seeking, wondering. These thoughts are all energy, these thoughts are all forming a pattern. Miracles cannot occur overnight they have to be worked for. Those on your earth that are experiencing problems are wondering what tomorrow will bring. My friends, you are creating the energy for tomorrow.

Your thoughts are creating energy and that energy is creating the vibration that is to come. You are existing at this moment within the energy that was created for you by those that sent energy before.

Much more is now known of energy that cannot be put under a microscope, that cannot be analysed. You see the results of energy, this has always been so. You see the leaves on a tree move with the energy of the wind but you cannot see the wind but you see the effect. You see your sea calm, you see the storm come and waves get bigger, there is an energy you cannot see but you see the result. You have times of unrest and you feel the energy of fear. You cannot see fear but can feel the energy that fear creates. You feel it in your human body, you feel the teneseness, you feel the agitation, the expression that your hair stands on end, you feel this. You cannot see it but you feel it.

So my friends what of energy that is much greater? The energy that drives your universe, the energy that is from spirit, the energy that brings healing that you utilise yourselves to help others. You cannot see this energy but you know it is there. You are spiritually aware and you understand that there is cause and effect. You understand that when you send love it has an effect. You also understand that when you send thoughts that are not so good this also has an effect but within your world there has to be a balance. There has to be a balance in everything that exists. To appreciate your summer you have to experience the hardships of winter and so it is with life to appreciate the good times you have to experience the bad times. Those that are struggling in your world at this moment are growing within, the light within them is growing through these physical experiences they are going through. When their time comes to go home to spirit their light is much brighter by the courage and fortitude they have found to overcome the hardships they have endured.

Be aware that there is a link of energy that flows through all creative force. You are part of creative force, so is your neighbour and so are those in other lands. Also other forces of nature, your animal kingdom and your earth kingdom all living even a blade is a part of creative force. All is energy everything that exists and will exist. A light can be extinguished but it will light again.

As you go forward into this new energy go with hope that the hardships that you have come through and those others have come through is adding to the energy that exists and this is building for the future. Be mindful that your world although vast in size is small because you are now all aware of what occurs in other parts of your world because of the communication that exists. You are able to tune in through your various methods of communication and witness events that are occurring in other parts

of the world. With this ability you are all becoming more aware of the problems of others and this is having a response because you are becoming more sensitive to the problems of others. Many are asking questions as to why these events are happening and state that this cannot continue. This is the response that is being sent by people such as yourselves. You are saying that these atrocities, this hatred one to another cannot continue. These thoughts you are sending are positive and they must have an effect, not overnight but ultimately they must have an effect. Your thoughts are playing their part in education and striving to bring about harmony. It will not happen overnight, I have said this again and again but gradually with positive thought there can be a change".
Given 26 March 2000

MORE TO PEOPLE THAN MEETS THE EYE

"I will introduce myself. My name is Martha when on earth I lived in Hampstead. I was a lady that had sufficient means. I studied people. I studied behaviour, personalities, how people reacted and responded. I still do this because I am very interested in how personalities are different, how we all function in our own way. When I was on earth there was what you call a class system where those that worked for you were perhaps in a different class to those that employed. Perhaps this is not so much in your world today but when you look at different people there is not so much difference.

When you take the trouble to understand people, to look within them, not at them but within them at why they behave as they do, what is the reason for their behaviour, what their background and conditioning is, you will be very surprised. You show to the world what you want the world to see and no one knows what is deep inside you. Sometimes you put on a facade for protection because you do not want to be hurt, you do not want to be despised and people may think you are very strong, very forthright, very forceful person but within you may be very timid and very apprehensive. Also the reverse; someone you think doesn't care and is very lack-a-daisical this also may be a way of protecting themselves because they do not want others to know what is deep within them. They do care, they are concerned but they do not wish others to know this. There is not so much difference, my friends, throughout your world.

Different races, different religions, different backgrounds but inside people are very similar. Those that live, as you think, for themselves, you do not know why they act such as this. You cannot know, you cannot understand but within everyone there is spirit. Everyone that exists on your earth is spirit within but that spirit is conditioned to live within the framework of that body with all the fears and anxieties that are buried deep behind the facade of that individual. Look at people, not just at their face but look in their eyes, look deep within, be aware on your other level of reasoning of their feelings and sensitivities.

It is difficult as your world becomes more busy and more populated. There is not space, there is not time for individuals to take for themselves and as they encroach more and more on each others territory. I am not speaking of land that they own but of areas around yourself. You know that your vibration extends outward from yourself and as you are in busy areas where there are many others your energies are intermingling and merging together. Sometimes you are not so happy in those circumstances because you can feel vibrations that are not compatible and this is when you automatically put a barrier around yourself and shut yourself away from others. This is happening more and more as your population increases and more and more people are going within themselves as a form of defence mechanism. As you do this you are understanding less and less of the others that are walking earth path with you. You do not have your communities as perhaps at the time when I was on earth where you took responsibility for each other. Everyone is now responsible for themselves and there is much loneliness. You can be in the middle of a crowd but you can still be lonely.

You say to me, 'Well, what is the solution? If I open myself up to all and sundry I am bombarding myself with all the various vibrations whether they are to my liking or not to my liking'. Yes, my friends, that is so. You need to somehow find a way through this jungle of humanity in which you live at this time. You have to keep your own counsel, you have to keep your own identity but do not shut yourself too much away from others. Be aware of others, be aware of their existence and do not always react to the facade that you first see. Give others a chance for you to link in with their vibration and decode the energy behind them. This does not mean that you take all to you and give all because that would be very foolish but you are consciously aware that you are spirit within a human body. Give your spirit a chance to link with the spirit of the others and decode the energy. Link with the spirit team that you work with and ask for their help and guidance. I am just saying be conscious and be aware.

I have learnt much since I have been back in the spirit realms. If I was as wise when I was on earth I would have been able to do much more for those that I came in contact with but that was my journey and that was my life at that time. I studied people, yes, and I am still studying people and I am learning much. I hope I have been able to give you something that will also help you in your search.

Thank you for our time spent together".
Given 7 May 2000

ENERGY OF THE PLANET EARTH AND OUR RESPONSIBILITIES

"Thank you for continuing to send your love to others, sending the darkness light, sending the beacon of light out into the darkness. We have said to you there are still problems to overcome but with your love and with this light of hope we can overcome but it will not be a while yet. There has to be cause and effect and all the problems your world has experienced has caused fear and anxiety and in turn these vibrations have to have their effect.

I was with you when you were researching energy centres and you noted there are energy centres within your world. You can perhaps understand now a little how vibrations radiate from these centres. There are problems in your world that are physical, I am not speaking of problems caused by man to man, I am speaking of problems caused by your planet itself, you perhaps say, 'natural disasters'. Deep within the centre of earth is the core of energy that is the nucleus from which the planet was created when it was but a ball of fire after the explosion. As this ball of fire, this ball of energy cooled your earth formed a crust and from this crust your planet as you know was formed Over many millions of years changes have occurred due to disturbance within the globe of earth. You still have problems at this time. You are aware of fault lines, you are aware of glaciers that move, you are aware of climatic changes beneath your oceans. There is much movement beneath your oceans. You hear stories of lost continents, lost countries.

To you your world is solid but within your planet there is movement of the energy within and this energy has to have an outlet through these centres of energy that you have called chakras. These are energy points that emanate from deep within the planet. These are centres that your ancestors, my ancestors were aware of back in aeons of time when they were sensitive to the vibrations of the planet. When the planet was revered not abused, when the planet was worshipped not ignored, when man was at one with his surroundings and could feel the vibrations of those he lived with and the planet he lived upon. Many years have rolled by and much advancement in your technology and science but the planet still has many secrets. You sail your oceans, you soar into the sky above but you cannot control the storms and the tempests, the upheaval, the drought, the dryness, the floods, the earthquakes. These cannot be controlled by man. Man has not harnessed these energies. This is just as well because these would be abused also and would be used man against man. From these centres of energy flow out much energy. If this energy is understood it can be used wisely but if it is abused it can cause many problems.

Your thoughts are energy, your thoughts are vibrations and when they are disharmonious in the range of these fields of energy there can be a magnification of turmoil but when they are harmonious within these fields of energy they can bring about much betterment of conditions. Man has to relearn how to channel energy, how to respect the planet he lives on, how to respect those that live on the planet with him. Most important he has to understand the consequences of his thoughts and his actions.

We watch, we try to help because those that walk earth path have all come from the realms of spirit to visit earth for a reason. We wish them success in their journey through the earth world, we wish them joy in their experience, we wish them strength to overcome the adversities that the earth throws at them but we grieve when we see the abuse that is there. It is to this effect that we ask for your love and your light to unite those that are disharmonious to each other. We cannot tell you that there will be a glorious time when everyone is at peace with each other because that is not the destiny of your earth world but we strive for perfection nevertheless. We strive to make those aware of their responsibilities because, my friends, they will all eventually return to spirit and we do not want these vibrations to come with them. We want them to return home to spirit to bring light, to bring knowledge with them so they can progress not to bring with them their mindful thoughts, their mindful conditions that those in spirit have yet again to work with, to overcome. There is so much more my friends than battling to overcome disharmony but your planet continues and spirit entities continue to return to your planet to learn these difficult lessons. So we continue to give strength and encouragement to those that are striving at this time to bring enlightenment and spiritual awareness.

Thank you for your work. Thank you for sharing your knowledge, sharing the knowledge that each one is responsible not only for themselves but for all those they share their existence with and responsible for the planet they reside on. You are living on the planet earth which has the vibration of those that have walked before and you are creating the vibrations for those that are still to come. As your world is a globe and a circle that rotates, your day and your night, your seasons, all in sequence so, my friends, your earth has its rotation of energy. It has its balance, not of your physical world but of something more infinite because it is part of a greater universe and everything within the universe has its purpose.

Blessings be with you. Go forward my friends, go forward in the knowledge that light must follow darkness as sure as day follows night".
Given 23 May 2000

A MATTER OF THEOLOGY

Religion is man made and is just a framework of understanding even the dictionary definition simply tells us: The belief in a superhuman controlling power especially in a personal God or gods entitled to obedience and worship. A particular system of faith and worship. A thing one is devoted to and this could be the football team because it is what is the most important thing in our lives.

The word Religion is derived from the Latin, Religare, which means to reconnect. Have we lost the true meaning of religion to connect our dimension with the spirit dimension?

From the earliest records written or handed down there is acceptance of an energy force that was revered. We are well aware that ancient civilisations worshipped the Sun, the Moon, Mother Earth, the Sea in fact any energy force that was beyond their control and comprehension. We also know that communication with ancestors was an accepted fact and considered normal in the Red Indian and African cultures. The Jewish knowledge recorded in the Old Testament is full of examples of communication with the spirit realms.

Do we ever think that any other religion is more acceptable than our own acceptance and comprehension of truth? Do we accept that everyone has a right to their own way of thinking and acceptance of a higher energy force, divine being or whatever they term their god?

Organised religion is comparatively new to our civilisation, The people that follow the Jewish way of thinking place the dawn of civilisation at 3760 BC or if you like 5761 years ago.

Religions have developed to suit the needs of the people. Remember that the New Testament was not written till some 300 years after Christ left his earthly existence, and the organised Christian religion developed over many years.

The Chinese and Japanese religion dates from prehistoric times and Shinto is based on the worship of sacred powers associated with natural features such as rivers and mountains. The traditions were handed down orally and it was not till the 5th century AD that Confucianism was introduced.

Religion can be defined as a framework that allows a particular doctrine to be recognised and allows adherents to identify with that particular way of thinking. It gives an anchor, a code of conduct, an acceptable answer to what life is all about. It is also in recent years a legal requirement to have a, "constitution", defining what you stand for and organise yourself if we are considering an organised religious based commercial activity.

There are many religions in this earthly existence, and many variations on a theme. How much do we know of others beliefs, creeds and dogmas? These are but a few :-

The religion and its basic doctrine
Australian Spirituality
Communication with the gods through art and dance, attaching much importance to dreams. Some go, "Walkabout" to help them contact the Universe.
Baha'i
They believe Bala'u Ulah was a messenger from God, and his followers believe that heaven and hell are states of the mind. They do not have public services but fast and meditate also read the writings of Baha'u Ulah.
Buddhism
Believers in truth and a way of life rather than a God or Gods. They say that the root of all problems and suffering is materialism. They follow eight laws - The Eight fold path of Right - understanding, speech, action, livelihood, effort, mindfulness and concentration.
Christianity
Accepting the teachings of Jesus Christ and his followers but there are many variations on this basic concept - Anglicans of high and low church, Roman Catholics, Methodist, Baptist, Seventh Day Adventist, Christian Scientist, Greek Orthodox, Russian Orthodox, Jehovah Witness, Salvation Army to name just a few.
Confucianism
A faith based on the belief and teachings of Confucius 407-479 BC. Teaches that the young should respect their elders and their ancestors. Behaving towards their elders as they would like them to behave towards the young. Stressing self-discipline, education, the importance of hard work and harmony in the home.
Hinduism
One of the oldest recorded religions with teachings in Bhagavad – The Gita that tells of a conversation between a person and God. Hindus believe in reincarnation and the system of karma. Karma takes account of past lives and reflects on future lives.
Islam
The Muslim religion based on all human beings having a connection with Allah (the Arabic name for God). Their accepted prophet Mohammed originally a business man who turned to a life of meditation and prayer writing the Koran c 650 AD.
Jainism
Like Buddhism it is a code of living. Jains say they are in touch

with all that is divine and that we can touch our spiritual side by releasing the soul. Their great vows include honesty and they do not eat after dark.

Judaism

The Jewish religion originating in the Middle East, teachings contained in the Torah. Believing that God created the World and predict a Messiah will come to save humanity. Linked with a traditional way of life but with many variations on a theme.

Kabbalah

Based on the Jewish way of life, The mystical aim of the Kabbalah is to unravel the mystery of God's relationship with the World through prayer, meditation, ritual and learning.

Kwanza

An African religion based on seven laws. God is seen as the mother and father of the Universe, and God is everything. Ancestors are seen as guardians of the spirit and pass on divine energy to everyone.

Maori

The original people of New Zealand with their beliefs steeped in legends and myths. Saying Mother Earth and Father Sky were the creators and their sons created the human race. All life force is a gift from the gods.

Native Americans

Belief in worshipping Mother Earth and nature, with respect for all forms of life . Contact with their ancestors through meditation and a hypnotic state induced by chants and dances.

Sikhism

Believing that there is only one God and that everyone is equal in his eyes. A belief in reincarnation. Once had ten teachers known as Gurus, each with a particular quality . They sing and pray from the Granth every day.

Shintoism

The original faith of the Japanese based on the elements of nature and the healing power in mountains, streams, wind and trees. They have four kinds of worship - cleansing, offering, prayer and fasting. They believe that the mirror is very important because when you look into it you cannot hide anything.

Spiritualism

A general name given to persons who accept continuation of life.

Taoism

At the height of Chinese Taoism is the balance between, "Yin & Yang", the negative and positive forces behind creation. A Taoist seeks to feel peace and calm on the inside, whatever is going on in his or her life. The "I Ching" or Book of Life teaches Taoist how everything in the World is connected.

Zoroastrianism

Followers of a prophet called Zoroaster or Zarathusta who fled from persecution of Muslims to India in the 10th Century. They believe when you die that you are sent to Paradise or the House of the Lie.

Voodoo

A combination of Roman Catholic and African beliefs. Believing that in pleasing every creation leads to health, wealth and contentment. A belief that the Gran Met, made the World but has long since returned to other worlds.

How many types of Spiritualism are there ? Perhaps as many as there are Spiritualists ! The Spiritualist movement as we know it was not developed till some time after the Fox Sisters had their psychic experiences, remember that they were not undertaking any conventional religious activities when the breakthrough of intelligent communication was made. The religion that developed was a format that gave some structure to the belief, some credibility that groups were working at a level of conformability. It's a bit like a restaurant menu if you see, "toad in the hole", you expect to get a sausage in batter and not a panting green thing looking at you !

Perhaps the moral of this story is to understand that everyone is different, every one has their own standards and the way they manage their lives, at a time in evolution of man. Look behind the doctrines and you see a common theme coming down from the ancient ways and understandings. The stories that were handed down were no doubt embellished to make the story teller's audience more attentive. Think about how you would explain or even understand complex truths, in times gone by. Today we accept that there are sound waves passing through our atmosphere, electricity passing through wires but we cannot see the electricity or sound waves, only the end result. However, there is much that we must just take on trust and know our limitation, but this does not stop us striving for a fuller understanding that meets our personal needs.

Spirit energy is not easy to explain, we can often feel power, energy healing forces, but it is a personal thing. We can experience the movement of objects by human energies controlled and manipulated by spirit . We can use the analogy of magnetism with the use of two magnets demonstrating the forces of attraction and repelling dependent on the poles of the magnet. There is acceptance that there are spirit energies but our human brain and language barriers does not allow us to fully appreciate or describe this phenomena.

We have a number of communicators who when on earth were in religious orders or were ministers, we also have a number who followed the

Roman Catholic religion. How does their religious understanding and perhaps the strong views they held when on earth regarding the type of communication we enjoy with our friends in spirit affect their understanding now? Interesting answers have been given. They tell us they realise there is a wider vista of knowledge, but they understand that the religion they followed developed to suit the acceptance and aspirations of the culture they lived it. It was their anchor, a way of making sense of their existence. On the other hand we have ones who would say that while they were on earth they were well versed on what the spirit existence was like, and they tell us that things are not as they comprehended. They could not begin to understand how much more vibrant, vital and real things are, but there is no way that the experience they are in now can be described because there are no words that adequately explain.

Joules who was a Frenchman who had vineyards on the Marseilles area was asked about the views of religion in the spirit realms and gives these thoughts to the following question :-

When you were on earth and you had your religion and if people talked about communicating, as we do, would it have been considered very wrong?

"We would talk through saints. They would intercede for us. We would say our 'Hail Marys' and 'Our Fathers' but we would pray through our saints. We all took on the name of a saint that was our own personal saint. We would very often pray through that saint. If it was St. Anthony I would pray through St. Anthony to help me with my problems. If I was going on a journey I would pray to St. Anthony to intercede to St. Christopher for me. This was respect and a system. It was our way, no problem. We accepted, no problem. We were not taught to question as you are taught. We would not think of communicating as you communicate. We had those that for fun would tell fortunes as you have. You have Romanies and we had Romanies. We would sometimes go behind church and go for a little bit of fun to see whether we were going to have a good harvest or not.

We had respect and went to church but we were not good all the time. What a boring life that would be! We had something you do not have because we could go and confess our sins and be forgiven! You do not have that. In some ways I would not like your religion. I could not be a good boy and then say a few 'Hail Marys' and 'Our Fathers' and say I had been forgiven. You know that you have to work your way through and forgive yourself. No one can forgive you because you have to learn to forgive yourself. It is different ways of thinking but I understand now.

Many people from your religion have gone home to spirit and they also have learnt that spirit is not as they expected it to be. We cannot explain to you. It has given you a faith and a purpose. As long as you lead as good a life as you can and do not go round hurting people deliberately with malice and spite causing problems, it is good. There are good and bad in all people. You get leaders in religions that perhaps should not be leaders of religions, but that is life.

I cannot explain to you how religions come together because it is a thought and that thought grows and becomes more material and it spreads. One person thinks one thing and another person will think another thing and then they do not agree and then they divide and make another religion.

You see we understand that we are above divisions. I do not now have to say I will not associate with another because they do not go to my church. I am not as blinkered as that now. So many wars and problems are due to religions. Why, why? We do not want to continue that now, do we? The religion of my life was something that I took on when I came to earth. I did not have that religion before I came to earth so why should I take it back with me? I have taken back the experience of that religion. I have taken back what it has taught me because it has taught me much but I have gone back to what I was before I took on that religion. Can you imagine saying that I am only going to earth if I can be a Roman Catholic? I am only going to earth if I can be a Protestant or if I am going to be a Jew? I am going to be Hebrew? I am going to be a Buddhist? I am going to be a Muslim? My friend, my friend, how narrow can you be? You would not grow. I will not say this has happened because it is not for me to say but it would be a very good experience for someone to come back to earth to experience all religions and when they go home to spirit they would know so much.

We were discussing previously the question why you can't recall things during your life on earth that were known to you before you came to earth. Imagine coming to earth and being a Roman Catholic but remembering at the same time what it was like to be a Buddhist! You would be very confused. This is why you do not want this information. You want the information for what you need at that time.

I hope I have not confused you too much. Do not worry about religion but do what you can. There are many that have travelled earth that have no religion but it does not mean they are bad spirits. There are some people that never go inside a church but they do a lot more good than all those that sit as priests or whatever. As long as you do what you can for others in love and do not cause harm to others, striving to understand and acknowledge that there is a creative force, you can do no more. It is important to acknowledge that there is a creative force, you are part of that creative force and every other existence is also part of that creative force. If it were not so it would not have life and it would not have the spark of the creative force within. Whatever colour your face, whatever church you go into, whatever part of the world or universe you exist in, you are part of the whole. By putting a barrier because one believes one thing and another believes something else does no good because you are shutting out another part of that creative force that is part of you. You are then causing problems for yourself. You are not in harmony with yourself. You understand how you are connected to everything and by shutting out others you are causing a back flow of energy to yourself. This back flow of energy will cause you a problem, maybe spiritually, materially or physically. If it rebounds it has to have an effect.

I do not say that you have to open yourself to everybody and all their silly ideas, taking them all on board, believing everybody and everything because that would be silly. You have to be wise. You have to have your own counsel but you have to accept that others are there, you may not agree with them but they have their right to be there. It does not mean that you have to take all their thoughts and ideas into your way of thinking. Just accept everything and say, 'God bless you, go your way.'

Thank you for listening to me. I enjoy talking to you. Do not get the impression that I went to church and was always good. Jules had his time! I did not cause too many problems and I paid my penance for the problems I caused".

PHOTOGRAPHS WITH "EXTRAS"
Mafra gives some thoughts with the assistance of Hanns

"It is energy, it matters not if you are using colour or black & white film. It is the ability to record images. When you take a photograph in your ordinary existence, what are you doing? You are recording a moment in your time, you are recording the energy of that time.

You are encapsulating a moment in your time onto the substance you call a film and then that is transposed through photographic procedures into a picture that is then printed on a sheet of special paper. You need to have special paper, you cannot have ordinary paper. Your cameras have become very technical and are able to adapt to light frequencies. They have been able to adapt to colour. The lens in your physical eye opens to the sunlight and closes to shield your eye from the penetrating rays of the sun. Your animals' eyes work in reverse because their pupils enlarge at nighttime to enable them to see when there is no direct light from the sun.

Sun makes everything visible. If there was no sun and there was no light you would still be able to feel forms and shapes but you would not be able to perceive, but that does not mean those object are not there. It is energy from sun that has the effect that makes these objects become three dimensional and makes them visible. If there was not light, your eyes would adapt as your animals' eyes adapt at night-time. Many of your animals hunt at night and for this they have to have very astute vision. There is no radiation from sun but they are able to perceive.

I will come back to your camera. The cameras in your world today are very sensitive to vibrations from light. They open and close their shutters to the right timing. Sometimes they have to be open wider than others, longer than others. If you place the camera in the wrong direction and too much light penetrates the divine energy, you then have substance on your finished picture that you do not like. Your picture is not clear and you have distortion.

Now we come to distortion. If the energy entering your camera, facing the source of light that is your sun, causes a disturbance in your photograph, what is this? It is energy from your sun impregnating the picture and distorting the picture. So what are your psychic photographs? In your historic photographs you had cameras with not such sensitive lens. You had photographs on glass and glass, again, is a sensitive subject and it reflects. When something hits glass it reflects back. Again, you have energy that hits the glass and you have a distortion. You have to be careful because, when these photographs are developed, it is how they are treated that can also cause a problem. It can be a physical problem caused by the developing of the picture, too much light in your dark room or too much exposure to certain chemicals. Not everything is as it seems. Sometime you have shapes and these shapes cannot always be explained. Sometimes there has been a problem with developing but sometimes it is energy being fed directly at the moment the picture is taken.

Unfortunately there are those that would like to draw attention to themselves and perhaps cause circumstances that are not completely truthful and some people with over active imagination. Also you sometimes have photographs where you can say that it is not a shape or a form, but you can actually see a face that may or not be recognised. You have to be careful that there are not two moments of your time captured on one space. You need to investigate thoroughly and when you have eliminated all possibilities, you can then say that this is something that cannot be explained. Explore all possibilities first and when you have thrown away all possibilities as not being accurate, you can then say that is something that cannot be explained.

If you have a picture with two people on one photograph who were in the same vicinity at the same time or who were on another frame on that film in that camera at another time before the camera was put away and taken out again, this may happen. When you have two people on a photograph who, perhaps, are not existing at the same time, then you cannot explain why their images should both be there. Sometimes you can have someone on a photograph that is existing at that time but was nowhere in that vicinity at that time. You know of thought energy and there may have been a strong energy field being sent to the one whose photograph it was at that time and the energy has thrown itself at this picture or at the event that the picture was encapsulating.

Explore. I am not saying that every photograph that is taken can be explained, but explore and when you cannot prove, then you know there is a question as to another possibility. Unfortunately many of your photographs are those that cannot be investigated because they have been handed down by others and you can only go from what you know. People may say that this was someone experimenting, perhaps not fraudulently but still experimenting and this has been misrepresented. These answers you will not know because you were not there at the time and do not have the opportunity to know. This is unfortunate.

The advice I give anyone that has a photograph that has been investigated and a solution cannot be found is that this must be written on paper and kept with the photograph, so that in future times those that look at the photograph will know the history behind it. If you have a photograph that you perceive to be not fraudulent but a mistake with the photographic process, again you should record this and explain what could have occurred. Everything should be recorded.

I hope I have explained energy. I have gone a little way around explaining about your physical eye, sun, your animals and how energy is absorbed in your physical world to help you understand what happens with energy from spirit. We are also energy although we vibrate to a different frequency to your sun but still you may perceive us as light. When you are developing mediumship quite often, before you are perceptive to decoding our vibration you perceive spirit light. So what is this on your pictures? It is energy depicted as light".

Given 13.07.99

PENDULUMS
Use of Pendulums for Spiritual Awareness

Pendulums can be any weight on a thread but for the best results the material of the pendulum needs to be of a dense material that is not contaminated with others vibrations or circumstances. The best materials for pendulums are crystal, diamonds, certain plastics and a dense wood like black ebony.

Some guidance in the use of a pendulum :-

1. Open up to spirit asking for the ability to channel spirit energies for the benefit of others, healing or your knowledge development. Make it as an affirmation that you have the confidence to channel the energies.

2. Ask for the White Light of Spirit to protect you in your communications so that you will only draw the highest levels of communication.

3. Know what is happening, that the spirit energies are entering your brain and energies flow through your body, down your arm and reflect in the coded movement of the pendulum.

4. Before you use the new pendulum hold it in your hands, get to know its shape and allow your vibrations to be absorbed by the pendulum.

5. The pendulum is your personal pendulum and should be kept as such.

6. Hold the pendulum thread in your fingers allowing the pendulum to be away from your fingers by at least six inches, or whatever seems comfortable. Tuck your arm into the side of your body to eliminate as far as possible movement of your forearm.

7. Ask your controlling spirit energy to indicate what movement of the pendulum indicates a yes, it could be from side to side, clockwise, anti-clockwise or something else. It varies from person to person. Then ask for the indication of a no and this may be no movement at all. With practice the way the pendulum reacts gives other coded responses such as a caution in a yes by moving slowly or a very positive answer by quicker movement, so that you will get to know.

8. Practise can be by the use of photographs placed face down by another person and asking if they are male or female.

9. Ask your question but don't expect to be told answers that relate to personal gain or something that is another's personal secret that that they do not wish to be disclosed.

10. The use of the pendulum is a way of opening up our latent ability to communicate with spirit as a natural function.

11. Pendulums can be used to assist with healing in indicating the area of the patient's body where the healing vibrations should be concentrated, which may not be where the pain is.

12. Witness pendulums have a small cavity that holds hair or a finger nail cutting of a person desiring healing and can be of help if developed for distant healing.

13. Always remember that you are using the pendulum as a device to assist with communication.

14. At the end of the session using a pendulum, even when you are practising close down the communication with a short prayer thought of thanks to your spirit helpers.

Compiled by Eileen & Trevor Davey with the guidance of the Spirit Teachers October 1999

SO WHY DON'T WE KNOW EVERYTHING ?

Ararmday a visitor from the higher realms explaining that we carry a vast amount of ancient knowledge within us, but this is not accessible to the human form.

"As your earth moves on from one era to the next new discoveries are made, new inventions are created. Your young minds are trained to grasp and learn much more than their forebears. Your mind is stretched in many directions to absorb so much. So much stretching out to learn and to seek but do not forget there is a multitude of knowledge within. Wisdom of ancients is within you all. You carry with you volumes of knowledge. Knowledge handed down to you by your ancestors of earth back into the mists of time and knowledge you have brought with you. Your eternal spark of knowledge of the spheres that is greater than any knowledge of your world. You question how you can access this knowledge. Everyone carries this knowledge within them.

Isn't that conflicting with the knowledge of our time? Of course, but there is a truth which grows and links as a chain all vicissitudes. You may dress your thoughts, your ideas, your ideals, your hopes and aspirations in forms of your era but they are no different from the hopes and aspirations of those that went before you. Yes, the presentation is different because your world is different but the hope and dreams that drive these desires are the same. It is a yearning for more knowledge. A yearning for more understanding, better communication with others and more a comprehensive way of thinking. A freedom from the barriers and the fetters that bind you.

This knowledge of ancients is within you and is clouded from you. However, you acknowledge without realising that there is more to understand than you are aware of and this is why you are seeking so many answers to so many problems. Have not your forebears been seeking answers to problems also and those that are to come will seek answers to their problems? However, deep within you know there is a missing link in your chain of knowledge and this is what you are seeking. You are seeking for that link but it is there, only veiled from your vision while you are in your earth existence. The knowledge that you so much seek is there within and can be released by training your mind to be quiet, to go into meditation, to release yourself from your earthly pressures, your earthly ties and pulls, the demands of your earthly world, your worries and anxieties. By training your mind to rise above these earthly conditions you are freeing your vision and you are able, with practice, to slowly link into that inner knowledge that is within you. This can only be achieved by dedication and gradual stepping back in time and unlocking that door that hides so much.

You ask, 'Why is this door closed?' This knowledge is so great it would override your earthly existence, your earthly brain would not be able to cope with the range of knowledge that you have within you. While you are in your earth condition and earth path walking from day to day you only carry with you the knowledge you need for that time. You are here on your earth for a reason; whether it is to learn, to teach, to care for others or whatever reason, you are here for a purpose. During this walk you are sharing with others their existence also. You have to be on a compatible level with everyone you meet because you are aware you communicate in ways not of voice. When your sojourn is finished and you are free of your earth ties, you are then free to unlock that door and unleash that energy and wisdom that lies deep within you. You are given glimpses along your path but only glimpses.

Have faith that you are eternal and you are part of the eternal wisdom that has been from time beginning and will continue through each generation that is yet to come. Go forward and share what is to be shared. You cannot share all because it is too great for your earthly world. 'Going forward' are very important words. So much time is wasted looking back at what you cannot grasp because it is not within your power to grasp at this time.

No knowledge is lost, it is continuous. It only appears in another form.

Blessing of the ancients be with you".

Given 11 May 1999

SPECIAL PLACES

In our travels in North Norfolk we visited the small town of Walsingham, which is famous for its shrine. People from many faiths have come to the shrine over many years to pray for healing, guidance and to give thanks. Michael, one of our communicators, talks to us about our experiences -

"Energy has to have outlets. It cannot just go and be no more but there has to be a result of energy, as it is with the shrine that you visited. There was a reason for the shrine being there in the first place and I understand that many have pilgrimmed to that area and many have come there in search of help for themselves or help for their loved ones and others they have associated with and their prayers have gone forward.

As with many religions candles have been lit and this candle is a prayer. The prayer itself is energy from the heart within and this is signified by a candle that has been lit and the flame that burns bright is itself energy. It is something that people can perceive that signifies their hopes, desires and prayers. You can pray, of course, without candles but to those in their belief it is an outpouring, it is something positive they can do for someone else or for themselves. They are actually seeing something that is happening. They are seeing their wish, their desire come alive. They are seeing the glow from the candle ascending and this is energy in itself, an outpouring.

So many prayers have been said in this shrine, so many wishes, so many hopes, so many desires. Sadness, yes, but also others come back and say 'thank you' in gratitude. You understand that energy cannot stay in that one place it has to go. We have explained to you before, there are no roofs or walls that make a barrier to energy going out. This particular building and this particular part of that building is the source of all those prayers so, of course, this is where the energy is strongest because it is a prayer from the heart. It is an outpouring of human energy mingled with vibrations from those from spirit that work in the field of healing.

A prayer does not need to be addressed to a certain named entity. If you were going to say a prayer, you would send a prayer as you have been taught. Those of other faiths will pray to their particular holy person, whether they pray through a revered person, a saint or they go through the one they call Mother Mary or they may go to the highest spirit. They may go to the God head. It matters not, it is the direction, it is the desire from within. It matters not if you ask a particular person to intercede for you or send wishes yourself because you are sending love. Those that work in our dimension for this purpose are able to send love to where it is directed. Of course, they cannot alter destiny. They cannot change destiny but they can give strength to those that are mentioned. Also there are many that have no one to pray for them. It is well and good to give a name, address, "fingerprint", or whatever identification but there are so many that have no one to pray for them. That does not mean that they are not also encompassed with this love because there are those in spirit that know of these ones and they are also included in this love and energy.

Many prayers are sent for the sick, for the bereaved, for those in war torn countries, for those that are suffering, those that have crossed the border from your world to our world and are in the in-between state and are not fully aware where they are. They can also be helped with this energy. It is not confined just to one or two special people that have people to pray for them. There is not a hierarchy as perhaps some of your faiths would wish you to believe that only those who are blessed are able to receive. Everyone is blessed, everyone is part of the creative force, everyone is conjoined to spirit and spirit energy and as you know, when you send love it is returned to you. You do not ask for yourself but it is natural law that when you send love in humbleness, in sincerity, not for your ego, not for outside pomp and show, the energy will eventually return to its source.

When you show love for a sincere reason do not question that love

will go. You may not see the result of which you pray because it may not be in destiny for that result to become possible but that one will somehow be uplifted, given strength of purpose, given strength to endure whatever there is to endure. The one that has sent the love will also be part of the healing process because love is manifold. You send love and it grows and it comes back to those that have sent with a sincere desire".
Given 12 July 1999

THE FLOWER
Inspirational words given when holding a spray of flowers

Life is part of creative energy
It has its own vibration it is part of Divine Energy
It is part of eternity

From the seeds of many other flowers that have gone before we have this one spray here
It has been nurtured, it has been cared for by the growers
It has been brought to our country from abroad, carefully tended
But energy is more than something that is manipulated by man
It is something that occurs deeper
Man cannot create, man can assist creation but man cannot create from nothing.

So it is with our thoughts and vibrations
We bring with us Divine Energy when we enter into a human body
We bring with us what has gone before
Our experiences, our strengths, our weaknesses
The love others have shown us and the love we have shown others
But added to this also we bring to a human form the traits of our human ancestors
Their weaknesses, their strengths, their experiences, all in our DNA

How can we divide what is spirit and what is human?
We cannot
We merge and blend together
We take from all and utilise at our will, our free will.
Whether it is for the good of ourselves or the good of others
Or for our selfish greed and the detriment of others
Free will is our choice but according to what we have brought with us we have the responsibility

How far we are on the Spiritual Path,
How much we appreciate what we have been given
How much we utilise this

As we tend our flowers and feed our flowers, give them water and food
Give them warmth and light
So we nurture our spirit which is us
We nurture those that walk with us and are given to us to help and advise
We cannot walk others' paths for them but we can share with them
And they in turn share with us
This is how we grow and gain knowledge

So as the bud of a flower opens out with the light of the day so our spirit essence opens out
With the light of spirit and the light of others
We must keep this energy bright
We must not turn from the light but walk with the light

As this flower has been given to us to enjoy, to cherish
So we must accept it with the love that has been given
We must accept other blessings that are given to us on our path and not take them for granted

Not all happiness
Some experiences we do not wish to experience
But they are there for a purpose and we must take them for this purpose and gain from them.
Always mindful that others are working with us and we share
We are all part of the Divine Energy
All part of each other

At times like this we can stretch out to those who are no longer in an earth body
But there are times when our feet are firmly on the ground of human existence
And in times like that we stretch out to those who are walking an earth path with us.

So we learn to blend with different vibrations
As the flower learns to blend with the coldness of night and the warmth of

the day
The darkness and the light
So we learn to blend with many vibrations

We cannot choose to always walk in a sheltered environment
But we need to spread ourselves to blend with many vibrations and share

Cherish the blessings that are given to us as this flower
Be responsible for it,
Be responsible for yourself
Walk always in harmony
Do not become despondent
Overcome the hurdles and learn from them

Blessings from spirit

Given 10 April 2001

THE LIGHT OF SPIRIT
Inspirational thoughts from Golden Ray

The spirit that surrounds you,
that protects you,
that walks with you,
That nurtures you,
That resides with you.

Open yourselves to the light of spirit that illuminates your path
whichever way that path turns
Whatever experiences that path has for you,

Open yourselves to the light of spirit
That is there waiting for you
Walking with you,
Shedding light to guide

Look forward, look ahead,
Do not cast shadows over your shoulder
But look to the future,
Look to the light ahead

Spirit is perpetual,
Spirit is eternal,
Spirit is you.
You are part of spirit,
There is no divide all are one in the light of love,
Keep yourselves to the true endeavours,
Strive upwards to the true path of dedication,
Knowing you are part of all
And all is part of you.

What has been is still there,
What is to be is there also,
No beginning, no end but continuous.

Send love out to others who are seeking
To those who are in a quandary,
To those who are perplexed,
To those who are stressed, unhappy, in turmoil not knowing which way to look.
Which way to follow.

Bring them peace,
Bring them calm,
Bring them into the light of spirit
Let them absorb the light of spirit so they too can be blessed.
And know they are part of all
All together walking forward with the light around them.

Blessings from those in the realms of spirit
Go forward knowing that all is as it should be in harmony

Yes, we understand your thoughts
Your world is not full of harmony
But we have told you that you are part of spirit and in that part that is pure spirit
Is peace and harmony
Hold on to this and try to shed this to others so they can also understand and feel the upliftment of these moments together
When you link with the true source of light and energy.

Each of you hold on to the token of light

Each of you will add to the beam so that beam will brighten and illumine
the path
for those who are seeking

Carry the light with you,
Nurture the light,
Keep the light above

Strength to you my brothers and sisters.
Given 3 April 2001

DO NOT JUDGE A BOOK BY ITS COVER
Good evening

"I may not have made your acquaintance my friends, I am Martha. When I was on earth I lived in Hampstead. It is of no matter now because I am of another home. I am interested in people, when I was on earth I was interested in people and I made it a particular hobby to notice people and the way they behaved and the feelings they had one to another. Now of course in the spirit world I am still interested but not in the narrow restrictions of my earth existence. I have a much broader scope of interests.

You know there are so many people in your world, (I will not speak of the spirit world at this time), you look at them and you form opinions of them by their backgrounds, their appearance, what they say to each other, how they behave, their mannerisms, what they show to the world, but you know within there is not a lot of difference between any of you. Some of you are more loving one to another, than others of course. Some live for their own greed, self advancements and do not respect others ways of existing. What I am trying to say to you there is behind the facade that many people show you a very different personality. They behave for a particular reason, sometimes it is defence for themselves because there has been hatred and they are frightened to open themselves up to others. This weakness is a vulnerability for them. So if you look behind and within as we can, people love, they fear, they grieve. they are impatient. They do care but sometimes they do not know how to show they care. So do not judge a book by its cover.

When we return to the spirit world, which is our abode, we of course want to leave behind the problems of the world. Sometimes it is difficult for us to do this, if we have built around ourselves a hard shell that our emotions and feelings can not penetrate through. So that when people come home to spirit it sometimes needs a lot of love and dedication by those in spirit to draw those ones through the shell that they have built around them. In the earth world you label people as to their background or as to the way they have behaved but within there is sometimes a very frightened spirit not being able to free itself from the encasement that the earth life has forced upon it. So when they come home there is a lot of work to be done, to help that one through towards the light. This is because they are still fearful, they still mistrust. Sometimes they acknowledge that the things they have done when on earth are not too good and they are fearful because they thought their life on earth was their life and that would be the end when they breathed their last breath. However, they have found that they still exist and all those things that happened on earth they have brought with them and they are fearful of their way forward. So you can imagine there is much work for us to do to try and help these ones forward to see through the problems that they have created for themselves or perhaps others have created for them because of the background they were born to and the life they existed within. So in your prayers please remember, not only those on earth that are experiencing problems but those that have returned to spirit and are still surrounded by the problems of earth.

So as I said to you I am interested and I am happy to come here and share my interests with you and ask you also to look at others who you come into contact with. Look at them and try to look behind the mask that they show you of themselves and send them some light to help the spirit within them to feed from the energy of light not darkness.

It is good to heal the human body that is sick, yes, this is a great blessing that some of you have, you are able to help others to relieve pain and suffering. Sometimes you know my friends the spirit is sick also because it is denied the bright energy of spirit that is its natural abode, so also heal the spirit".

Given 10 September 2000.

THOUGHTS BEFORE WORDS

Greetings it is I, Running Bear

We had a question from our friends in Portugal they asked that when they talk on spiritual matters they have been advised that their spirit friends tune into those conversations. Is there a reason for this? Can you tell us more?

"There is no need to talk, spirit is on same wave length no need to talk, thoughts come before words. Before words are uttered there are thoughts to form words, before thoughts to form words there is a thought pattern forming quandary, forming the whys, the wherefores. This is when spirit are attuned because we are also part of investigation process. We also are always learning, we do not know all the answers. We know more answers than you because it is not clouded for us, as it is for you.

I will try to explain. You know many answers to your thoughts but in your earth body you are not always able to bring answers to the fore but you know inside there is answer. Your human brain is asking question but your mind, which is more than your human brain, knows the answer as we know the answer. It is not always possible to draw from the mind energy because whilst in a human body it is not always wise to know so much. You say, 'Why, it would be good to know answers'. Yes, but there is a reason why you are on earth in an earth body, learning again. Some information is clouded from you whilst you are in a human body but you still know that there is answer and you are trying to get answer from mind energies. This is when spirit links because we are part of energy link. We are part of family group, not earth "blood" family group but family group of spirit, so we try to help. We recognise your confusion knowing but not knowing. We try to uncloud as much as we can for you. Sometimes it is something that we wish to learn also, something that has happened during your earth existence which you have experienced which has brought these thoughts to the fore. It may be an experience that you have had but we have not had that experience ourselves.

As you struggle to find an answer to your questions, why this happens? why that happens? why we go this way? why we go that way? If we do this it causes effect but if we do that it causes different effect? This is your experience of your earth life and we as helpers who walk with you are also interested in your answers. Of course, we link with you. Although it is good that you sit quiet to link with spirit it is not always necessary. Spirit communication is easier when you sit quiet but sometimes you have a different energy, busy energy. You are busy people doing many things and your energy is vibrant. You may think sometimes it is too vibrant but there has to be different energy. We also link with this energy force because we are not always calm, as in this moment here. We are sometimes very busy people! Helping here, helping there, doing this, doing that. We do not just work with you but work with others. Many call on our healing, teaching and we try to respond where there is a need. Need from those on earth, need from those in spirit existence who are also searching.

You find it difficult to understand how we can do different things at your same time but our time is not your time. Our existence is not your existence. Not in compartments as your existence. You have a set time to do something but you plan in an hour's time to do something else, but in two hour's time you do something different again. This is not the same with us. We are all the time giving, taking, drawing energy, throwing energy to others and giving out what we can. You understand our energy fields are very multiplicited on different levels at once. We work with earth vibration because we work with you. You are a spirit within an earth body and you are in earth vibration so we work on that vibration listening to your words but also linking with your thought energy which is a different vibration than your word vibration. Your thoughts are much deeper than words. You work with your brain but you also work with the mind, another energy. As you are working as such you are linking with others who do not have earth body. They are finding similar questions to you and wanting to know answers so again we are working with them. This is why I say multiplicited. We are working on many levels at once.

The basic level is your human level when you talk but your thoughts are much deeper than your talk and we have link with you before words come but we follow through. We don't just absorb thought energy but follow this thought energy through to your human existence. We are not in a hurry as you are in a hurry, we wait for you to go through the process of talking and discussing. You are then either becoming clearer or more muddled depending on your thinking and reasoning. We come through this process with you trying to help and assist but sometimes also learning.

However, we will not intrude. If it is something very personal and you want to keep it between two people or just one person, yourself. You may not be ready to discuss your anxieties, your worries with others and want to keep to yourself. Yes, we want to help but you know we are there waiting but we cannot intrude if you do not desire us to intrude. We wish dearly to help, yes, but sometimes you need time on your own so we do not intrude. We are not in a hurry and we wait until the time when you wish to open to us and we can then give energy to assist. Sometimes fear shuts out vibration, something happens that brings fear to heart and you are fearful to open up your thoughts to others. This is not good for you because you are keeping fear inside and that is destructive energy, negative energy. It is good if you recognise fear for what it is and open up to other vibrations that can help but we recognise that you have free will and your free will is yours. We are there when needed. It is your choice and we will not intrude.

You say, 'How do you know whether it is something that we want to share with spirit or do not want to share with spirit when we are talking and have not said?' I say to you friends that thoughts go before words so we understand your thoughts whether you wish to share or not wish to share. We are not there to solve all your problems. It is no good you saying, 'I have problem I will ask Running Bear and he will tell me the answer'. Running Bear may wish to help but Running Bear knows that you learn by experience yourself and sometimes you have to go through something yourself to be able to understand, rather than Running Bear do it for you. Sometimes the lesson is hard and you have to learn the hard way. We stand by and wish we can help but it is part of your path of progress that you need to learn in a different way. We give strength, we give energy, and encouragement but we cannot walk in your moccasins for you! You need to walk in your own to feel pebbles under feet, to feel thorns in path, to see signs on your path, signs of danger, signs of friendship, signs of healing, signs of destruction and signs of progress. Many, many signs. We have told you before to look for signs not through your physical eyes but your spirit eyes.

Yes, friends we link with you and feel your frustrations. We feel your wanting to know and your impatience because in a human body you become very impatient. Time is something very important and you wish to put as much into time as you can. For us time is forever, so why hurry? For you time is forever if only you could see but your vision is clouded. Coming back to what I said before, you know the answers but your vision is clouded while in a human body and you cannot grasp that answer that is as an apple on top of tree, just too high to reach. You know it is there and you wish to take fruit but just out of reach you cannot grasp tree of knowledge. Not until the time is right and that fruit comes within your grasp when the time for you to grasp is there you then take fruit and eat and devour knowledge when you have earned the right for that knowledge. When you have gone through obstacles on your pathway and learnt lesson of human existence because not only are you learning so are others with you. You never, never, learn anything on your own.

All the time you are sharing knowledge with others whether with words or thoughts and others share with you. Perhaps you are thinking over something that is puzzling you and these vibrations go from you out into the ether. Others also have similar questions and you attract those questions, those thoughts to you from others because they are similar to yours. So you have your question but added to your question you have others' questions which are similar but a little different. Your questions are forming a pattern and without knowing you are sharing information with others, learning from each other and we learn with you alongside you. Sometimes it is something we can help with, sometimes our hands are tied behind back and we are not able to assist until the time is right but we give love and encouragement.

I hope these words are of help".
Given 1 May 2001.

SPRING IS IN THE AIR

There is a change in the air.
There is a new awakening.
As your days roll on and you approach the
Springtime of your year.
There is new energy.
A new stirring.
A new vicissitude.
Growth, rebirth comes to your part of the planet.

You watch the sky.
The formation of the clouds.
Not always a blue sky.
Some clouds, some greyness, some rainfall.
You need the rain to bring forth what is to come next.
Your blossoms, your fruit, your harvest later in the year.
All in its cycle, all in its turn.

So you too must look to the change in seasons of your life.
Not always sunshine, some cloud.
As your planet needs refreshment of the rain.
So you need refreshment and recycle also, of your existence both material
and spiritual.
Because, you have blossom time and harvest time.
As your earth shares its harvest, so you share your harvest with those you
come in contact with.

Look forward to this new energy, strength, the brightness, the joy and the
laughter.
Always striving forward.
Always working towards the light.
Enjoy this energy, absorb this energy, share this energy.
It is a gift from spirit.
You are part of spirit.
You are a part of this energy.
Take this energy wherever you go and share.
Because it is in sharing that you grow from strength to strength.

Blessing of Spirit be with you.
Go forward in love knowing we are ever close.

Share these words with our friends

It is Golden Ray as part of the team of communicators,
with a strong influence from Running Bear because he understands the
strengths of your planet and the strength of Spirit.
One linking with the other as it should be in harmony.
Given 25 April 2001

SILENCE - A VALUABLE COMMODITY

"Greetings to you my friends

You sit in quiet, you sit in calm serenity linking your thoughts above the noise, the commotion, the frustration of your earth world. So many do not have this opportunity. So many are unaware of the importance of silence. What is silence? It is something your earth world does not appreciate. Yes you have a busy world much noise, much commotion but within you there is a strength, a silence of infinity. Even when you shut away from your earth world you do not have total silence. You perhaps take yourself away from busy roads, busy towns into a natural environment surrounded by nature's bounty but my friends still no silence. Different kind of noise, noise of nature, noise of earth, even noise of man encroaching but listen to vibrations around you. Be in tune with your world of nature. Be in tune with your own body noise from your body, your heart beats, throbs, pulsates, blood flows around body. These functions of your body occur so that you can exist, you hear, you breath in and out, you hear noise of your skeletal frame, bones, muscles, sinuses sometimes these make noises. The noise of thoughts within your brain, you recall events, you recall music, voices and these are not heard by your physical ears but you hear in another level of consciousness.

So as you tune with spirit you also hear not perhaps the sounds as your earth world makes sounds, but vibrations that you are tuned to so there is never total silence. However, there are levels of silence, levels of conscious awareness. Know the difference of those vibrations that are destructive and inharmonious to yourselves and those that you can attune to and be in harmony with. Many vibrations around you, you are not aware of perhaps but they are there. As you are aware of sound waves making noise, how sound travels on sound vibration so there are many other vibrations around you which you are not attuned to but you can attune to if you disassociate yourself with the inharmonious. You can learn to attune to spirit, you can learn to attune to natural vibrations but only very slowly. There will be much more depth if only you would pursue and sit quiet for many moments of your time. You sit quiet and noises intrude from your world but you learn to shut these noises away and go deeper and deeper into vibrations of harmony. In this time you are perceiving spirit around you. You may say that you are not aware of spirit around but brothers and sisters you are perceiving and this is linking with your consciousness that is not of the earth world. So do not think you sit in silence and nothing occurs, you are communing, you are learning all the time to open to harmonious vibrations. So give yourself time. Time is something not of spirit but of earth, but give yourself space to link and go deep into this meditation so that you can delve deeper into communication and vibrations of our world linking with yours. This is because you are spirit within and your spirit hungers and thirsts for links with its natural abode. As your earth body hungers and thirsts if you deprive it of nourishment and vitality of earth provisions, so your spirit hungers and thirsts for links with the energy of spirit from which is its natural food. This is a word you use to explain, nourishment to sustain, to give energy, to give strength, as the food you absorb from your earth world nourishes your earthly frame so the food of spirit kindles the spiritual flame and strengthens the spirit within. The spirit within can give strength to your entire body, both earthly body and spiritual body, for the work you do and the tasks that lay around you and before you on your path of progress. So value the time that you link with those that walk with you. Your natural spiritual family who encompass you with love and dedication.

Your earth body tires and needs rest. It is at times such as this that spirit draws close and can help your spirit sustain your earth body. You have the ability to draw strength to sustain you on your path but if you neglect this ability not only will your earth body become frail and imbalanced so will your link with spirit because you are moving away from your natural ability. This ability is natural to all but as with other senses if you do not use them they become slow and non functioning. Keep this link with your inner spirit open and give your spirit opportunity to recharge itself from the light of spirit that we all share. Send your thoughts and love to those that need support and strength at this time but also retain energy for yourself. Wrap yourself in the light of spirit and take this into the very centre of yourself. Absorb deep into yourself the radiance of spirit energy that is there for all who open themselves harmoniously to the vibration.

Look up as to the rising sun and absorb rays of energy. As your sun bathes your earth world so does the radiance of spirit permeate your spirit form. Drink from this energy, breathe in the energy, flow the energy around your body, recharging, vitalising deep into your inner depth that you cannot imagine. You can imagine your earth body with all its frame, organs and functions but you have a problem visualising your spirit which is greater and more powerful and lasts longer than your earth body. It has come from aeons of time and will continue when your earth body is no more. It is important to keep the energy flowing so that it is radiant and can endure.

Blessing to you honourable friends it is a pleasure to be with you".
Communicated from K-Chee
Given 30 January 2001

MEMORIES OF AN EARTHLY EXISTENCE
E-OM-BA on his life and work in Abyssinia (Ethiopia)
Commences visit with his usual chant. "Did you hear me bang my staff in the corner? It is not just a piece of wood it is a symbol of strength and has a meaning. I had carvings on my staff which are signs of power".

E-OM-BA introduces himself to a new friend. - "Greetings friend I am from the continent of Africa. This was a long while ago, there were no white faces in my land then. The strength from that continent is good, there is very old energy in that continent. It goes back many, many years before other areas were inhabited. There was much strength and knowledge, Much knowledge has been lost but you still cannot take away energy that we put into the land. There have been many troubles but strength also. Troubles make strength.

We gave knowledge to others. They took our knowledge to other areas but it has all changed. When you take from one area to another you have different energy in different areas so it has to be different. We give teaching of our way. Some of our tribe travelled from our land (Ethiopia) taking knowledge to other lands, to teach. Not to teach as your white men come to teach black men their religion. That is not the same. We just went and others copied our ways because we took with us our teaching, our way of living and others copied. We did not convert but if others wish to copy they could. It is not our right to come to you to say that you do this wrong and must change to our ways. That is not the way. We just existed and followed our path and if others wished to take some of our knowledge they were welcome. We tried to help with others' problems, with illness, famine, when there was not love one to other but dispute we would try to bring calm and togetherness. We would not say. 'This is what you should do' but they should want from within. It is no good copying others to be like them but you need to desire from within.

It is the same with you when you wish to develop your skills to contact the spirit world. Some do it because it is the thing to do, it is good, it is the thing of the moment but others, as you, desire from within. It is desire from within that helps you in making a stronger link with spirit. It is a coming together. You are spirit no different from me except you have an earth body at this time. You are spirit and I am spirit. It is natural communication but you have to learn to throw off your earth world for a short while".

Did you do this when you were on this earth?

"We went into time of meditation but not as you, noisier than you! We would come as tribe and chant, also noise with drum and stick. It would last many hours not just few minutes as you. We would go long while into dream world together. We would all go as one and come back together. We would go as group but older wiser ones would stay away longer".

Could you bring information back?

"Of course, we communed with ancestors when there was a problem. You have meeting around table in your world and you thrash out your problems. We would do the same but not around table we would sit on ground because vibrations from ground was good. We would go together to commune with ancestors and bring knowledge back with us. Not everyone would go because others had to stay and protect because of surroundings. Dedicated ones would go because it would not be any good just elders going because there had to be training of young ones to come up when we were there no more. We would take younger ones in group and teach them as well because they would be the future for the tribe. When we went home to spirit they would commune with us because then we would be ancestors.

It was part of ritual to train young ones when they showed interest. We would not push them but when they had desire from within that was time to teach. Of course, we would guide from little ones. As they became older and into manhood leaving boyhood behind we would guide them in our way. Some would rebel. You say that boys and girls rebel now but boys and girls have always rebelled. This is not new but we would understand and wait for them to go through their immature years. When they became more interested within we would then take them into group and they would sit with us and we would teach".

So they would make the first part of the journey?

"They had to sort out their problems first. Elders would be there to guide. Also they would be taught other things concerning survival, to hunt, to exist, to look after their mothers and sisters. It was important that they were part of community. There had to be time away from tribe on their own, hunting but also time to explore and discover then come back to tribe and initiated again as member of tribe. They learnt this way, survival of physical body but this gave strength of thought to help them develop other thoughts also.

As each country exists, each has their own way and each generation is different from the past generation. Many, many years have rolled by since I was on earth but, you know, your boys and girls are still searching. The questions may be different but they are still searching for truth. Sometimes it is more difficult in your world because there are too many things coming to them now and alas, links with families are not so strong. You may be fortunate in your families and have boys and girls that know they are loved but many of your boys and girls, young people, have nobody to love them and they are wondering what their life is about. This makes them rebellious and they put a barrier around themselves so they cannot communicate with other people on your earth so how can they communicate with spirit? They shut themselves away because of fear. Send your love to young people of your world. You send love to the planet, you send love to children, you send love to sick people but also send love to young people who are trying to find their path at this time because they need guidance".

Do you give guidance to animals?

"We would commune with animals in thought. Our communication was not as your communication, yes, we spoke to each other but not as you speak. It was necessity. We would not talk, talk, talk as you talk. This no criticism but I am explaining how we existed. We often communicated by thought one to other. When members of tribe were away we could still communicate. Also we would understand when animals were fearful and we would be able to sense when animals were coming close to tribe. We would hear because our hearing was more acute than yours, we would hear noises that you would not hear. We would also know by our senses. In this way we would communicate with animals. We knew fear, we knew when smaller animals would sense bigger animals and they would be fearful. We would understand the animals' fear and in this way we would know there were other animals approaching.

You have these senses but because you do not use them they do not work so well. Each sense you have in your physical body, you have five that you use everyday, but you have the equivalent of these in your spiritual senses. You may say that you smell perfume but this is not through your nose but through spirit nose. You see but you do not always see solid figures. You see a form, a shape or whatever. You hear but not with your physical ears but with spirit ears. You sense touch. This is also a spirit sense of touch. Speech also, you speak but you commune in other ways as well as voice. You know that if you walk into a room, if there is fear, if there is happiness. You know when members of your close family are angry or excited. If they are not well you sense they are unwell. It is a sense you have and the more you use these senses the better they will become".

Do you still go back to Africa?

"There is no reason. I can but it is busy, busy now. There are many buildings and much noise and communication. Under all those buildings, all that soil there is still energy of those who were in that land many, many moons ago. You say that you put roots down. We all put roots down and we leave something behind. This energy is there for others who can attune to the vibration. This is not just my country but all countries in the world are the same. The older ones when there were not so many people in the world have deeper roots than newer lands. Those that you call newer land also have old roots, many lived there that are not known of. Their history is now gone from your notice but their energy is still there. All buildings, whatever you put on ground to cover ground cannot take away what is there. It takes time to permeate but it is there".

Please tell us more of your way of life when on earth
"We would have drums that we hit with our hands, they were round and covered with animal skin that we would have between our legs as we sat on the ground that assisted with our communication.

I had a staff, I carved my staff with signs as I became more mature in years and more senior in tribe overcoming many problems. Each problem would be signified as a sign on my staff. It was made of a very hard wood that I carved myself. When a young warrior came to tribe to learn more mature ways as part of his initiation he would be given staff and as his years progressed his staff would change according to his life and experience. There would be signs that meant things to him on his staff, this was the story of his life. When we went to our ancestors (passed) the staff went with us on our journey, a burning journey (cremation of the earthly body)".
E-OM-BA used to communicate through Trevor's grandfather, Albert Fruin, many years ago in the home circle, he would transfigure and create knocking sounds with his staff but at that time did not speak.

Is there anyone left in Africa still following your way of life?
"There is but in different ways because as you in your part of the world follow a religion it is not the same as your ancestors. It is the same with my country there is truth still there of old religion but it has been altered because white man brought his religion and others have brought their religion and so it is a mingling. I am not saying that these other religions are not as good as ours. It is a different way of worship, as long as they worship in love, with love in heart for the good of others to a superior energy it matters not what they call themselves. It is when they work with "black" powers and darkness that it is not good. There is still this activity in Africa and other continents but more so in Africa. There has to be light over darkness. I still believe in showing the light, go to the light always, I would not be speaking with you if it was not through the light, I would not be allowed to come.

I visit other groups to listen but I do not speak, remember we are all part of a much bigger group, including yourselves".
Given 14 January 2001

A MATTER OF TIME

"Time is a necessity of the human existence to regulate the way we all live and work together. Our concept of time developed from the cycle of day and night, the sun being overhead once in every cycle of day and night. Over the centuries man learnt how to recognise the movement of the stars and planets in relation to our own earth and to know there was a yearly cycle and cycles of the movements of the universe that were predictable. We find it difficult to grasp that in the spirit realms there is no such thing as time, no day, no night or seasons and a lack of measurement in years.

One of our communicators, John Lyon, gave the following insight into the way spirit measure progress linked with cycles of the universe. He was talking in early January 2000.

"You have now rolled into another year of your earth time. You have rolled into the year that many looked towards as a time of change, a time of great happenings but you are looking around and saying, 'where are the happenings, where are the changes?' Every new year brings changes, every new year brings different vibrations but this one has been marked for a while by the thoughts of those that have existed in the earth plane looking towards this figure with hope and desire that it will bring about a change. Also that it will bring about a golden age with new opportunities and a new way of thinking. But you know there is no magic wand that can be waved so all that has happened can be wiped out enabling you to start afresh.

Everything happens in its appointed time and everything that occurs has to have an effect because every vibration is alive and every vibration is a form of energy. Whether you perceive this as good or not so good once set in motion it has to have an outlet. Yes, you have been hoping for new things. When I was on earth we looked towards this figure that you are now at imagining great occurrences and you can imagine all these thoughts and desires from all those that were struggling for something better for those that came later. There has to be an effect but what is time on your earth?

Time is something that is made by man to fit your calendar. You have to have a marking point, you have to have organisation, and you have to have dates, times and calendars. The more advanced you get in your reckoning and calculations the more you need time and dates. You say, 'You do not have time in spirit, John, so why do you refer to time?' We do not have time as you have time but we have a cycle as your universe has a cycle: your universe, your planets, your stars and your suns. I say suns because you know of your sun but there are more that you are unaware of. These are all working within a system, within an orbit. There has to be some kind of balance. Yes, time on your earth is made by man for you to live by but originally it was ordained by your seasons of light and darkness for your days and nights. You have taken this a little further to adapt to your way of thinking and your way of living. You have to live within confines.

When you are free of your earth body your restraints will be different. You will not be confined to earth time because you will not rise with the sun and go to bed with the moon. Your existence will be a lot different but you will still have cycles. You will have cycles of development, cycles of rest, not rest as you know on earth sleeping and restoring your energy, but times of recapping, reviewing and deciding which direction you wish to travel next. Cycles of learning, progress and cycles of duty to help others. We do not have time as you have time but we do work to a system and to a routine. This does not mean that we are confined as you are. We are able to encompass different energies at the same time. You are confined to earth and you are only able to work within the time span of your earth but we are able to look back into time past. I will try to explain this to you; if I say memory bank and we can relive whatever we wish to relive in time gone by if we need to relearn. We do this if we need to recap but we are still at our own stage of development. We just regress for a short while to take something that was important and bring it forward with us. We are also able to look to the future, not in a crystal ball as you imagine but we can organise our energy so that we are planning for future progress and preparing for what is to come. An example to explain this for you would be that you are aware that there are those that return to earth from spirit at a dedicated time for a dedicated purpose. This does not happen by chance but is planned for and is foreseen. This is why I say to you we work in your present, we work in the past and we work in the future. We are infinite, we are not bound as you are bound by your time and your sequence of events.

I will come back as I was talking to you of your year that you have marked as such a change. Yes, there are changes. You have seen changes in the years coming up to this time. As you roll forward you will not expect to see all the changes in the first years of this century. There has to be change but it has to be gradual. There has to be a clearing of vibrations before you can step forward into new thoughts and new energy. There is a rethinking, many are rethinking their thoughts and their teachings and this takes time. It will not occur all in one generation but seeds are being planted now for generations to come, as you are reaping the benefits of seeds planted in previous generations. There is now a new energy, a new going forward, so do not be disillusioned that you have come over the threshold and there are still disasters occurring, still tragedies and you cannot see this golden light that you have been promised. Do not despair and do not let others despair because you are going towards a brighter time ahead for all but it will come gradually. Lessons learnt gradually are absorbed more than those that are absorbed instantaneously".

It was interesting listening to you speak about the cycles in spirit.

"We do not exist just wandering and roaming but we have to exist within a pattern because we exist with others. Our work is inter-linked with others. Those that are higher ordained than ourselves know of a system, know of the future more than we know of the future. They are preparing us for the future. Your future is linked with our future, it has to because we live alongside you. We do not live on a planet many light years away. We are living with you now in a way you cannot see us but our vibrations are inter linked. You are confined to your earth vibration, which is as it should be, because you are on earth and you are existing as an earth person. This does not mean that what affects us does not affect you because we are alongside you. We feel your sorrow, we feel your happiness, we feel your anxiety, your doubts and frustrations but as we are not encompassed with your earth condition we are not affected as much as you. We can still feel these conditions but we have a lighter 'overcoat' around us therefore we do not absorb it as much as you. This is why we say to you when you are in need we are only a breath away because we are living alongside you. We are not looking over your shoulder all the time, we are existing in our way, in our dimension alongside your dimension, but because our energies are linked when there is a problem or anxiety we feel this and we are drawn to you. If you send a thought to us and ask us for healing, for help, we are there. I will try to explain; it is as if we are living in two houses, you in your house and I in my house and there is a thin wall that separates us. You have a problem and you call to me, 'John' and I hear you through the wall. I will not be there with my ear to the wall all the time listening for you but I would hear your voice. If you compare your voice to a vibration thought, I will feel your thought through the wall. This is the best way I can explain. We do not intrude because you have chosen your earth path and you are here to learn but it does not mean that we stand back and watch you struggle. If you want our help we are there and are only too pleased to assist".

John, We are often fearful for the future and face it with trepidation due to all the problems there are in our world. What guidance can you offer?

"Do not face the future with trepidation because this is negative energy. Yes, it is natural to be apprehensive but know there is a pattern in all things and there has to be a way through. When I was on earth if I could see what would be occurring within the next hundred or two hundred years

I would be as you very fearful, but the world has rolled on and it still exists. Mankind has adjusted and coped with many situations that I never foresaw and I could never foresee in my wildest dreams. They have found the courage and strength to work through these problems. They have taken on many onerous tasks, they have taken on greater responsibility and endured many hardships and they have come through. By doing this they have learnt and progressed, not for choice because you would not choose this knowingly, ha, but have they chosen it before they came to earth? I am not going into that at the moment because I am going away from your question.

Do not be fearful for what is to come. There has to be changes in your earth, you cannot go through the same conditions and vibrations as those that travelled your earth before you. You have to have different challenges, you have to have different disasters, different circumstances to learn how to overcome and to learn how to deal with them. If you had the same you would just look back and say, ' Oh, that was dealt with in such and such a way and I can alter it and do it in a different way.' That would not be the same learning process as facing something new.

Through the years that lie ahead for your planet there are going to be many changes, many things that you may be fearful of but this is part of human existence, change, disruption, learning to cope, learning to live side by side with others through disasters and tragedies, learning to share, learning to grow together, learning to give love. There will never be a solution during earth life, there will never be a golden age because you are existing in earth conditions and you are all here to learn. There will be changes, there will be advancements in communication in your world and with our world. There will be times when the link between us will be easier than it is at this moment because it will be acknowledged and once there is an understanding of when you shed your earth body you are still existing. This will come, there will be an awareness that there is life after death but not on a far planet sitting on a cloud playing a harp. This will come but this is a little while yet. There are those that are aware of it now, I am not saying that it is not known, but it will come. Your scientists fight, as they should because scientists are analytical and they need proof, they need rows of figures they can add up and balance but how can you do this with something that you cannot perceive?

There will be many questions and many testing times but there is enlightenment ahead but this does not take away the problems of earth because it is problematical because it has to be for you to exist. Each generation will face new challenges and new obstacles".

LOVE IS THE MOST POWERFUL ENERGY

"I come from the realms of light. I am vibration only but I give you a name so that you can know me. I come from realms of light to join with you and share our love with you. So, so many questions but this is good because it is an awakening. Awakening from the sleep of centuries of thinking and living existence on the earth plane under the doctrines of fear. Man on earth is now awakening to vibrations that have been shut from his vision for many centuries. It is not a new vibration, a new experience because this was your natural way of existing many centuries ago. It is natural for you to share your energy and vibrations with each other and it should be natural for you to share your energies with those from the realms of spirit and for those from the realms of spirit to share their energies with you. There has been this barrier of fear built which has come between what should be a natural communication.

You know, you are aware that you are spirit so why is it unnatural for you to link with others who are spirit? Whether they are of your earth existence or whether they are free of earth existence. One of you is part of another. You all share energy. You share your thoughts of earthly matters so why is it so different to share spiritual thoughts with those that have not the vibrations of earth because you are free to link with others of compatible energy.

I talked to you before of the energy of a particular number. This is a number you have used in your earth world but it is more than your earth existence. As my friend who came to speak to you and told you about energy of numbers. He tried to explain to you that you look at written words, you look at written figures and you just observe but before these were marks on paper they were energy thoughts in someone's mind. Before they were thought they were pure energy that was absorbed by the thinker. This energy is not just confined to your earth world but it is part of us all. We do not sit at tables and chairs writing down rows of figures as perhaps you do in your existence. We work with vibration and what Erik was trying to tell you numbers are more than something written on paper. They are energy as is everything that exists. Energy that is used in an earth condition is slowed down to a slower frequency because of the conditions of earth but it is still energy.

It is difficult, perhaps, for you to perceive the difference of spirit and earth but try and just look at your earth existence for a moment. On your planet of earth resides yourselves who are human people living and breathing, existing within your time frame of whatever allotted years you have been granted to achieve your destiny. Within that earth world there are others existing who have different time spans. You have those of the animal kingdom, the insects, and the plants. They all have their time span, many shorter than yours but you are existing side by side. Existing as a vibration and because another member of creation has a shorter existence on your earth than another, their perception of time must be different. They do not think and reason as a human brain because they are of a different species but they exist, they survive. They have their instinct how to survive, how to reproduce their species and this has to be done within the framework of their allotted time. They have their energy frequency and you have yours living side by side. So, my friends, can you perceive spirit also free of earth existing in a much faster, quicker, more vibrant energy but we do exist side by side together. We are sharing existence but as you cannot understand how your butterfly exists and how your butterfly views the earth existence, neither can you with a human brain understand spirit, even though you are spirit. This is because you are confined to the human condition at this time. Does this explain to you a little of energy and existing side by side with one another? Do not worry too much because this knowledge is known to you but, as we have said to you, it is not possible for you to carry this knowledge with you within the confines of your earth existence. You share your existence with so many because we are all vibrations, we are all part of creation just at different levels at this moment.

As you sense and perceive the vibrations of others; you are saddened, you are enlightened, you are uplifted by others vibrations, so, my friends, we share also your vibrations. We share your laughter, your happiness, we feel for you when you are anxious but we have problems coming close to you when you are fearful and most of all when have negative thoughts. This builds a barrier that is difficult for us to work with. We are not saying do not question everybody and everything that occurs, or you read, or you perceive but with an open mind. When in your earth existence you come close to someone that you feel is incompatible with yourself, I am not saying one is higher on their path of evolution than another but just walking a different way. However much you wish you feel you cannot draw close to that person and exchange love with them. Love not in a human sense you understand. This is how we feel when we wish to draw close to those in the earth world to help them and they throw negative thoughts at us. Rise above negativity, rise above those that throw to you negative thoughts.

Each of you serve in your own way and each of you shares love and tries to help others who you share your earth life with. Some will accept that help, some will not but those that will not, it is their path. You have served, rise above and when their time has come to accept the love you have shown them that love is still there because although it is retarded with negativity, it cannot be destroyed because it is a powerful vibration. Love can overcome many hurdles and obstacles. Keep your vibrations higher than those that try to cause problems in your earth world. Send them love. Love that they will understand one day and be able to put aside their malice, their brutality one to the other. Do not feel pity because pity is a negative vibration. Send them love and strength and enlightenment. Send them a ball of energy to surround them so that little by little this ball of light will penetrate the darkness they have built around themselves. Imagine a person surrounded with a film of darkness, greyness and around this is a circle of light. Imagine this light gradually penetrating this greyness and bathing them in a light of spirit so they will gradually become aware that there is more to existence than hatred one to the other.

You are in a human world in human conditions and I know it is not easy to do what I have requested, but try. You will not always succeed. Do not chastise yourself for this. Be aware that this will occur. You may not succeed but that does not stop you trying again and by doing this you are growing and you are learning because you cannot help others without reaping some of the benefit yourself. This is natural law.

Blessings be with you. Light shine on your path. You are aware that at any time you can look for this light of spirit and raise your vibrations to this light. When you are experiencing problems with others who are so negative and so destructive one to the other link your light with our light and we will draw close to assist you in your endeavours".
Given 2 July 2000

LIFE IN THE SPIRIT DIMENSION

The communicator is Doris Davey, Trevor's mother

Answering a question about when people pass to spirit being encouraged to progress. When Jimmy talks about being woken up was he in a kind of stupor for a long time after passing to spirit?

"He was just not wanting to do anything. He thought he had gone to sleep and that's where he was going to stay because that is what his Bible had taught him to believe. He thought he was going to sleep so he did".

Would he have been aware that he was in the spirit dimension?

"He was aware that he was somewhere but he wouldn't have known where. He would have known that something had happened to him and he was just waiting. I was lucky because I knew where I was going and what was going to happen. Well I thought I did but it wasn't as I had imagined. I knew that I was going to another life and I was going to be alive and doing things but he conditioned himself to believe that he was going to sleep in his grave until he was called and that was what he was doing. There are a lot like that and there is a lot of work being done to encourage them to find a way out".

Is this merging of energies?

"It is trying to get a light to them for them to see and go towards it. If they don't want to see then they are not going to see it. Sometimes it is easier than others. Sometimes someone of their own can get close to them and that helps. If there isn't anyone or they are in the same state they are all sleeping together".

On that same theme - where you have got some religions that believe that they will be reincarnated directly after they die does that put them in a different way of thinking?

"They have an idea that they are going to live, so that is not quite so bad for them because they know there is something and they are not going to sleep. They acknowledge that there is another existence that they may not stay in but there will be an in-between time. They don't believe that they are going to sleep. It is the ones that believe they are going to sleep that have the problem because they don't expect to find anything else. They surround themselves with a mist. Sometimes it is helpful to use energy from people like you on earth because your energy is very near their energy. Sometimes they can see your light but not spirit light. A lot of work is done when people are asleep because in sleep state they can sometimes help others. You are free of your body to travel but you still have earth's energy and that can help those that are in that state. When you think about it you are in a similar state to them and in that situation you can help them.

It is a problem and until their religion changes and openly teaches them that they are not going to wait until the trumpet goes until they wake up. It is drummed into them because it is a religion of fear and they are frightened to think of anything else. They are taught that it is only the special ones that are buried in consecrated ground laying in their graves that are going to hear the trumpet. It is not a religion of love but of fear and they are taught that they have to keep within the confines of that environment. There is a lot of work being done to try to help. You think that it is a waste of time but it is not because it is nothing and they are in suspension. They are not hampering their progress because they are not going back but just staying there and there are many in that state. When they do come through and see the light enabling them to go forward, for them, it is like yesterday - one day they were on earth and the next in spirit. The time in-between is nothing as you go to sleep at night and wake up in the morning. If you sat still in the armchair for the same amount of time you are asleep you would be really unhappy, but when you go to sleep you lose track of time. In ordinary sleep state you do not realise how long you have been asleep".

Explaining about communicating and asking spirit to work.

"Don't doubt yourselves when you get spirit communication. When you get something don't start thinking but just go with it. Don't be satisfied with just something but ask for a little bit more. If you get given something, say it and then ask for a bit more. You need to make us work as well because we need to learn as well as you.

This is complicated because I didn't understand it when I was on earth. We work on such a different vibration. The best way I can explain it is as if you are working on a thought vibration and you are sending your thoughts to people. I am trying to explain to you how we communicate and compare it to how you would communicate in an earth body but were communicating the same as spirit. You wouldn't open your mouth and talk. If you wanted to tell another person in this room something you would just throw your thoughts at them and that person would pick the thought up. They would then throw their thoughts at you without any words being spoken. Therefore, when we give you things we are throwing things at you and you pick up, perhaps, a name and then you could acknowledge the name but then ask us for a description, where they lived, how old were they or other questions. Make us work as well.

You think of talking to your earth friends as being natural and they reply to you in their natural way. You don't realise that when you are speaking words you are also communicating on a thought level, but you are not thinking about that because you are just thinking about the words. Communication with us should be natural as well and it was in your earth world centuries ago but as we all became more reliant on physical conditions our communication changed. We had to have words written on paper to send a letter to somebody or we had to look at them face to face to tell them something. You know that sometimes you have hunches and have a feeling about somebody. That may be when somebody is thinking about you or you might go to bed and dream something and you can't understand why you dreamt of somebody you haven't seen for ages. That person may be thinking of you, whether they are in spirit or on earth and you are picking up their vibration. It should be natural but because the balance in the earth world has got more reliant on material things so communication has become more reliant on material things".

Is that why, way back mediumship was more physical. Do radio waves interfere with spirit communication?

"It is not so much that as your attitude of mind. The mediums that I knew when I was a girl were more down to earth. If you had them on the earth today you wouldn't give them a second look. You wouldn't think they were sophisticated enough, that they didn't dress the part and they didn't know so much about communication but they were just straight forward ordinary people. They had no airs and graces. Of course, there were some that were showmen or show-women you always get that, but a lot of them were just ordinary folk who wanted to help others who were in need.

These mediums gave their time and dedication. They sat in circles for much longer than mediums today and they were trained differently. Those that trained them were much stricter. The education system in the world has changed. When I was a girl school was very strict. I am not saying that your children should have the same schooling as I had but it made us a different kind of person than your children are today. That was the same with the mediums that were trained. Their teachers were much more strict in the circles and the demanded more of their pupils in the circles. If a pupil sat there and wandered off on their own they would be brought back and asked what they were doing, what they were thinking, what were they perceiving. They would not be allowed to go off on their own so much and were required to come regularly to circle. If you belonged to a circle in those days you had to come every week. This is how circles were in those days and everyone was different. That was the training ground and that is why the mediums in those days were much more developed. Now people sit in a circle for a year then they go on the platform and are mediums. They don't want to learn any more, they know it all. That didn't happen years ago. I am not saying that years ago was a golden age and marvellous but you were asking me why it was different then to what it is now.

I am all for free thought and free speech. I wouldn't liked to have sat in some of those circles because I wasn't a person that would conform. I didn't like to be told what to do and so I developed in my own way. I sat in circles but as I got older I sat in circles where I took the lead but I was very lenient with those that sat with me and I would encourage them to do their own thing in their own way. If they didn't want to come one week that was their choice. I don't believe people should be frog marched and told to stand to attention but I was just answering your question because you asked why there is a difference between mediumship then and now. I think people develop more willingly if they give of themselves what they want to give and not because they are frightened of upsetting somebody. That is my way but some of the mediums in the olden days were a lot different. You couldn't have those people running circles today because no-one would come to their circles. This is why mediumship has changed".

You say that you are interested in the Lyceum and other things as well. May we ask what other things?

"There are so many things I am learning now. I want to learn so much and you say, 'You have the opportunity but you haven't got time but there is no such thing as time in spirit'. There are so many opportunities that I don't know what I want to do first. I am interested in the Lyceum and also in education wider than the Lyceum. I now realise that the Lyceum is not on its own but part of a much bigger system of education. We divide ourselves up when we are on earth into compartments. This is our way of thinking and that's their way of thinking, but it is not like that. There are a lot of similarities between religions and beliefs. People that haven't got a religion still have a lot of links with people that are very religious but they are not always aware of this. They believe in something, perhaps they don't believe in a God or a supreme power but they know there is some force and if they are in trouble and are pushed to the limits they ask for help. They don't know who they are asking help from but they will call out to somebody to help them. There are links.

I am interested in the Lyceum because that was my work on earth so of course I am still interested but my interest is now of a much wider scope. I realise that people living in various countries on earth might call themselves by a certain religion that is practised universally. Let's talk about a religion like the Roman Catholic religion because you know that religion is nearly all over the world and is dominated by what the Pope says. All Catholics believe what the Pope says. I am not here to preach whether he is right or wrong but just giving you an example. They all go to mass and take part in the same prayers that are written down and have to say the same words but when they go out of their churches and lead their ordinary lives they all take a different part of their religion with them. They all live in a different way. Yes, they all come under the same umbrella but they all walk a different path but come back together again for their service.

It is the same with the Lyceum. It is said that it is not so uniformed as it was years ago when they all sat there around the Lyceum Manual and took every word, talked about it and discussed it. Now they are much wider in their vision. They have their exams and studies if they want to get diplomas and certificates but besides that they are much more free to explore different ways. Those ways are often quite common to other religions that are doing their thing, studying the words in their bibles or books but coming away from their bibles and books they're living their lives and there is not a lot of difference except they call themselves by a different name. If you said to one that you are very similar to the other they would disagree. I am beginning to understand that there is not so many compartments but many more similarities between people.

People are the same the world over. They are frightened, they are happy, someone goes to spirit/dies whatever they call it they are sad, they cry, they miss them. A child is born and they look at that child and however much that child is wanted or not wanted they see something in that child that is a miracle, it's a new life a new birth. Some people put a steel overcoat around themselves so that they don't become sensitive to vibrations and conditions but if that steel overcoat was taken away inside they would be the same as everybody else. Everybody is the same within but they wear a different mask to the outside world".

Has your perception of God changed since you went to spirit?

"I never believed God was a man sitting on a cloud. I believed he/she was a driving force, a driving energy but my perception is different because it encompasses so much more. You become so blinkered on earth because of the earth way of thinking. We are all part of God, God is us because we are all part of that energy. It is not a system of some energy. It is a driving force but we all create energy and we all make the effects of the energy that we give out. We build up our own problems, we create our own problems, we solve our own problems but there is a balance. There is an overall energy above us because if we override our balance and start to effect others then we are pulled back. We have a certain amount of freewill to explore and do what we want, but when we start affecting others' progress we are pulled back because it is against natural law to affect others. We have to go back on ourselves and alter the way we are thinking or sending our energy force because we are making an imbalance. There is enough of that in the earth world. As we are all so close together, perhaps you don't realise this but we are, we are affecting each other. You are affecting us and we are affecting you because we are close. I can't explain in a way you would understand".

How do we affect you?

"You are all the time sending energy, sending thoughts and vibrations. I will try to give you an example; if we are trying to help you and you are rejecting it because you don't want our help, you are sending a negative energy to us. This rebounds on you because it is cause and effect but it also is restricting our progress because we want to help but we can't. We have to learn to be patient or learn how to cope with that situation. If too many people in the earth dimension are sending too much energy of one kind at one time that energy effects us. There maybe a time when a popular person goes home to spirit and everyone sends so much grief and sadness that is a lot of negative energy and we feel that change in energy and we experience problems. In this situation there needs to be a change in balance to adjust.

We are all progressing, whether it is you on earth or us that are not in the earth condition. The natural law is of continual progression and it is everyone's opportunity to progress. Not everybody wants to progress but they have the opportunity to. By your negative thoughts you can stop somebody else's progression and that causes an imbalance and that rebounds on the person that has sent the negative energy. It is very difficult for me to try to explain".

Is somebody telling you what to say?

"These are my own experiences because I have experienced things since I have been here and I am trying to explain. I remember what it was like to be on earth, to think with an earth brain and to puzzle and question because I used to puzzle and question to make sense of things. It was my job to try to teach and talk to people on earth during my lifetime. This is what I am trying to do now. I am trying to talk to you as if I was still on earth and explain to you my experiences. This is how I tried to teach people when I was on earth. I was no teacher that could teach about this, that and the other. I would teach through my own experiences and I would write things down for people about my own experiences. You all experience things that are similar. You think you are unique and what you go through nobody else goes through but what you are going through people have gone through before and people are going to go through afterwards. If I can help people by my experience and tell them about how I experienced things it might help them when they go through a similar experience".

For example, talking to somebody about death would you write down your own experiences?

"My reaction as experiencing death or my reaction as being on earth and losing somebody. Which do you mean?"

You said that you used to write down your experience to help others.

"That is right. You know I used to edit the Banner. I used to do that once a month and send out stories in that. People also sent me things of their own to include but I also used to put my own thoughts in as well. I used to talk to people who were going through events that I had experienced. I would not tell them what to do, I can't tell you the way to lead your life but I can tell you an experience I have been through in my life that might help you. No one would want to do exactly the same as I did because I was different. You are different from the next person. If you wanted to cross the road you might want to cross it on one corner but your friend might want to cross it on another corner because you see things in a different way. You can only tell people the way that helps you. I just tell people how I have experienced things and if they can find something that helps them, good, but if they can't, they can find out for themselves".

What happens when there is a large imbalance of energy caused by thoughts from the earth world?

"We all feel the imbalance, the drawing back of energy. We feel the pull of the earth vibration. We feel the earth condition that people send out. This pulls our vibration down because our vibration is a much lighter and quicker vibration than yours is. Although we are walking alongside you we are living and existing in a different energy zone. When many people on earth send out sadness it slows our energy and vibration down. The effect being we would exist in a slower frequency than our norm so we wouldn't be able to do as much in our way of helping others because of this pull. There are those that are much more evolved than me and those ones work to alter and diffuse this energy, changing the balance. Gradually we would feel a lifting of vibrations and our energy would not be pulled down. Then we would be able to add to that energy to help others".

It is incredible that it has that effect on you.

"We are existing with you but on a different level. You are spirit, albeit in a human body and of course, you are linking with us because spirit is your natural abode".

Are you planning to return to earth?

"Not yet. I haven't made any plans. There is too much I want to do here yet".

Have your spiritual beliefs helped you enormously in spirit?

"Yes, I was able to know where I was going and there was no fear. I didn't fear death. Fear is negative. I was upset for those I left behind but I was ready to go at the end. I wasn't ready to go until the end. I would have liked a bit longer. Life is always sweet and you always want a bit longer but when you realise it can't be you have to accept it".

Were you a medium when you were on earth?

"I wouldn't call myself a medium but I used to be able to communicate and give them some words that would help them. I wasn't a medium that stood on a platform and gave messages because I didn't hold with that".

Why?

"I was more interested in education than telling the future. That is what a lot of people want they just want you tell them what is going to happen to them and I wasn't interested in that. Don't get me wrong, I was interested in helping people to stand on their own feet. Let them know their loved ones were there and they were all right but you have to go on with life. You can't hold on all the time to what has been and gone. It is not fair on those in spirit to feel grief for ever and ever, you have got to let them progress. By letting them progress you are able to progress with them. I wouldn't have made a very good medium standing on the platform because I might have said some things I shouldn't have said but I helped people in other ways. I tried to help those that stood on the platform to give a good address, to give good knowledge to people, about spirit and about their lives on earth and the opportunities that were open to them. Also the opportuni-

ties that are open to them in spirit and teaching that they were part of something that was much bigger than they envisaged rather than just go to church to get a message. I used to try to teach those that were teaching, those that stood on the platform, often very good mediums, but sometimes they weren't very good speakers. The important thing is to get the balance, to have a good medium that can give a good address as well. That is important because people come for messages, but if you can give them a bit of truth along the way that stands them in good stead and makes them not frightened of the future, it takes away fear".
Given 16 November 1999 & 27 February 2000

SOME EXAMPLES OF OUR SPIRIT FRIENDS' LEARNING.

We tend to think that our friends that come to give us guidance and teachings are able to do this without having to go through some form of learning. From our experience we have witnessed this "learning curve", taking place in some cases over many months or just a matter of a couple of communications.

Katie comes to us as an 8-year-old girl who has of course progressed in the spirit realms, but communicates as a child. While in Portugal we were undertaking a trance event and there was a lady whose husband had recently passed. This is part of what Katie had to say. The simplicity of a child gives us all something to think on.

"I try to teach children that come home to spirit to be happy. You can all teach people to be happy, it is not special you know. It is not just something that I do. You can all teach people to laugh.

Don't be sad when people go home to spirit. You miss them because they are not there to touch, feel, cuddle, kiss and make a fuss of but they are not a long way away. They are only just next to you but you don't see them. You can still talk to them. If we come to see you and you talk to us it helps us too because when we go home to spirit we are sad as well because we have left you behind. We are happy to have no pains anymore but we are also sad because we cannot talk to you and we think you cannot see us. We want so much to tell you that we are with you, we are all right, there is nothing wrong with us and we are happy. We can't do this because you close your eyes. Talk to those that you love that have gone home to spirit in the same way as you would when they were with you in your room at home. Do not think you are being silly and people will say you are strange because you are talking to somebody that is not there. Don't worry about other people but talk to them. Talking helps them to come closer to you. You will feel thoughts in your head that you may think is your imagination, but it is not always so. This is our way of communicating.

We cannot always come to talk to you through a medium but we do come to your homes. I wouldn't come to your home because you are not my mummy and daddy but your family would come to your home. If you talk to them you will learn to feel their vibration and learn to recognise them still being there. Some people feel silly talking to nothing but you are not talking to nothing".

The second example is Jimmy who tells us that Trevor's grandfather came and woke him up to encourage him to, "get busy". Now Jimmy came from Devonshire and was a farm hand, but would often go down to the docks at Plymouth to see those "mat lows" (slang for sailor).

Jimmy comes to speak with a strong Devonshire accent from the time he was on earth about the early 1800s. This is the first serious teachings he has brought. Talking about links with our ancestors and communication.

"All the folk that have gone before ye you have got part of them in ye but only part of them. You have only got the bit of them that was here when they passed on the seed that made you and those that come before ye. You haven't got all their experiences, only part of them. You have got the bit in you that is discovery bit when they were just sorting themselves out. Sometimes if you have got older folks that have youngsters, later they have a little bit more knowledge but usually they are not that old so they haven't got themselves sorted out very well. What a mixture you have got! It is up to you to take a bit of this and a bit of that and sort it out.

As you have a bit of them within you, if they want to make a link with you it makes it a bit easier because you have got a link. If ye do that ye can get a little bit more knowledge from them that ye haven't inherited. Only if you both want it. If you don't want it, you don't get it. There are a lot that go home to spirit that don't want to know what goes on afterwards. They are happy there and don't want to come back even if you are part of them. They say that their time has gone and they have gone home to other things or go to sleep for a hundred years! One that has gone to sleep for a hundred years won't be much good to ye unless you are strong enough to sort him out by telling him to wake up because you want to learn from him. That could happen if you were stronger than he. It wouldn't be very good at teaching because he would be all asleep!

What I am trying to say boy, is if ye have got someone that ye have got part of in ye and that one wants to come to give you a lot more knowledge that he has learnt since he has been in spirit because ye have a link there, it is easier for ye to make that link. This can cause problems sometimes for some folks because they might have someone that want to help them and they don't want them to help them. If they don't raise their vibrations to a different level they can link in with somebody that is not going to help them for their good. You know what I am trying to say, they could cause them a few problems. If you don't raise your vibration you could link with somebody that were not as good as they could have been. We have all got them, haven't we? That's what makes it interesting, boy!

I have said to ye that they can come to help you with what they have learnt since, but if you have learnt a bit more than them, they can come and ye can teach them. They link with ye and ye can share some of your knowledge with them. That John Lyon comes and learns new words from you. Your world moves on with new discoveries and new things that we never thought of. We would never go to bed and dream of things that ye know of and take for granted. Never, never in a thousand years would we dream of things ye have got. When we come back we have got to know a little bit about it because we want to learn as well, you see, boy. If we want to come back to talk to ye we have got to be on a similar vibration to ye and your vibration is nothing like our vibration was. We have got to update our knowledge. This is how we come and learn from you. If we want to work with the energy ye have got on earth at this moment, we have got to understand it. We have to not only understand things in your world but we have got to understand your energy. We have to 'update' - *that's a word I've learnt* - our energy to your energy for us to come and learn and do things with you.

I don't know what I am talking about. It is a muddle and a puzzle to me I hope ye can understand. I will have to go and have some baccy and have a think about it! If I go and have some baccy, I can have a think and perhaps it will make sense.

I wouldn't want to come and learn to do some of the things ye do. It is all too fast. I wouldn't want to fly in the sky, not in those aeroplanes! I wouldn't like that, that tiny little box. No, boy, I wouldn't like to do that. Ye folks take it for granted. You say, ' that is what we do and that is what we are going to do.' I wouldn't do that, it don't seem right to me, boy. I much rather see you there, that's easier. I will go there in my dreams. That the easier way of going in your dreams".

When we are undertaking our Spiritual Awareness events the demonstration of table movement is a very positive example of the power of spirit to communicate in a visual manner. On this same tour of Portugal we were with a group sitting around a massive heavy wooden table that would take at least four strong people to lift. Also the floor was rough stones. The table started to vibrate and this was visible in the bottles of water on the table, the table then slid about the floor and just as we thought the demonstration was over the table was lifted twice to everyone's amazement. When talking to Mafra later his comment was simply, "O you of little faith" !!!. Given October and November 1999.

ENERGY LINKING WITH COLOUR

"Consider colour that brings energy to you, Kimyano works with colour but you think of colour and light, it helps build energy. We give you coloured green grass because this reflects and is more vibrant than just saying blue, green, yellow. You just think of picture, the picture has not energy but grass is vibrant. That is why we give you colour in grass, so there is more energy for you.

You need energy at this wintertime because vibrations are low. Your time of year in your world it is not so bright now as other times of year. You may have bright days but you also have grey days and cold days. You have problems with your health which makes your resistance low so the energy in your body is low. That is why we give you something to help you lift your energy levels. Think of your body and the energy centres in your body from the crown at the top of your head to base energy centre and link all of these with colour. Let colour flow from one to other so they balance. It is no good having one bright and the others dull because this drains the level of your energy. Sit quiet and think of these colours going around your body, recharging each centre until it flows up from your head like a fountain and brings energy to all those around you. It is important to charge yourself first because that is important. Think of dancing and your energy dancing throughout your body. Dancing from one energy centre to another round and round linking and giving you energy.

I say to you think of colour and you all think of a different colour or different shade of that colour because you all need something different. You all need something a little different than the person sitting next to you. Perhaps you sit in big room, a church, library, school room, office or shop where there are lots of people and each person thinks of different colour or different shade of colour. You are all together and because you are near each other you are giving off your own vibrations to others but each of you is individual and each of you needs a different energy. You can share your energy but keep some for yourself. You think of colour green, blue, pink, mauve but how many different shades are there of that colour? So many. Just think of all colours dancing round as if they are ribbons dancing giving energy. You take what you feel is your colour to yourself and drink it in as if it was a flower and you could smell the perfume and take that into your system, as it is lively not just as colour on a piece of paper. You look at glass and say that it is a pretty colour but when you see the sun shining through it, then it is a different colour and it adds something to it because the sun has added its energy.

We give you energy. Take this energy with you when you go out of this room into the world and share it with others. Don't forget, go into the quiet yourselves and charge your own energy centres and give yourself lots of colour because you need it at this time when your energy is low. You are of the earth world at this time and you absorb energy from earth world and your part of earth world is in its time of sleep and so much is dormant. There is life there waiting to spring forth. Do not misunderstand, but it is time of rest for your earth world. Your animals and birds sense this. Birds are noisy sometimes and sometimes they are quiet. They are looking towards warmer days and their cycle also because they have cycles of breeding and bringing forth young ones. It is time for preparation for them and there are times when you hear their notes when they are singing one to another, but there are times when they sense the earth is going to be quiet and they are quiet also. You have weather patterns that change and they foretell weather patterns. They know when it is time to snuggle up warm somewhere and not fly from tree to tree. They have their preparation to make as you have your preparation to make, but you do not realise how closely you are linked to the energies around you. It is natural for them because it is their way of existing, but you with your mindful thoughts do not realise how much you absorb the energy from the earth vibration. So when the earth vibration is gloomy and dull, try to think of things that are brighter, days when the sun shone and flowers grew bright.

You have it in your memory so use it, do not discard it. Draw from your memory because that is what memory is there for. Everything is there for a purpose. You have memory. Use your memory when you need it. Travel to wherever you were happy whether it was on mountaintop, sea shore, in field of corn, in woods, in green pastures or perhaps in a busy city with many elegant buildings, which you look at and admire. Travel to wherever in your memory and relive and take with you the thoughts of that time and those that shared those thoughts with you. This all adds to your energy and you feel more relaxed but also more vibrant. You say how can you feel relaxed and vibrant at the same time, but you can because you have put aside worries and frustrations from your present time and you have absorbed the energy of a previous time in your memory. That has given you the energy so you are relaxed and vibrant at the same time. It is learning how to use energy. Energy is so important".

Given from Beda 7 January 2001

VISITORS FROM SPIRIT

This is just a small part of a much longer conversation but the sound quality was very poor .

The following is the only part that could be accurately transcribed. It was this lady's first attempt at communication but she was anxious to reassure people on earth that existence in spirit is something beautiful and not to be fearful of death.

"It is difficult to talk. I wanted so much to talk but it is so difficult. I was with you when you sat with others and was trying to let you know I was here. It is so difficult. I come to talk. I listen to others talk but now I am here it is not so easy. There is so much I want to say. You see, when I was on earth being so puzzled as to why I was there and what was going on, I heard of people talking to the dead and I thought that was peculiar and thought that was not something I should do because it was witchcraft. I was fearful what would happen to me or my family if I became involved in this kind of communication.

I know a little more now. There are brighter souls than the dark ones, but I didn't understand that because I thought they were all bad because good ones shouldn't come back. They should be in that place that was beyond earth and they should be allowed to rest and not be disturbed. That is what I understood but here I am talking to you, but I don't think I was so bad. No one has asked me to come back. I want to come back. It is not being called back but I want to let others know there is nothing to be frightened of. Everything is beautiful, so much light, no pains, no worries, so much better than you could ever imagine. So don't be frightened because it is such a nice experience. There are so many here with me.

I didn't know what to expect. I used to say my prayers and ask for God's love. I can understand why you are told not to talk to people who are dead because it can cause problems if you don't link with the light".
Given 5 April 2000

SPIRIT WORKING IN UNISON

John Lyon discusses 'where do we go from here?' When talking to our home circle group of friends. The information is shared as an example of how spirit work hand in hand with us.

"We have walked quite a way together. You ask 'where do we go from here?' What can you do with knowledge we have given you? So much knowledge you have already, so much knowledge we have brought to you. This knowledge has been written for others to read.

So what now, what else can we bring you? Much more of course, but of what use would it be to you? You only need to know so much of what occurs in our dimension. There are those who wish to ask questions of the whys and wherefores of existence in spirit. We understand curiosity, in some ways it is reassurance that there is another existence, that there is a status quo, that there is a law of cause and effect, that this life of earth with all its tribulations is for a reason, that there is something at the end of it. You go through so many problems and there must be a reason for them, so much of what happens on your earth is not understood, you ask why? Why?

We can bring you knowledge, we can tell you of eternal existence, we can tell you of eternal progress, we can tell you of spirit return to visit earth either as I am returning to you, or as the companions who walk with you and guide your steps with inspiration, or perhaps returning to earth for another existence. We can tell you so much, we have told you so much but then there are questions about

What else there is in the spirit world?
What levels are there?
What dimensions are there?
What work is there?
What do you do with yourself all day?
Do you carry on earthly pursuits or is there something else, if so what is this something else?
What is there to occupy yourself?
If you do not have time what is your existence?

So many questions. We have tried to answer many questions but there is a danger of giving surfeit of knowledge. There is only so much you need to understand at this time in your existence because if we give you other knowledge it is beyond the comprehension of the human mind. This is where we have problems with communication and we have problems explaining to you the conditions of our vibration in our dimension.

To bring you these answers we have to make a comparison to your life on earth and give you explanations in a way that your human brain will understand. When we do this there is a danger of distortion because we are finding words to fit something that has no words. This is why through many generations and many books that your people have read there are so many explanations and descriptions of the spirit world and spirit existence. Those wise ones that have brought this knowledge to you have tried to explain it to you in a way that the human brain will understand and of course this is very difficult because we are explaining something that is not explainable in words. This is why now there is confusion. Some say yes, there are houses, there are buildings, there are gardens, there are trees, there are people with black faces, red faces, yellow faces, there are children, there are old men, old women, there are nurses, there are doctors, there are teachers. Yes, my friend, there are but not as you perceive them. It is so difficult for us to bring this knowledge to you, so very difficult.

We are bringing knowledge to you that you know of already but for the purpose of your existence on earth this knowledge has been clouded so that you do not retain this knowledge. We are not coming to teach you have come from spirit and you know of this, so we are not teaching. We try to answer so many questions. It is curiosity but also a desire to know and understand. As you become aware of those spirit companions who are with you, yes, of course, you want to know more of their existence and their work in spirit. We do try sincerely to bring knowledge. We understand that yourselves, your group are aware and have, perhaps a more in-depth knowledge of spirit but perhaps those who read your words, or you will be speaking to, will not have this knowledge. We are conscious that we do not want to paint pictures that will become tradition. This has happened with so many of your faiths, I will not use the word religions but I will use the word faiths, on your earth.

Knowledge has been brought because there has been a desire, a thirst for knowledge, and so as to give an understanding, a description has been given and these have been taken literally. There are words in the Bible that says 'In my Father's house there are many mansions,' spoken by Christ. Of course, there are many mansions, but so many people take it literally as houses. This prophet we are speaking of gave these words to try and explain to those who were listening of levels of the dimensions of spirit. I say the word 'spirit' this again is a word I am using to try and explain to you the existence but what is spirit? We are back to words. If I speak to you in English and you translate this into Norwegian, Spanish or whatever language you will put another name on this and there again it may not be exactly the same as your English and it would get distorted again. Of course, generations previous there was the language of Latin that was useful, at least different nationalities were able to understand the same word in whichever country they lived in because Latin was a language they understood through their church. Now there are no universal languages as such except in your professions and in your clergy but there again it is diminishing.

We come to you, we try to bring you knowledge and you say 'well, where now?' We continue to come and talk to you, to continue to bring you knowledge because we need to keep the communication between us because while we are using words there is a stronger communication also, your spirit is communing with ours. If we did not make this communication through words your other communication that is much more important would not be taking place. So yes, we will come, we will answer questions that you perhaps think are trivial and we will try to address questions that others give you. This is education and we are trying to bring enlightenment, we are trying to break down the barriers that have been built up over the years. There have been barriers built up by your religions, your orthodox churches but there is also distortions been built by your spiritualist's churches. You cannot blame one religion or the other. Wherever there have been words brought from spirit there has been distortion because of what I have just detailed to you.

What we say is yes, we will keep communing with you because this is valuable time. You may not credit this as being valuable but believe me the time we spend with you is so because you do not realise now but in future times when you look back you will realise how much you have perceived. Do not be concerned that you do not remember everything that is said because we come again and give this knowledge to you in another way, it will be the same as we have told you before but perhaps a little more in-depth. The more we tell you the more you understand because you are linking stronger in the higher vibration.

What we want to develop is harmony. It is a fine line we tread, we know that you are human and as you are human you wish to experience human affects. You will appreciate movement of your trumpet and table or the other vehicles in your room because you are human. We do not want to discard this because these are building bricks for us all. This opens your awareness in learning, it opens the door of learning and from this opening you are going deeper and you will ask more questions. There are what you call physical circles where many things occur but my friend, this proves there is a possibility of movement of objects, materialisation, de-materialisation, there is a force beyond matter that can move and create. What this doesn't bring to you is knowledge, wisdom and education. You can have all these things, you could sit, link with spirit and have all these things but at the end of the day you are playing party tricks. You are proving spirit is here, you are proving that spirit exists and perhaps with materialisation you can observe spirit that is marvellous, especially for those who wish to see their loved ones. We are decrying this as it is very important for those groups but your group is for education so we are not using the energy so much for that purpose.

This is for you to decide because it is free will. If you decide, yes we have had education how much farther can we go down this road, is there any more we can learn? You may say 'well, thank you spirit we appreciate the knowledge you have brought us but we feel that we cannot learn much more with the capabilities of our human brain, so can you give your energy to the movement of objects?' This is your choice. It is not for me to advocate one route or another route but we are, of course, interested in education. When you go home to spirit what you have learnt so far will be of a great benefit to you. You are not just thinking of your material life but you are thinking beyond. Even though we have given you thoughts that perhaps you do not understand and you cannot comprehend this wisdom is there with you and when you are free from the constraints of the human brain you are open to so much more. We are not advocating which route you should take but we are showing the opportunities that are open to you.

Not only are we bringing to you knowledge through a mouth we are hopefully educating those who sit with you that they are perceiving for themselves. Also, we are bringing many from spirit to learn with you. So you see we are not only speaking to you, we are communicating on another level with so many more that are in your group with you from spirit. You ask why do we need to bring them here, why can't we educate them in spirit? We do educate them in spirit but there are two reasons;

1. There are some who are very close to the earth vibration so they learn better in a vibration where there are mortals because their thinking is similar.

2. We are teaching teachers, so they are here learning how to teach. They are learning how to perceive your thoughts, how to perceive those that are seeking. They are learning how those more experienced teachers are giving words and how these words are being received and how we react.

There is much more to your group than perhaps you realise.

I have not answered your question 'Where do we go from here?' I have given you the question back for you to answer for yourselves. You do know but you need someone to tell you but it is not for us to tell you. You need to make your own decision because there is free will.

You are constrained in the human body and human condition. You have your earth life to lead and you are here to lead your earth life. You cannot spend days, hours with spirit because what would the purpose of your being on earth? There are many who do this but what is the purpose of you being on earth? You have to balance your energies, you must not neglect your energies for your earth life because you will come to the end of your earth life and you will find you have not achieved in your earth life what you desired when you set out. Once you are in spirit there is infinity to learn but you have come to learn on earth, perhaps what it is not possible to learn in spirit. You must make the most of your time on earth. It seems a long while you are on earth when you are a child and at your age you still think you have quite a time left on earth. I am not saying this is not so but compared to infinity it is no time at all.

It is your free will. You have earth life and you must live your earth life and we appreciate the time you share with us but we understand it has to be limited. There are many who do not limit their time and this can cause problems with concentration, it can cause problems with the way their mind thinks and operates because you have to disconnect. You are thinking on a different vibration, a different level. You must realise you shut down and put to one side and pick up again when the time is right".

Given 28 July 1998

Explaining how information has been built up.

"You look back on your records and perceive what was foretold in the very beginning when you first started to sit as a group. We told you of the plans for the group how you would be the hub and from this hub your team and our team together much would go forth to others who were seeking. At that time you could not visualise how far your words would go but now you are beginning to see a little of what we were speaking about. We were not foretelling the future because that is not our province but we were giving you encouragement, trying gently to guide you so that you would record words that were spoken. It is very important that this is done so that others who are to come can read our communication. We gently guide but do not lead, we give you suggestions but you have the free will it is your decision how you follow these instructions and guidance.

You say, 'yes it is free will but is it ordained?' You can change your mind and turn round and say 'enough I will not continue' but if it is in your destiny you will eventually come back to the same situation. It is your free will how long a route you take and how many roads off the main path you decide to wander but if it is in destiny you will continue. We do not want you to feel you are restricted and this is your path and you cannot step from your path. If you wish to take diverse routes this is your free will, explore other avenues this is your free will. We will not depart we will just stand and wait for you to return, as we have done in the past.

Everyone has those who wait to work with them on their path of destiny. Sometimes people become a little impatient and wonder why spirit is not using them more, why things are not happening. Perhaps the time is not yet right".

Given 1 November 1998

FAIRIES - AN EXPLANATION

Reference was made to the Sir Arthur Conan Doyle records of the Cottingley Fairies that described how two young girls saw fairies at the local beck and were able to allegedly photograph evidence of their existence. This has also been made into a film called 'Fairy Tale' and had subsequently been issued on video. While watching the video there were noticeably rappings in the room indicating to us that our friends from spirit were taking an interest. John Lyon was asked about the phenomena that the children perceived.

"It is decoding. You were talking of children. Children's perception is not clouded because they do not have preconceived ideas as it is natural. They bring this knowledge with them when they come but over time it becomes clouded and distorted. More so in your more recent years where there is so much visual communication to put images in one's mind. A few generations previous whence we are talking of, your children were free to use their imagination so much more.

We must not think that this was imagination. As children use their imagination they are drawing on a part of the brain that is not usually used, it is a part of the brain that is usually dormant. The more you use your brain, the more you stimulate your brain, the more impulses are reverberated so that it is a chain reaction. If you do not think, question and stimulate you become very dormant in your thoughts, you just believe what is put in front of your face. Children used to play and imagine. They used to imagine many things, whereas your children now, they have their dream world, they have their imagination but this is tainted with ideas that are put before them. From a very young age they are shown pictures from your television and films. This all the time is going into their subconscious so when they are playing the pictures that have been created by someone else are brought to the fore and they stifle the pure imagination of a child.

When a child comes to your world they bring with them so much knowledge, so much wisdom because, as you are aware, they are spirit. They quite often are spirit that have been in your world before. Some may not it may be their first visit but they have so much knowledge. Gradually as the years go by and they become more of your world this knowledge recedes. They have pure knowledge of how to communicate with spirit and often have invisible playmates, a friend whom they talk to. Perhaps unenlightened parents will chastise them and tell them not to be silly as it is their imagination. The more enlightened parents understand this. They do not push them but they just accept that they are able to perceive spirit and accept this. They do not put thoughts into their mind but just acknowledge that this is possible as long as it doesn't disturb the child. If the child becomes worried or distressed this is another matter. This should not occur there must be a reason why the child is distressed. In natural development the child will bring this ability with them and for their first few years on earth life they will take this as normal as talking to their earth family. As normal as meeting other children they are introduced to in their earth world. Gradually, gradually, as they become more of the earth world this ability recedes.

The children depicted in the film decoded spirit as images of small people. Those of you who have seen spirit lights and witnessed how spirit manifests itself where you have spots of light going around your room, darting, swirling. Tiny pinpoints of light. Can you imagine a child who is not clouded with all the trappings of earth they perceive spirit so much more clearly than yourselves. You perceive light but a child will perceive this light surrounded with colours that swirl. It does not take much imagination for this perception to turn into a fairy because in the child's imagination they are imagining something that they can explain. They cannot explain a swirl of colour. They are perceiving with their spirit ability but also they are decoding this through their human brain and their human brain in bringing in the conscious reasoning. The conscious reasoning is trying to explain something of which it does not know. This spirit light that the child is perceiving swirling and dancing that is full colour is being changed into a small person in their decoding because this is logical. As they are in a human body logic has to be involved. A talented child is able to draw pictures and because something flies around it must be similar to a bird, it must have wings so the draw wings. As it is something they have to explain they add because their conscious reasoning has told them if it is a fairy it must have arms and legs and gradually over the years this has evolved.

Now this does not occur so much because your modern world has put images of many other things to your young ones and they are not perceiving naturally. They are perceiving what their conscious reasoning has told them to perceive. Sometimes this becomes distorted and frightens the child because it is something unknown, it distorts into an image which man has made with pictures on screens.

The innocence of children is something to be treasured and to allow a child to retain its innocence for a few years is very precious. Unfortunately, in one way, your world has evolved and your children have to mature and become aware and protective of themselves much younger.

I understand questions that may be raised. Your children are maturing younger and are becoming more of your world younger but going back to many generations your children were deprived of their childhood. They were not allowed to be children but we have gone full circle. Your world revolves in a circle. Generations ago your young ones were not allowed to be children they had to work and be part of the work pattern of the family. Then gradually the pendulum swung and they were able to be children in their innocence they were able to use their imagination.

The pendulum has swung the other way now, your children are not sent out to work for their living but they are being deprived of their childhood. Everything goes in a circle. You think you are progressing and evolving, you are, but, you are still going in a pattern. The problems one generation faces another will not face in the same guise but the will face in another guise. This is history. You have seen diseases come and go. You have diseases that have wiped out generations then your medical men have discovered a cure but then another disease occurs and then they discover a cure for that. So it is with other discoveries in your world. You suddenly stumble on an invention that is going to save so much time and make your life so much easier. Why, my friends, if you have all these marvellous utensils that make your life so much easier, your homes are warmer, your way of living is so much easier, you can travel so much easier, your communications are so much easier, your education is so much more advanced, why are you still frustrated? Why are you still striving to achieve what you cannot achieve in your earthly world? I am not talking of spiritual values I am talking of earth world.

You are on earth and have taken on an earth body and whatever befalls you on that earth journey is there for a reason. You cannot travel the same path as your ancestors because each generation comes with a new vibration, a new level, a new vitality but also they face new problems and new obstacles. They have to strive themselves to overcome. It would be no good having to face the same problems as your parents and grandparents because you would know the answers, you would know how they overcame those problems. So you have to have your own set of problems that have not been surmounted before so that you can learn how to overcome them and grow. You each come as a new generation with new vitality, on a new wave length, a new structure of vibrations to cope with what befalls you because your earth is forever changing.

I have not answered the question. Yes, the children we were talking of in this particular age were free to use their imagination, free to stimulate the knowledge of spirit they brought with them. This is not so of your children today because they have another way of coping. These children in the story were decoding spirit but in their own way, in a natural way. As the story unfolded it was altered and adapted to make it into a story because however you tell a story whether it is by words or writing you have to present it so that it is enjoyable for the reader or in the case of a film the viewer. So you have to add a little bit of yourself and artistic licence to the story. If you look within there is much truth.

The ones that were depicted, the learned men of that age, their stories are well documented. They are there to be researched. They were well known in their time and are still well known now. We have mentioned the pendulum swinging around, it is coming again, when there will be people who are well known, who are able to put their name to advanced learning. This was advanced learning at that time. The world has moved on and you have coped with many things since but there is now another time of awakening coming. You are already on the threshold of this.

You have been told there are many wise ones coming to earth. There will be many ones who will have well-known names and they will be able to put their names to give credence to very useful information. If only others will listen it will be of great benefit to many, not only for those on earth but communication between the dimensions. There is a breaking down of barriers that you now know of, your world, our world. You know there is no barrier, we are inter-dimensional but, alas, there are many that do not have this wisdom. When you try to explain this to them they will look at you as if you are a little unbalanced and think you are dreaming. If someone came who could prove facts and figures, write them down, put their name to them and explain in a way that others could understand. Today's generation are being educated much more scientifically. When I say scientifically you are thinking of science as you knew it at school but I am not talking of science as such. I am talking of a different kind of science, a science of inter-dimensions, a science of communication. You are now aware of frequencies that are in your world, how you can communicate with people on the other side of the world not by putting pen to paper but instantly by other means. This was unknown to people one hundred years ago but this is not a mystery to those being educated now it is natural to them. You understand it can be done, you can pick up your telephone or look at your screen and you accept that you can communicate but if you are truthful you do not fully understand how this occurs, you have learnt to accept that it occurs. You may have a vague notion of wires, frequencies, aerials, satellites and whatever but it all comes together you are happy with the result. Your young ones are aware of how this happens it is natural for them, they will give you chapter and verse of how this occurs. It is natural, it is not a new discovery it is something they have grown up with. As you grew up with discoveries that were unknown to your parents so another generation on is going to be even wiser and this will bring about a new understanding. This is exciting that there are frequencies and wave lengths that you can link with not just with people who are alive and breathing but of those who have trodden your path on earth but have left that path and have moved to another dimension.

This exciting, this is something that is to come. I am unable to go any farther at this time but this is the going forward we have spoken about. It has to be handled very carefully because you can imagine, this information and knowledge is used for good but it can be used other reasons. You are aware that inter-dimensions and we link with you from our dimension but there are other dimensions that could cause problems. You lift yourself and ask for protection, you ask to be lifted to a level where we are compatible but there are other that are not so compatible and there are many who would wish to contact those on earth who left their work unfinished and would love to return to earth and cause havoc. Although your men of wisdom are aware now of this information it has to be guarded and protected so it can only be used in the right hands. There is so much more to investigate before it is unleashed for others to learn.

I hope you find this exciting because we find it exciting. So long we have worked to contact the dimensions, to break down the barrier and we can now see step forward. So for us it is exciting and hope it is exciting also for you because you will also be involved in this. I have gone a long way from the question of fairies".

THOUGHTS AT THE BEGINNING OF A NEW YEAR

"So you are starting again another cycle of your year. There has to be a time to mark seasons, to mark events, to mark the cycle of your earth's rotation. There are so many thoughts at this time of year that you go forward with new challenges, new ideas, new hopes, new aspirations and new desires. This is good but why just this one time of your year? Take these hopes, take these desires, take these intentions forward with you, do no lose them persevere, continue. It is a good time to look back and recall what has occurred but also to look forward with hopes for the future. So often a few weeks of your new year have passed and where are you? Back to where you were before.

You think of time as something that is restrictive. You have to live within this time span of your earth, this is accepted because you are of the earth but you are also of spirit. Spirit is timeless. Your earth is timeless. You measure your earth its cycles, its years and its events but before time was marked your earth still existed. You speak of time as of all importance. It is becoming of greater importance as your generations increase, more and more you are restricted by time. There are events that occur and these are markers for you. There is a sequence of events that you go through in an earthly body. You go through your years. As a child you understand spring, summer, autumn, winter and you grow with this but as your time on earth matures you do not mark so much the seasons as your years. You look at events in your life and you say 'That happened before' or 'that happened after that event.' You are still restricted by time.

Time is infinite. Time is something that we do not measure. Time is as long as its takes. You have two people walking side by side on your earth; for one time goes fast, for the other time goes slowly but they are still walking on earth. They are still looking at your time pieces, they are still looking at the seasons of your year but they are balancing time in a different vibration. This gives you a little insight into how we measure time. Time is something that is an allusion. There are events that occur which you look at and as they unfold you say 'When this occurs I will be a little wiser, when this occurs I will be a little wealthier, when this occurs I will be a little healthier, when this occurs I will have more freedom.' These are just some examples. All the time you are restricting yourself to time. You are waiting for something to occur before you can step forward, before you can go another pace on your path. Do not wait for these milestones but start your voyage now. If there is something you desire, if there is progression you desire do not wait for a milestone, go forward now. Lay the foundation for whatever event you wish to occur. Of course I am talking of your spiritual progress, I am not talking of bricks and mortar. I am not talking of your mundane world.

So many that walk your path link with spirit, they are aware of spirit, they know of communication with spirit, they say 'If only I could learn more of spirit if only I had time I would dedicate myself to spirit if I was not tied down with whatever.' You have the free will, you have to live the earth path, you have to feed yourself, clothe yourself, you have to live within the confines of your human existence. We understand this because we have walked the earth path also. You also have those that make demands on your time that is part of the travel through your earthly voyage. You are here to interact with those others whom you are either related to or come into contact with because this is part of your existence on earth. It is through this existence that you are progressing and learning. Do not use these as obstacles. Enfold them in your existence, accept them for what they are, they are part of your existence. Encompass them and show love where it is needed. Do your duty where you have to do your duty. Also encompass spirit at the same time. Walk hand in hand with spirit. Do not be restricted by these obstacles where you say 'If only I hadn't got to do this, if only I hadn't got to do that, I would have more time.' You do have time. You can expand time, you can shrink time and you can manipulate time.

If you think of time as a bag and into that bag you can only fit so much and you have filled this bag with all your obstacles, all your problems and there is no room for you to fit spirit into this bag, it is full, it is overflowing. Turn this bag inside out, look at this bag, look at the hidden corners, look at the expansion, move around all your obstacles you have put in this bag, re-pack your bag and you will find you have more space to walk with spirit also. Spirit can become part of your life. You don't have to keep it separate. We know that when you walk your earth path you do not want to shout from the roof tops 'I am talking to spirit.' You can walk with spirit and also continue your ordinary existence, you can meet the demands on your time but you can work together with spirit. You can involve spirit in your earth life. We are here and are happy to do this. You already do this when you do your healing, when you meet people who have problems and ask you questions we know you are linking with spirit. Perhaps on other occasions you are shutting spirit to one corner. In some cases it is good because you have to have freedom and space. Spirit cannot overtake you. You are yourself and we come when you request us to come.

As you walk through your life and overcome obstacles and learn, spirit can come in and learn with you. You are meeting challenges every day. Do not take these on your shoulders alone just send a thought to us and we can near you and assist. As you come across whatever it is you do during your day time, your night time, your eventide, your morning, be aware that if you so wish we can assist. You can all the time link and send thoughts to us and send thoughts to others. We know you do this with your absent healing, your distant healing but when you see someone you may not know walking, sitting and you can see there is a problem. Perhaps you cannot go and talk to them because they may think it would be strange if you intruded in their problem. Send your thought on the higher level of communication that you are aware of to that one and you can link with that one on their higher level of communication. Everyone has this higher level of communication, you are not special, everyone has this, everyone is spirit. You can link with them and all the time you are communing with them and your communication hopefully is giving them some help in some way. They may not realise but it is not the singer but it is the song.

As you are look at your animals do you realise they absorb your energy, they know what you are thinking. Do you also realise that these animals are also communing with other animals that you cannot see? Do you sometimes wonder why your animals behave strangely? Why do they behave out of pattern? What is the reason?

Stretch your thoughts, stretch your imagination but if you wish to call it imagination. What is imagination? Imagination is shutting down your conscious reasoning and opening your higher reasoning. At first perhaps you daydream, you make pictures and you use part of your conscious reasoning to do this. You sit in circle and are given a meditation that perhaps takes you on a spiritual walk. Initially the leader of your group is drawing a picture for you, he is suggesting perhaps you draw a picture for yourself and to do this you are using your imagination. Slowly your imagination recedes and you are then free, you have shut down you conscious reasoning and you have opened yourself to a higher level of reasoning that is not part of your earth reasoning. Why is it not part of your earth reasoning? Why do you shut this away? You cannot go around on a cloud all your life on earth you have to have your feet on the ground. You have to beware, for your own safety, what is going on around you. For your own livelihood, your own protection of your human body and for those around you, you have to use your conscious reasoning. You cannot wander off and drift off because you have to be aware physically of all that is occurring. That does not mean you cannot be spiritually aware at the same time. You come back from your spiritual journey but the link is still there. You have come a little closer to spirit, you have touched spirit, they have touched you and each time you do this the link is a little stronger. You can withdraw and your attention is for your earth world but when there are moments when you can slip away that link is there waiting for you.

Do not be restricted by your time. Of course, you have to live within the confines of your clocks and watches, your seasons and years but be aware there is a greater value, a greater existence that is not measured the same. When you walk your earth life you have a certain time to complete a certain task, whatever that task is. For example, if you choose to dig your garden you may say 'I have got to do this before the weather changes so I am confining myself to this time.' This is not so with spirit, when you work for spirit you have not got to confine yourself to a time limit. You do what you can, when you can and if your physical demands crowd in on you and you cannot complete the learning you have put aside for spirit, the part of you that you have put aside for spirit, you cannot say 'I have failed spirit because I have not completed my learning and I have had to return to my duties of earth.' There is not a ceiling on this you can go forward later and can continue. It is not as in your garden because you have done your spade work before your earth has become frozen. If you have not done your spade work for whatever spiritual task so continue with the spade work later, the earth will not be frozen, it will be waiting for you to continue. Do not confine yourself to the aspect of physical time when you are involved in the work of spirit. Do not feel that you have not achieved because of your time restriction because you are achieving, you are achieving every moment of your existence.

What you may not understand is the knowledge you have within

you already which you think is shut away from you but when you are freeing yourself from the confines of human existence you are opening yourself. Not only are you learning from spirit you are learning from yourself because you are spirit. You are spirit with much wisdom. You have wisdom within you that is timeless. It goes back I cannot say the word 'time' because it is timeless. You can draw from your own wisdom as well as stretching out and absorbing wisdom from spirit. Here again, your human mind, your human intelligence is restricted to what you can absorb. You have the tools for your walk on earth, you do not want to clutter your walk on earth with other information that is of no use to you while you are here. While you are free from your earthly world you are then free to expand".
Given 3 January 1998

TASKS WE PERFORM

Responding to a question regarding putting part of ourselves into the tasks we perform.

"We are a teaching group and in so being we are bringing those to you who are learning to teach and we are assisting them. If we, who have been with you for a long while, came all the time and spoke to you these others, whom we are training, would not have opportunity and who are we to decry opportunity and progress for others? I am here now so do you have any questions for me?"

Modern day communication on earth takes place very quickly and with the aid of modern technology. The thought process and the personal input seem to be less than in days gone by so does that mean that we as individuals are putting less of ourselves into our daily tasks? Does this impede our learning and our path of progress?

"You perceive that when you have a task the more of yourself you put into the task the more influence you have, the more of yourself is being given to that task. In your modern world you still are putting yourself forward to innovate your ideas and set in motion the wheels of industry, whatever the industry may be, but you are channeling the process. This is progress of your world because you cannot stay the same. You have to change, adapt and go forward with progress. You cannot stay in your isolation and continue using the same methods forever because it would not be compatible to your world. There are so many more of you in your world and there is much more communication between countries, peoples and populations. It is necessary for you to go forward.

When a craftsman worked on a piece of wood, carve, manipulated and created something that would last for hundreds of years. Those ones have long gone home to spirit and that carving is still there. You look at your books that were written by your scribes who have long since gone home to spirit but these books are still there to be read if you are capable of reading the language they were written in.

Yes, I understand but you are still putting your thoughts, you are still putting your own spark of yourself within each task you undertake. Just because you are not perhaps seeing the end result you are not getting the satisfaction that a craftsman would have had when after many years of toil in front of him was this marvelous carving or whatever. As the pace of your life has increased to encompass all that has happened in the world of yours and because of communication with other parts of your world you have had to adapt. This is progress with a question mark perhaps, but it is progress.

A craftsman would have spent years making one item of furniture but an item of furniture can be made within hours now. What is happening to the time you have saved? You are still filling your hours, you are not sitting there in idleness because your task is completed. You are filling your time with other tasks, other duties. So perhaps, in one way, you are giving more of yourself because you are giving to varied tasks instead of just the dedicated task. You may think your skill is not so great as the skill of those craftsmen. Perhaps in some way your skill is greater because it is more diversified and you are having the opportunity to partake in many skills and having influence in many directions. Also you are having the opportunity to not only give but draw from others' ideas and others' skills and there is a greater interchange. You know you are interchanging physically but also while you are interchanging physically you are also interchanging on your higher level of communication. In some ways your thoughts are more active.

Alas you may not have so much time for meditation and contemplation this is perhaps a failing of your world today. If you are wise you make time out of your busy life to take time aside, albeit a short while of your day, but wise ones dedicate a short while. If you care spare greater time, so be it but to put aside a short time from your busy life each day to go into the stillness and the quiet absorbing your own thoughts and vibrations. The true spirit from with and the essence from within and link with those that are close to you.

To recap; yes, those ones going back, maybe just a few years ago in your own century, perhaps put themselves into their tasks in a different way to the method you are using today. You are still putting yourself into each task you do. Perhaps you are not seeing the end results but they did not always see the end result either. They had more time to ponder on what they thought was occurring but if you are wise you can make time from your busy life to give yourself time to ponder and not be swept away with the tide. This is a failing to be swept away with the tide. Give yourself time to think and contemplate what is occurring in your mundane world. It is good to shut yourself away from your mundane world and to link within but also give yourself time to think of your mundane world and what you are doing and what you desire to achieve.

If you are not happy in the situation you are in it is not practical to turn your back and run away but turn it around and ask yourself why you are in that situation? Why are you doing what you are doing? Is there a reason behind this? Is this something you have to work through rather than turn your back and escape? Face it head on. From each obstacle that presents itself you can learn something. Each opportunity that comes to you take it with open hands and walk through it with the thought that you are walking through this and you will walk through to the other side and will be wiser after the event. Treat the problem as an opportunity, adventure, whatever word you wish to call it. If you are wise you are putting part of yourself into every task you undertake. Alas, there are some that do not do this, they just work routinely and work with the idea they will finish their task as soon as they can and then be free to do whatever they wish to do. This is their choice. It is the wise ones that give of themselves because by giving of yourself you are, in fact, growing yourself and learning.

These words will give you some thoughts but they will not answer your question because that was not my intention. I am giving you thoughts to enable you to answer the question yourself".

Given 7 February 1999

CLARITY OF COMMUNICATION

Earlier this evening a new communicator who gave the name of Jeremy had briefly introduced himself speaking through Trevor as the medium. John Lyon was asked if he could give more details regarding this visitor who had introduced himself as a barrister in the City of London also served as a Judge at the Assizes. He gave dates of his existence as between 1800-1859.

"Jeremy was a man of precision and he still has this attitude. He wishes things to be correct. He is anxious that when you link with spirit your mind is uncluttered. We know you have a procedure where you shut yourselves down from your normal thoughts and mundane pressure. You come within this environment and you open yourselves to spirit. This is good but when we come and try to make ourselves known on your table it is difficult for you not to bring in your conscious reasoning. You are eager to assist us when we are trying to make ourselves known to you and all your the time stretching and trying to find a way of making this link easier for us. It is difficult in this instance for you to shut out your conscious reasoning because it is 'trouble shooting' you are trying to solve a problem. You are bringing thought in this instance. It would be better if you tried to take a step back and then link with the one that is trying to make themselves known on your table at a higher level of communication. Then try to confirm on the table what you have perceived. The initial link would then not be through your thought process. It will be through a higher level that you may call intuition or perception. When you have perceived do not elaborate on what you have perceived, do not paint the picture. So often it is easy to perceive a thought, an idea, an image, a sound, a sensation and link that perception with some other experience you have gone through. You then elaborate on that perception. Hold on to the initial perception, whether it be a sensation, sound, vision, sense of touch or whatever. When you have this perception hold onto it. Then, if you so wish, confirm this on your table and then you can go a step further.

I will give you an example; you perhaps perceive a black cat and your mind may wander to someone who owned a black cat, your mind may wander to an area where you knew a black cat, you may perceive that this may be our friend Hannah because she is connected with animals, you may perceive it to be a product that was associated with a black cat as its trademark. There are so many interpretations. Instead of just linking with the first perception your conscious reasoning has become involved and you have moved into other areas causing confusion.

I am not criticising but you were asking me why Jeremy has introduced himself and this is an instance where he is trying to direct the communication for you. He is assisting in a clearer definition of your communication. Also he is anxious when you relay to others only what you have been given and do not elaborate and 'gild the lily.' Quite often when we come from spirit and we give you words just enough words are given to stimulate your own thoughts. If you stimulate your own thoughts and put your own interpretation and you carry this to someone else you are not giving them the words of spirit you are giving them your interpretation. If they heard the words of spirit themselves they may interpret in a different way. We like to give you so much but still leave space for you to do some work yourselves because this is how you learn. Children at school used to learn by rote but now the aptitude is to learn by discovery. This is a better way of learning because they are learning through their own process".

Given 21 March 1999

THE AGE OF AQUARIUS

John was then asked a question regarding the Aquarium Age, the length of its duration and influence on progress.

"We are speaking of something that is not confined to a fixed number of years it is a cycle. What to term Aquarium Age is the position of planets in your solar system and influences. You do not open your eyes one morning and say 'today is the Aquarium Age.' It is a gradual move and has been for the last two decades, gradually moving into action. Each cycle of your year you are a little bit further into what you term the Aquarium Age. An age of enquiry, awakening and rebirth. So many people on earth at this time are looking towards what you call the Millennium and once your clock has ticked from one minute to the next minute into your next millennium so many have the great expectation that from that minute onwards much knowledge will be available to everyone, everything will change and alter. This is not so because it is gradual. There are already changes, there have been changes over the last two decades in preparation for this event but it will gradually continue into the next century. It will not be instantaneous everything has to go in a cycle, has to be worked for, has to be lived through. It is not as you go to the theatre and the scene is set when you pull back the curtain. Each generation has to go through their experience. The Aquarium Age encompasses more than one generation. You already have perhaps two generations that have been born in what you term the Aquarium Age and there will be more still to come. Each of those generations will be slightly different because they will have come to earth with a different energy, a different vibration because you are all the time moving, altering and changing.

Everyone is becoming more spiritually aware but at their own pace, in their own time of evolution. Everyone will not reach a certain stage of evolvement at one time because it is gradual. The more you put into this the more you will learn. Those that sit back and say 'this is a new age, I am waiting for it to come and all will be revealed' will be sitting there for a very long while! The more you go with this, the more you will learn and more that will be revealed. You have to go through one stage before you are ready for the next.

It is exciting for you to live through this time on your earth. I was happy when I was on earth (during the Elizabethan age) because I too lived through an exciting time, a time of great change. A time of advancement, a time of great discovery but you are going through yet another pattern of events that are similar in a different way. You are also witnessing much change and discovery. You are privileged to be part of this because you are part of this".

Are you referring to communication in particular?

"I am referring to awareness, learning, discovery. Communication is one part of this. One part of your world is communicating with another part of your world. You are communicating with others on a different level that you are perhaps not aware of but this is just a small part. It is becoming aware of your abilities. Many are becoming spiritually aware but would not accept this awareness as communication with spirit. They are becoming aware in another way".

What sort of another way?

"It is interpretation. Some would say they are becoming more attuned to earth vibrations. Some would say they are becoming more attuned to people coming from outer space to talk to them. Some would say they are becoming more attuned to their inner self. Each interprets in a different way. Some would say they are becoming more attuned to scientific discoveries, to advancement in communications through scientific discoveries, mind power, the power of the mind. It is all into interpretation because of the restrictions of your world, especially the western world where you are perhaps blinkered in your religions, you may be told you must not communicate with those that are dead and it is evil. Many would taboo spirit communication but they may be perceiving spirit communication without realising the source of the information. They are perceiving ideas, linking in with the universal mind, drawing from the universal mind, linking with its creative vibrations. Perhaps writing music, designing fashions, building structures but it you told them it is all connected with spirit they would not admit to having any connection with that because for them it would be taboo. They are linking with something beyond your earth. They are connecting with something that is linking with their true spirit within. It is freeing itself from the trappings of earth and is able to explore further than your earth condition. It is very complicated".

You are really saying they are opening to their intuition.

"They are opening to their potentials and linking with a force that is greater than anything you could have on earth. The creative force that is the creative force of all not just for the chosen few who can link with it. The great creative force that permeates down through many vibrations to all aspects of existence. More and more are becoming attuned to this and are able to link with this and draw from this. If you said to them that they were linking with spirit they would disagree. Spirit is part of the creative force as you are part of the creative force. Your universe is part of the creative force. You are all intermingled and linked but this is all part of discovery.

The more you come into what you call the Aquarium Age the more you realise you are all intermingled, there is no isolation. On your planet

Earth so many countries are confined within their boundaries and will not accept those living in the countries next to them. When your men go up on their voyage of discovery into space if you could see what they see and how small Earth is and how two countries so close to each other could perceive they could be isolated from each other when they are part of something much greater and much wider. That is only from their spaceship can you perceive the universe as a whole? These barriers will have to come down, they will have become more aware of each other and how each other's thoughts can effect each other. Not just words but thought, how thoughts can effect and cause problems in time to come. Thoughts that are now are causing problems for those not yet born. You can see this in the history of your world. Countries that fight one another, they solve their problems, they sign the pact but the next generation take up arms and fight again because of all these thoughts that are positively creating something. In this case creating are not good vibrations. There has to be a long while for stability to come. The more aware man is of he is not just a man in a human body but he is of something greater the more responsibility he would take for his thoughts. It is all part of awareness, not just awareness of spirit but of something more vast.

I hope these words help".
Given 21 March 1999

COMMUNICATION ON A THOUGHT LEVEL

Responding to a question 'We have been told by spirit that when sitters are negative in their thoughts this makes it difficult for the more evolved spirit visitors to draw near can you please explain this a little more? People can give the impression that they are positive but deep down there are negative attitudes or the opposite giving a negative impressions but really understanding.'

"We communicate on thought. We see beyond the facade. When you are in an earth body when you first come to your earth existence you come and have no pretense but gradually over the years you build up a defense system. You only show to the outside world what you want the outside to see. You have had many knocks and bruises to yourself, not physical, but because of this you put a shell around yourself and put on a facade to the outside world so that you cannot be hurt. You do not want others to know you too well because by knowing you too well they know your strengths and weaknesses. By knowing your weaknesses they can hurt you intentionally or unintentionally. This is the problem the more you develop your spiritual assets because the more sensitive you become, the more in tune you become to spirit, the tune you become to your fellows whom you walk along side with in your earthly existence the more sensitive you are becoming. By being sensitive you are opening yourself up to the pitfalls of your earth world. Not only your earth world but other vibrations that are near to your earth world so this is why those that are taught wisely are taught to put on a white cloak of protection to protect themselves. It is not a physical coat but it is an awareness you put around yourself. Not the defense of your physical world that you put on. It is not a pretense it is an awareness, a knowingness that you are linking with a higher level of existence and you are closing down to the baser elements that can cause you problems.

As you walk through your physical world you meet many but you cannot say to yourself ' I am only going to talk to those that I am on the same wave length with.' What is the point of being in an earth world, you have come to an earth world to learn alongside others of all stations in life, in all experiences. There are many that shut themselves off to those who they believe to be inferior. Who are you to say that another mortal is inferior to yourself because they come from a different station in life, have had different experiences and a different background to yourself how can you say you are not compatible? You are what your earth world has made you while you are in your earth body but within you are all spirit.

When there are groups sitting to unite with spirit the communicators wishing to answer questions and trying to establish strong links to impart knowledge that can help those that are seeking truth but not necessarily giving proof of survival. We are talking of deeper communication something richer more finite. We are talking of progress and education. We can leave aside proof of survival for those that wish to travel that path. Of course, we also come to bring to you those loved ones but this is not our main intention. Our main intention is to bring you knowledge for progress. I am not talking particularly of this group because, as you know, we do not talk of identities. We are talk of 'a group' who are joining together to link with spirit. Spirit in turn are linking their vibration to a compatible vibration near to your earth vibration to make contact. Those mortals that sit in 'a group' they may come from many walks of life it doesn't matter because we are not talking of your human vibration. We are talking of the vibration that is within the human body that is seeking and stretching out for knowledge. It does not mean that they have to be well versed in your education or that they do not know how to write their name or read because it does not matter.

We are not talking of a physical condition but we are talking of the spirit within that is asking and seeking for knowledge. There are those that sit who open themselves and in sincerity are asking. They are asking physically with their physical tongue, 'I want knowledge of this' or 'I want knowledge of that can you give it to me?' Within they are asking the same in their spiritual vibration. There may be others in that group that are sitting and voicing the same words but when words are given from spirit they are saying that they agree but behind that facade they are not agreeing but believing something totally different. They are therefore doubting the truth that spirit is giving. We tell you to question and not accept everything that is given to you because we want you to question and prove for yourself but not to be negative. It does not mean that you have to accept everything but accept with an open mind by saying,' Yes, I understand what you are saying but I have read something that is slightly different and I will examine both ideas and come to my own conclusion.' This is different from thinking, 'It is different from what I have read so you must be talking rubbish.'

On the other side of your coin there may be someone in that 'group' who whatever is said they will dispute and down cry but this is their way. Whatever befalls them on their earth path they will dispute and not accept but behind that facade they are accepting. There are two sides to each coin and when you are not handicapped with an earth body you are able to perceive a lot more clearly. You are able to link with the true vibration of that one and see through a facade.

It is similar to children when you look into their eyes and they speak to you their thoughts. They do not wrap their thoughts up to confuse you. They learn this as they become older in their years. Gradually through childhood they become a little artful and they think cleverly because they can tell you one thing and mean something different. This is the way of life on your earth. It is your defense mechanism you are putting around yourself. You are becoming insular in yourself so that no others can touch you and know the true 'you.'

The very advanced ones from very high realms come to speak to you or to other groups come to your earth vibration there has to be a total adjustment of their vibration because they are so far removed from earth. There has to be a bridge for them to come. If they come are met with this negativity it is pulling their vibration down lower than the bridge so they will go back. They have worked for the position they have reached in their progress so why should they allow the negativity of earth to draw them from their advanced level because at that advanced level they are very wise and can help so many with that wisdom. They would be attracted to those that seek with positive thought not with negative thought.

I hope that explains a little some of the vibrations that are experienced".

We are told to send positive thoughts in healing conditions. When people send sympathetic thoughts not hopeful thoughts does this have a detrimental effect on the healing process?

"When you as a healer offer your services to others and others seek healing or someone asks for healing for a friend or relative who is going through a period of illness, unease or whatever you link with that vibration. As in your physical world your doctors and nurses attend to those that need help wear a white coat or uniform of their profession so do you put on the white coat of spirit but I do not mean a physical white coat. With this you are stepping above the normal vibration. You are putting on a defense mechanism and it is similar. As much as you want to assist others you want to remain strong and you need to give that one your love and energy to assist them to overcome whatever they are enduring at that moment in their existence. You must not be dragged down by their condition and take on their condition. By doing this you are not helping yourself and you are not helping the many other who in time will come to you.

One of the first things you learn as a healer is to give love but not to take on the condition. You feel sorry but you do not feel overburdened. You give love for whatever that one is enduring at that time whether it is physical, mental, social condition or whatever. You address that condition and give healing but also the greatest gift you can give is the gift of hope and upliftment. You cannot promise a cure because it is not in your power to promise a cure. It is beyond your control and is in the control of destiny. You cannot give false hope because that would be unkind. It would be unkind to raise someone's perception that you are going to cure all their ills and they are going to be free of their illness if it is not in destiny. You can give to them hope that you will be able to give them strength to endure whatever it is they have to endure. You can give them the knowledge that they are not enduring this on their own. If they understand spirit you can explain to them that there is spirit with them uplifting them and upholding them. If they do not understand spirit you can demonstrate that you are giving them strength and are there to share their burden and they are not enduring this on their own. By doing this you are giving them hope not despair".

If there is a hospital bed and people are standing around it who are sad, worried and unhappy does this affect the patient?

"In that situation it is not so good because they are draining that one. They are giving negative thoughts; for example 'that one is looking so terrible they are never going to get over this.' They are no voicing these words but you are all sensitive whether you know or not you are all accepting other people's thoughts. If you are in the state of illness you are drained to a lower vibration because of your physical condition and these thoughts can handicap your recovery. Sometimes there is another complication. If it is a member of the family that is in that bed and that member perceives that the visitors are worried and anxious, not only are they perceiving the negative thoughts about their own condition but they are being given another burden because they can sense their family are unhappy and sad. They do not need this burden because they need their strength for their own recovery.

It is difficult when you visit those that are sick especially if there is a family link. I explained to you that as a healer you put on your healer's white coat, not a physical white coat, but doing this you are highering your vibration. When you are dealing with someone close to you it is very difficult to do this because you can see through the facade and they can see through your facade. This is why in your medical world quite often doctors do not treat their own family. It is not good in some instances for a healer to treat those who they are too closely involved with because it is difficult to keep the distance that you need to give the strength and encouragement.

One gentle word of advice is as a healer if you encounter this problem does not only just send love out to the one you are sending the healing thoughts to but also ask for upliftment for their family. By doing thus you are assisting the patient".
Given 23 April 1999

ENERGY - CAUSE AND EFFECT

"Everything that exists whether it is yourself in a human body, pure spirit that does not have a human body, animal kingdom, your earth or anything that exists is part the creative energy that has come from the creative source. You all have something in common because you are all in some way connected. You are all vibrations. You are all an energy in different forms because I am not, for one moment, saying you are the same energy as a blade of grass, a tree or mountain but you are all part of creation. Within everything that exists there is a part of creative energy. A blade of grass is alive and it grows. You are existing as a spirit within a human body. We are existing without the encumbrance of a human body. Your animal kingdom, your birds and fishes they all exist and are all part of creation. All of you are an energy because you all have your own energy field. As you know, you are all the time generating energy to exist. You create heat, sensations, and your electric impulses that flow through your body to allow your body to function it is all energy.

You are also producing energy from your thoughts. As you know, your thoughts leave you and go from you. You are producing now sitting here as group your energy is mingling with the energy of others who are in this room whether they are in a human body or as myself pure spirit. We are all merging energy. We cannot exist on our own because we are all part of the whole. The thoughts that you emanate, of course, effect those whom you come into contact with as do their thoughts affect yourself. Your energy merges with the energies of others that are giving energy at the same time because you are emanating together. In a normal circumstance in your world there are those that are emanating thoughts of happiness, there are those that are emanating thoughts of sadness, there are those that are emanating thoughts of fear and there are those that are emanating thoughts of peace. If your world is balanced one energy is counteracting the other.

In a normal existence your world is balanced because you are all emanating different energy because you are all individuals and are all existing in your individuals lives. You all go through periods of happiness, sadness, fear, panic, pain or frustration but all in your own cycles and usually there is not an overbalance because while someone is experiencing one emotion another is experiencing another emotion. In normal conditions the scales do not tip too much one way or the other.

You may recall an event that happened in your recent past where there was much emotion, much sadness, unhappiness and in some ways fear, negativity and the sense of loss. Not only in your country but throughout much of your world because an international personality was involved. At that time the scale was tipping too much one way and there was an imbalance. This is not the first time this situation has occurred because many other instances similar to this have taken place in your recent past and more distant past. You do not always see reaction instantly. You think of time as now, today, tomorrow or next week but of course outside your human form there is no such thing as time it is energy that is there.

We have told you that when you send out thoughts of love and healing when much is sent out the excess energy is used again for another time when there is another occurrence. This other emotion of sadness and negativity also does not have an immediate effect but it makes an imbalance of energy. I am not saying that would particularly cause an earthquake or another disaster but when disasters happen, when there are problems they are usually caused by an imbalance.

Destiny has written that some events are to happen and whatever occurs, occurs for a reason. Sometimes human emotion and freewill takes over and too much energy is created in one particular form. Sometimes we try to assist to bring a balance by diffusing energy. Energy has to have a reaction because it has to have an outlet. You know that when you send love it goes and it has a result. You may not see the result straight away. There may be someone there that you wish to send love to and that one does not immediately show a response to the love you have sent but when you continue to send love eventually you can see a result. It does not always happen as you wish because destiny is also involved but natural law is that when an energy is produced it has to have a reaction.

We come back to the problems in your world. You mentioned earthquakes but there are also other problems. Your world also goes through cycles, cycles of events and energy. You look at history and see times of unrest and times of peace. You see times when there has been a reverse, t when there have been dormant times followed by an awakening. Destiny is ordained and these things occur but when they occur as in a cycle and added to that cycle there is an imbalance of energy that causes a greater problem than destiny ordained.

You were told that at this time that you call millennium there is a change of energy in your world. It is part of the cycle of the history of your world that is being written at this time. As 2,000 years ago there was another change, and so on, and so on, throughout history. It is ordained at this time that there is a change of energy and there has been a build up of this change. It does not happen instantly overnight when one day of your world there is one energy and the following day there is another. Everything occurs gradually and as you look back over your last three decades of your earth world you have seen many changes gradually becoming stronger as your decades have grown.

Now you are coming to a point when a lot of people in your world are expecting a change because they have been told this is an event when something is going to happen. The very thought of all these people thinking that this is a great event in their calendar when something is going to happen creates energy and adds to the change that is ordained. You will have effects. Some of these effects are part of destiny but also the energy that people have produced also adds to this. One person is not personally causing an earthquake no person must take that responsibility on their shoulders. You know that thoughts have an effect and you are able to guard your thoughts. As a human your thoughts wander and stray but you must not be too hard on yourself. You are able to pull them back and be aware of what is happening and be careful with the thoughts you send. You are in a human body and it is human nature that you show reaction to events. If someone is not so pleasant to you it is your normal reaction as a human in your world to show that reaction back. After a while when you have had time to count to ten and bite your tongue you are wiser than some others and able to diffuse the situation. There are many in your world that do not understand because they do not have this knowledge.

This is how there becomes imbalance but do not blame yourselves because there are cycles of events all through history and you are now going through another cycle of change. You will see many changes occur but not instantly because they will be gradual. As the clock chimes and you go into a new year, a new millennium, you will not go to utopia and everything will become wonderful and beautiful because change has to be gradual. There has to be a clearing of vibrations because when there has been a build up of energy, and as you said, there was a build up of sadness, hysteria in some cases that energy has to be diffused. It has to be used up and taken away or burnt up before there can be a new energy for your new millennium. There has to be a leveling and these events are clearing the vibrations. You may say in some ways these are the birth pangs of a new age. There has to be a clearing before there can be an introduction of a different energy.

You are aware that when you send out thoughts they have a reaction but do not be too harsh on yourself and blame yourself for causing events because you cannot change destiny. You can help diffuse situations because of your knowledge by sending love but you cannot alter what has been ordained".

Given 5 September 1999

PRECONCEIVED IDEAS - A PROBLEM

Explaining that what we have been taught by our religion on earth effects our awareness when we go home to spirit.

"So many in spirit wish to make their presence known to their loved ones and it is with sadness that they are not able to do this because their loved ones are not aware. This is very sad. Those ones that come to you are happy that you know of their existence and know that this bond is still with you.

When we make the passage home to spirit some find the passage easier than others because of what we have been taught. We had been taught that there was another existence but it would not be until we were called from our rest that we would be awakened. This is sometimes difficult for us to accept. When we are in another dimension we feel it is wrong to stretch out and look for light because we expect to be in darkness so we stay in darkness. Our loved ones that wish to greet us have great difficulty because we do not want to accept because it is indoctrinated in us that we well be asleep until we all resurrect together. There are many now that are not shackled with these thoughts.

I understand that religion still exists but there is freedom of thought within religion. There are still those that follow a religion of fear because it is the way they have been taught, the way their ancestors have been taught and they follow the same path. Gradually your world is becom--

ing a little more enlightened. As your world becomes smaller because you are mixing with other cultures, other thoughts and beliefs. Gradually these beliefs are merging together and it is making thoughts. As you know thoughts are a living vibration and this living vibration links with other vibrations. Gradually it is opening doors and you are able to perceive that there is something a little different than your blinkered religions.

It is not progress because you are returning to the way of thought before religion held sway. Deep within you have memory of a more free way of worshipping. This is dormant within but it is there because you have inherited this knowledge in your genetic blueprint from your ancestors way back beyond formal religion. Linking this with the spirit that you are, the true you, there is a way forward for new thoughts and new ideas. It just needs the door to be slightly ajar and that will gradually open wider as you seek higher thoughts. Fear causes many problems. Fear is negative. Fear suppresses love and growth".

We had another experience the other week when Mafra was talking when he was picking up on another one in your dimension's vibrations and describing that vibration. If he wanted to merge the knowledge of that other entity with his own to give us information such as the person name or the knowledge they had gained would that entity have to be in close proximity?

"What is close proximity to us in spirit? It is vibration. It is a compatible vibration. We have no difficulty communicating with the rest of our group because we are compatible with each other. We are on a similar vibration and we have worked for many of your weeks, month, years, we have no time, together but when we are not speaking to you we are also a team. We do not wait until we come to visit you here and join together as a team. We are a team and our visit to you is a short aspect of our work. We merge energies as we work together in spirit dimension, as we help those in the field of education. We are all the time linking with each other and each other's vibration. As you witness when one of us is talking and you ask for information that we can explain but some other member of our group has had more experience that information is with us directly because we are merging but the one that is speaking is giving the words.

Now we will walk a step forward. If you are asking of someone else in spirit who is a visitor, who perhaps is a loved one, friend or companion of someone else in your room and you wish to obtain some more knowledge of that one. Of course we link with them on their energy field and depending on their vibration because it varies as to how compatible we are. That one may be new to communication, I am not saying new to spirit, but new to communicating and we have to bridge the span between us to merge to the right vibration. You have frequencies in your world on your radio machines and just because you turn your knob it does not mean you can pick up all the signals that are flying around your world at this moment. You have to locate the vibration and be sure that your energy from your receiver is compatible to the energy that is being sent from the radio wave that it wishes to communicate with. It is similar. We are communicating all the time with others in spirit because we are not an isolated team that just contact each other. We are all the time contacting others of different vibrations, those that have just come home to spirit, those that need our help, support and strength. We are linking with those that are of a higher vibration than ourselves in wisdom and we raise and alter our vibrations to tune with those.

When you say to us that we had a visitor and were not sure whether that visitor gave all the information that they wished and ask us to help. Of course, we endeavor to help and we link with that one who may not have had contact before with the earth world since their journey to spirit or it may be one that has returned several times. We adjust our vibration. They are also individuals and are different. Maybe, counting your years and days, they have been in spirit a long time and they have shut away their earth memory. We are linking with the spirit entity and we can tell you what we are perceiving. We are perceiving them as spirit, their vibration. Perhaps a description you would understand is their personality. If I was thinking of you, my friend, I would explain your character, your way of thinking but perhaps I would not describe your physical appearance because that would not be your true essence. Your physical appearance would just be something you borrowed when you were in a human body and you would have left that behind. Of course, you would have taken the memory with you and if you wish to share that memory with myself you could. Sometimes the one that is linking is wanting to get over some vital piece of information and the memory of what they looked like, their name or location is not so important as the essence of their message.

We make a link and explain to you the condition we are linking with, whether that person is a gentle vibration or a more illustrious vibration. Whether they are a vibration that is patient or impatient. I am just giving you some examples. We try to explain the character. If that one has returned before the link is easier. As you meet a new friend on your earth the first few times you meet that person and communicate with them you are a little guarded in what you say. You are a little apprehensive of how they will receive your thoughts and ideas. Gradually you give them a little more information. When we first contact someone in our dimension it is the same because we do not suddenly change. If when we are on earth we are a person that wishes to withhold information and only give a little of ourselves we do not suddenly change when we go to spirit. If we are a person that exaggerates on earth and we tell you a very exaggerated story of ourselves we do not suddenly change when we go to spirit because we are the same. There is no magic wand that alters us. We learn and progress but initially we are very similar. If someone has returned several times they then will give you a little more information and communication will be that much easier. They will be more relaxed, we will be more relaxed and the information between us will flow and we will be able to give you more of their thoughts perhaps giving more information of their earth life. It would then be easier for then to relax and draw the memories of their earth life to the fore and relay them to you.

We do not suddenly change. If we were a person on earth that liked to tell a grand story and exaggerate ourselves we will do the same in spirit. If we are of a modest personality and do not give you the full worth of our character we will not suddenly change when we go to spirit. What we give you is the essence, the vibration that we are perceiving.

Be wary when you are told that a particular person is present and they are saying certain things because if it is someone you have known on earth and they give a similar personality that is evidence for you. If it is somebody you have not known personally but have heard of via another person you may not recognise the description because they describe themselves within their character. i.e. a modest person would not give you a full description of their good points".

I have been given understand that there is a date set for when we come to earth but is there also a date set out for our return home to spirit. I also understand that we have a path of destiny and if we take our own life that is a mistake and we have to come to terms with this experience.

"There is an end to your existence on earth but dates and times are man made. The duration of your stay on earth not exactly to a certain day is determined but around about a date. You are destined to experience so many things during your existence on earth. You are here to experience for yourself and to learn but also part of your path of destiny is to teach others and to share with others. You are learning and experiencing but also you are destined to touch other paths while you are on your earth journey.

Sometimes those on earth become very weary and question why they are still here because they have experienced all they want to experience and they want so much to go home. They understand there is another existence and they want to go home to spirit. You are not isolated because you are touching many other lives at the same time and in your destiny there may be an experience of meeting someone you have not yet met. That one also has free will so sometimes there has to be an adjustment until your two paths come together.

This goes much deeper. Many of those that you touch during your earth existence are those you have known before you came on your earth journey. You are destined to come to earth at the same time, walk your own path, experience your own existence but sometime in that journey you are destined to meet each other as an earth entity. Sometimes there has to be an adjustment until your paths cross and you give each other something.

Is it also true that we are judged by our own conscience?

No one is judged. You judge yourself. All of us abide by natural law. We are all part of creative energy. We are all linked one to another because we have all come from the same spark of creation and what you do affects another because another is also a spark of the same creative energy. This is why it is important not to send out thoughts of harm to others because you are linking each other together. You are walking the same path and sharing the same existence with others but you do have your own thoughts, ideals and path to travel but you are all the time sharing".

We are also told that we see our whole life before us when we come back home and see the mistakes we made and judge ourselves. We can see our mistakes and we work in spirit to atone for those mistakes. Our own conscience is the judge of this. Is that right?

"We all come home to spirit and we all have experienced things during our earth existence. We do recall what has happened during our life but we have to learn to help those that we did wrong to but we also have to learn to forgive ourselves. You cannot carry guilt with you. You can blame yourself and say that you did not do as well in a situation as you should have done but you must see why you behaved as you did. Everyone behaves in a certain way for a reason. If you are repentant and you feel guilt you are not growing and progressing. You have to acknowledge and accept that you behaved in that situation for a particular reason. If there is someone that you did something to that you are unhappy about you then have the opportunity to ask them for forgiveness. By asking them for forgiveness you are making a positive thought towards them and by undoing the unhappy vibration between you, you are acknowledging yourself. You can then forgive yourself. If you carry that repentance forward you are not progressing. I am not saying you will throw that event aside saying you should not have done that but it was the situation you were in at that time. You cannot expect someone else to forgive you because you have to learn to forgive yourself and understand why you behaved as you did. You can look at the situation and try to overcome the situation".

It is not true that we are told where we went wrong?

"You know this yourself. You understand natural law. So much is clouded from you are in an earth body but you are all part of the creative force that has to live within natural law. If this is not so there is an imbalance. If there is an imbalance this is when you have problems. There are problems with your planet, with countries, with nations and individuals. This is why we say to you, my friends, it is good to send thoughts to other far lands to help other people that are in need but start with yourself. Look at yourself, accept yourself for what you are. You are not perfect, I am not perfect, your fellow sitters are not perfect but we all aspire to be perfect. Accept that you are an individual that at this moment is spirit within a human body and you are stretching yourself and aspiring to progress. You have your faults and we all have our faults. Love yourself for what you are. Accept that you have faults but wish to improve on those faults. Acknowledge that you are weak and are not always able to overcome your faults but you sincerely wish to. Love yourself for who you are. Do not despise your weaknesses but love yourself and you will grow. Once you have learned to love yourself look at those around you, your nearest and dearest. Sometime it is difficult because it is easier to see the faults of those that are near to you than those further afield. Therefore, you are more critical of them because you can see similarities within you. Love them for their faults and for who they are. In turn respect them for loving you. Stretch your thoughts then to those a littler further afield. If the whole world did this the whole world would be in harmony but, alas, the whole physical world would not be here because it would not be a physical world anymore. Start with yourself and love yourself. Do not be too critical of yourself. I am not saying ignore your faults and not to try to improve on them but accept that you have faults. Try to overcome them but do not be too harsh on yourself".

After some deep discussion regarding earth problems John continues by reminding us to count our blessings.

"We cannot alter your path of destiny or take away your problems. You are here experience. Do not look at them as problems but as experiences. You are here to grow and to experience. If you did not have these hurdles on your path you would not experience. If you can imagine any event in your life that you have gone through; it can be a vast hurdle or a small stone on your path but something that has happened to you. Can you say that when you have experienced that you are the same person as before you had that experience? Has it altered you? Has it changed you? Has it broadened your vision? Have you touched others during that experience that you would not have touched normally? Have you shared something with them? Have they learnt something from you? Have you learnt something from them?

We cannot sweep your path clean so that you are just walking on clouds. What is the point of coming to earth? When you go home to spirit you will see how you have grown and how your experiences have changed and altered you. Also how those that you have met and shared your existence with have shared with you and you have shared with them. You have learnt from each other. You do not know what your path is in the future. You do not know what you wish to achieve when you go home to spirit or what path you wish to tread. You may wish to assist others in a certain way and what you have experienced in your earth existence will give you the tools to be able to assist those ones that you wish to help. This is because that experience has helped you.

I hope I have given you something to think about. Do not be too concerned about the whys and wherefores so that you do not enjoy your existence. While you are taking on so many problems and hurdles you are shutting your eyes to other experiences. You need to open your eyes to what is around you. In your part of the world you are surrounded with much beauty. Your plates are full with food and you are not hungry. You have companionship. You are enlightened ones and have knowledge of spirit that many do not have. You have companionship of friends of your human existence, your animal existence and you have friends that walk with you from spirit. You have many things to be grateful for. Do not be so overcome with your problems that you cannot be thankful for the many blessing that you have that others do not have".

We do take on other's problems that we cannot walk away from.

"You have taken those duties on and are helping others. By helping others you are learning and growing. You are giving strength and support to others. This is all part of your path on earth. What I am saying is do not be so overcome with all these conditions that you cannot enjoy your existence. If you look around you have many things that you are happy to experience. You may have health problems but all humans do but just look at your hand. Your hand is a marvelous instrument of creation. How many movements your hand makes? What can you do with your hand? That is just one part of your human body. Think of the rest of your human body, all your organs working, all your senses, your sight that you see, your ears that you can hear, taste, smell, so many sensations, colour, warmth, cold even is a sensation. Do not be so bowed down with your problems that you do not experience the pleasures of your existence also. Just think of music whether it is someone singing or an orchestra playing. If it is the song of the birds, the ripple of the water. Whether it is the ocean or a stream. So many things that you just take for granted. You are so surrounded by problems you do not notice. If those things were suddenly not there you would wonder where they had gone but they are there everyday but you do not notice.

Thank you for your love. Please continue to send your love out to so many that are at this moment in need in all parts of your world and those that have come home to our dimension. It is a time of change. We have told you this and continue to tell you and we are working and striving to help those that are coming home to spirit. Please send your love but do not be bowed down with all problems because there is light and hope. There is a change of direction and there will be more harmony and love brother to brother and sister to sister but there is this time of change that you have to go through. Help us to help others and by doing this you are helping yourself.

Love be with you".

Given 3 October 1999

NEW ENERGY AND THE PATH OF PROGRESS

You are aware that we have been working for a long while in your earth time to bring about peace and harmony but you wonder where this peace and harmony is and why it is not here. You send thoughts of love out as have so many others. Peace and harmony does not come instantaneously. There is a balance in your world. As with your scales sometimes they tip one way and sometimes they tip the other way. If they tip too much in one direction it causes problems in the opposite direction so this has to be handled carefully and this is what is occurring.

You know of changes with new energy. Mr. Go Forward spoke on the 23 November 1999 of much change of energy at this time:-

LOOKING TOWARDS THE NEW MILLENNIUM

"Just a few words. So you are approaching the time in your world that you call the millennium, a time of change. We have told you of change. Change is occurring, change is ongoing and wheels have been set in motion. There are still many in your world that need prayers.

Many of your people believe that once the clocks chime and you enter a new millennium there will be a different world. Alas, this is not so but it heralds a change of vibration. As your year unfolds and your flowers open in your springtime to a new vibration, a new energy so your world will feel a breath of tomorrow but this has to be striven for. The energy is there but it is for man to use in whatever direction they choose. Yes, there is destiny written for all but there is also free will. This is a new energy, a new vibration and if used for the good of others can bring a new awakening, a new response from human hearts for upliftment and working together to bring peace and love for fellow man. If it is not used for this purpose there could be more problems. So I say to you, in your thoughts send thoughts of hope, upliftment, send thoughts of progress for betterment of all not one supreme over others but harmony and going forward in light.

So much has been worked for, so many lives on your earth have been dedicated to bring peace, so many have worked from the realms of spirit to bring harmony this cannot now be lost. There has to be progress. Light must overcome darkness. Fear causes problems, fear of what might be brings despondency. Face the problems, look them in the eye and say that you can overcome. Light must overcome darkness. For the children of tomorrow there must be hope.

Continue to send your thoughts of love, light, upliftment. Talk of the future as a future of opportunity but not to sit back and expect it to unfurl before you. This has to be striven for. Encourage others to whom you speak to strive for the sake of others towards the light. There is no time to sit back and wait to see what unfurls because you create your own progress. You need to desire from within to go forward. Yes, you read of what might be, you read of what can be but you have to be part of the action yourself with your thoughts. Those ones in your world that are unable to take part in physical activities can still lay foundation for future because they have energy that has been created from experience and this energy can be sent forth to others giving them hope and encouragement. Everyone in your world is important, everyone has a part to play, no one is so insignificant that they have no contribution to make. Encourage all to look forward to the future with hope and each one to do their own part in going forward.

There are many years ahead, many centuries ahead for your world. We cannot foretell and write for you what is to occur but it is important that you are playing your part in leading the way at this time when there is a change of energy and vibration because you are laying the foundation stones for progress. The future will not be always rosy, it cannot be because it is an earth existence but you can sow seeds to help those ones that are to follow to ensure they are carrying the light of truth forward. There will be a time when spirit energy can come closer to earth energy because it is together now, we are not another world away.

You look up into your night sky and you see billions of stars many of your earth years away this is not the same with spirit. We are here with you now, we are sharing your existence but in a capacity man has not been able to define. We have told you that in spirit we do not change, we have similar thoughts, similar desires to when we were on earth so we come to you with love and encouragement for progress. There are many others that would come to you for other reasons so this is why we say to you lift your thoughts, lift the thoughts of those that you come into contact with to a higher vibration so that when that link is made with spirit you draw a higher vibration of light not a vibration of darkness. There are those on your earth that would attract darkness if they desired.

Go forward with these words, highering your vibration to that of love and sense of purpose that you know you can strive upwards towards light. You can enfold this light with others that wish to walk the path, encourage them, give them enthusiasm that there is so much more than the problems they see at this moment. Go forward with love and harmony, always looking ahead, always striving towards light and carrying the beacon with you.

Blessings be with you".

John Lyon continues

"This is a new energy and a new vitality but we have to work together with you and those ones from the realms of spirit to bring about a balance. There are upheavals in your world, there are changes but this was foretold. You look at this with human eyes and you worry and fret. Do not worry and fret. Of course, send out love but send out thoughts of hope, light and upliftment because this is positive energy not fearful energy. This is energy with which we can build to help bring balance so that this new energy can bring progress and wider understanding, wider awareness and spirit can link closer with those of you that are spirit in a human body.

I hope I am not repeating words that have been said before but it is important that they are echoed again, not as reassurance but as a positive statement that things are progressing. You are walking your earth path as so many others are walking their path but you are all walking in destiny, all playing your part. You cannot see the pattern emerging but you have to trust there is a pattern for progress".

A visitor to the group mentioned they had been sitting in their circle and had witnessed 'Mr. Go Forward' transfigure through a member of that circle and asked for confirmation.

"This gentleman links with you, he links with many that are striving for truth. You are part of many that are working together. You do not realise that you are working together, you individually come together in small groups sitting together. You are also linking with many other groups and beyond these groups there is a much vaster network of energy from spirit that are working and coordinating this new change that is occurring.

I have spoken of the balance and this is being coordinated by a team in spirit and this gentleman is part of that team. As you are aware, he came to earth at a time previous to a crisis that was to arise in your land and, in fact, the whole of your world. He came to an earth body, he matured in that earth body, as you all do, destined to be at the fore at the times of darkness in your world. He linked with other leaders in your world that had also come at that time from spirit to be in an earth body to lead your world through this dark period. Of course, he was spirit within a human body when he was on earth, as you are, but he was also spiritually aware. He was aware of spirit and he did link with others from spirit and guidance was given to many at that time. He returned home to spirit but he is still continuing his work steering a course forward, linking with those that work for peace and harmony. He is linking with many groups because you are all joined to each other in a common purpose. He will not call himself a figurehead, he will not call himself anyone of importance because he wants to be part of team. We are all part of team, all playing a role and he is joining with you.

To answer your question, he does link with your group and at that time he wished to make his presence known".

Will he return to earth at all again?

"When the time is right. It may not be for many of your earth years but should a need arise that you need his expertise he will again return but that is for the future. Many say he came to earth to serve a purpose, that is so but he came to earth as a very wise counselor to serve at that time and he continues that work now".

I have a puzzle; as we approach the millennium are we just going to drift over into it or are we going to see some major changes in the first days and weeks?

"The millennium, as you say, is a date on your calendar. It is a date that has been aspired to for many centuries. When I was on earth, we would talk of another era that was so far away we could not envisage it. There is a change of vibration and energy but nothing is instantaneous. You have seen many changes over the last few decades of this century that you are now in, gradual change and as you are approaching the millennium the changes are escalating. There are many occurrences that you wish would not occur because they are causing problems but his has to be. As you approach the actual day, the actual time there will be no instant unfolding of something different. There will be a change but it will be gradual.

Those sensitive ones of you will feel a change of energy, a change of vibration. Many are asking questions, many are seeking, many are wanting a change in their earthly lives, I am not talking of spiritual awareness. Many are feeling, enough they want a change of direction and want to do something different. This is your perception of a new energy, you are sensing this and feeling the change of energy. There are also many that are questioning why they are on earth, what is the purpose and what happens when they are not on earth any more. They wonder what has happened to those that have gone before them where they were before they came to their life on earth. So many questions and this is why we have said to you that we are training teachers because so many questions are being asked.

Also there are many wise souls that have already come to your earth and there are more that are coming to your earth to exist in a human body who will shoulder these responsibilities and they grow and take on adult status. They will be wise ones that people will listen to. They will speak words of wisdom that people will be able to understand. They will be in positions of prominence and people will listen and accept their words. This is all for the future but it is happening now and you are living through this and are helping by laying foundations stones.

Your new year heralds your new millennium. As the days of the year go forward and in your part of the world you approach the springtime there will be a change of energy. Your plants will feel this, your animals will feel this and also you will feel a new awakening. It will not be from one day to the next but it will be gradual. From the despondency of the year you have just experienced with all its problems you will be able to see just a spark of something better, something encouraging, something that you can build on. It will not be instantaneous but you will think that you are going forward and putting some of the problems behind you.

You have to be very careful because there will be many that will expect wonderful things to happen at the sound of your bells chiming in the new year and when they find there is no evident change they will be unhappy and depressed. This is not a good energy. There may be despair because they are looking for something that is not there. Try to send thoughts of upliftment, thoughts of hope and thoughts of light to uplift and to keep up the momentum of hope. As this energy unfolds spirit draw close but, as you know, in spirit we are similar to what we were when we were in an earth body and not all in spirit are enlightened. Those ones that are in despair, those ones that surround themselves in gloom and despondency they can also attract those vibrations and it is important at this time that the energy is used for upliftment and higher energy. Therefore, try to send your love on a beacon of light. If each of you sends a beacon of light those lights can join together and grow much brighter one to the other. Everyone is important, everyone can carry this light forward".

It would be nice John if you could give this message to every circle that sits so that we can all do it.

"Every circle that sits have their ones that come and talk to them. Everyone that sits who wants to go forward, not for selfish reasons but for betterment of others, already knows this".

The snag is that the expectations are being raised so, so, high that there will be many that will be despondent and will need help.

"Mankind want things now! Spirit are aware of this.

Thank you for listening to me".

Given 28 November 1999

LINKING AND GREETING SPIRIT COMMUNICATORS

"You were aware of many here this evening from spirit, my friends, there were many more. It is difficult to synchronise so many. Each comes on their own energy vibration. You each have an energy vibration which you throw to the centre of your room. Each of you blending together. Those that wish to communicate with you from spirit also bring their energy and it is a merging. It is a mass of energy and as one comes and goes another comes, and again there is an adjustment because each one is different.

We try to assist those that come for a particular purpose. There are some that wish just to come to say,' Greetings' and that is good because it is a way of communicating, it is a way for them to make a link. Also, there are others that wish to come for a deeper purpose, with an intent, perhaps to ask for help for elsewhere, perhaps to make you aware of some area of concern. Perhaps they are linking with someone at this moment in an earth body and your thoughts linking with that one from spirit you are able to send your love to that one on earth who is in need of perhaps healing, upliftment, guidance at this time. This may be something that you are not able to do in your ordinary earth world but in this time here together, joining in thought with their loved one from spirit, you are able to send love on another level of vibration.

It is good to greet your friends, your loved ones, helpers, companions from spirit. It is natural, it is a time of enjoyment but it is for a purpose. Energy goes from here out to where it is needed and this is very important work".

John replies to a question concerning a family sensing a spirit presence within their home. There was concern because there were young children within the family and the parents did not wish the children to be frightened.

"Children have very vibrant energy and they are not so much weighed down with the vibrations of your earth world. They are open to spirit much easier to the more senior members of the family who are obviously concerned with the mundane running of their existence. Children come with a lively, vibrant energy. They are spirit, as you all are spirit, within but their spirit is more vibrant because of the circumstance of earth, the worries, the cares, the frustrations have not dulled their energy and their spirit vibration. They are sensitive to vibrations that are around. To them it is natural. It is only when fear introduced, fear perhaps from people outside the family speaking of events, fear that they perhaps perceive from others. Fear is contagious, it is a vibration as love is a vibration. If there is a spirit in this home that wishes to make their presence known ask mother to send love to someone in spirit that she respects, who she has love for, who she trusts. Ask her to send love, perhaps to a senior member of the family who has gone home to spirit and say, 'please assist in this condition, if there is one here in this home please surround this one with love.' No ill feeling, no fear because this is a negative vibration but surround this one with love and send this one on its way.

There are so many in spirit that seek love. They have gone home to spirit but they have perhaps had lives on earth where they have not been loved and they are still seeking for that love. Instead of leaving behind the problems of their earth life they are still looking to solve those problems, not intentionally to cause problems to others but it is a lack of understanding, a lack of knowledge that there is so much more open to them. Perhaps they have been taught whilst on earth that when you die you go to sleep and you are woken when the time is right, when everyone shall arise from their sleep. These ones have come home to spirit but they are still in a mist, they are still in a in-between stage, not able to take that step towards the light to meet their ones that are waiting to greet them because of the condition of their mind when they went home. Instead of going forward they are looking back trying to find love. In your thoughts of healing also send thoughts to those that are at this stage to help them on their way. It is a mindful condition that they have taken with them from the earth world and they are locked in this 'time warp' where they cannot break through that barrier. Eventually their loved ones are able to reach them but if we can help them on their way and make that easier for them it is so much better".
Given 21 April 2000

ORGANISATION OF SPIRIT - AN INSIGHT

Mafra explaining the organisation from higher levels and the known spirit links with other groups.

"We are all being organised. This is above our group. You know that Mafra (myself) and Running Bear are perhaps, fathers of group, we have been with you from the beginning, we have been protecting, watching and guiding you. We are guardians of your group but other groups have their own guardians of their group, but above this are the organising team and they are the ones who are organising us. It is all part of the plan. They let us work and find our own level together until we come to a point in the road where we have to link with others, then there is a higher level of organisation. As you have learnt to be compatible with each other in your group, different levels of understanding coming together we on our part have also drawn other from spirit to come to you. There again, we have learnt to work together but we still bring new visitors to you and they are learning to link in harmony with the rest of the group. We as a group have to learn to work together with other groups, so this is where the higher level of organisation is coming into force. Looking above that level, there is a still higher level organising. Each one has some other vibration organising them.

We are still here as a group and will continue as a group, bringing to you new ones because this is important for teaching. Not only are we bringing you those who wish to teach but we are bringing others who just need to learn and they learn here with you".
Given 15 July 1998

SPIRIT CHILDREN

Mafra explaining about a young spirit called Katie who has started communicating with us. We have ascertained she was about 8 or 9 years of age when she went home to spirit.

"You will think why does a child come and talk? It was previously explained to you how spirit is created. The information given was that these spirits sometime come to earth and lead an earthly life. Other newly created spirits may go to a level in spirit dimension that is close to the earth vibration but then they develop, mature and evolve in spirit. The still have a lot to learn in other ways but this is a question for another time.

What I am coming to tell you is that Katie is a young spirit who came to earth for a very short while, a few years of your earth time. She did not grow to be a woman but she went home to spirit after a few years of earth time. She touched earth, she has earth memory but because she is a young spirit she is now evolving in spirit dimension. Part of her evolvement is to touch earth again but she is touching earth through coming to talk to you. As the only memory she has of earth is as this child she comes as this child. She cannot come as a lady because she never grew to be a lady on earth, but of course in spirit she is evolving. As a result of only touching earth for a short while she is not tainted with earth's problems as others of us who grew to more mature years. She is a very sweet soul, very pure soul but to help with her evolvement she is touching earth again to learn from you, also to learn with you. This is why she comes as a child.

You know that while you are on earth you are a spirit within a human body, you are spirit who happens to come to earth and live in an overcoat of a human body. When you go home to spirit your spirit is then free and your spirit then returns to the level of evolvement that it is compatible with in what you call the spirit world. If a child on earth goes home to spirit they will not always stay as a child because they might be a very wise spirit that came to take on that child's body. Once they have become acclimatised to their spirit condition they may not stay as a child because they are much wiser than a young spirit, they are more mature so they go to another level of evolvement. Katie is a lively, bright, young spirit and she is evolving in spirit so to help her evolvement she comes to join you and learn with you".

Mafra was then asked 'Will she gradually evolve to become an adult communicator?'

"Gradually you will see a little change, gradually she will become more accustomed to the earth condition. She spoke to you telling you she had been with you when you had younger earthly people visiting your home earlier today. As she touches earth she sees other people on earth and she links with their vibrations, she is not attaching herself to them but she is linking with them, so she is able to gradually mature as an earth child would. Of course, she is not an earth child she is spirit. If she wishes to continue to visit and talk, perhaps bringing knowledge from spirit she may gradually evolve into a more mature personality. If she wishes to come and give deeper words of wisdom she will need to do this because she cannot do this in the framework of a child. Although this child is pure and brings a lot of love there is a limit to the knowledge a child can bring. You can learn a lot from a child, simplicity, but if she wishes to bring deeper knowledge she will need to evolve, creating a different personality. We do not know yet which path she wishes to pursue it is her choice.

She has evolved in spirit, she is no longer a young child in spirit but because she is touching her earth memory she is coming as a young child. You are all children, you can all remember your childhood and at times of revelry you can go back to that childhood in your dreams. You can daydream, I do not mean unconscious dreams, I mean you can daydream and member things you did as a child. No one can take that memory away from you because the feeling of being a child is there inside you".
Given 19 July 1998

BLESSINGS GIVEN BY SPIRIT

We had been reading an article that stated that certain spirit helpers had earned the right to bestow blessings and we asked Mafra how this is organised.

"Who has got the authority to bless? You all have the authority to bless and you all can bless each other to a certain level. You are talking deeper, as for example when Brother John comes and blesses you. Someone with more advanced wisdom, someone who has evolved to a higher level of progress. You all can bless, children come to you and you have them on your knee you talk to them, you love them and you do your best to give them your love, in a way that is a blessing but you are talking of a blessing from a higher level.

Those ones that have come from a higher level of evolvement to touch earth, to communicate with earth, to share their wisdom, these ones bring with them a blessing. This is because of the dimension they have come from. I will give you an example; on your earth you go through many trials and tribulations. As you go through these various events you come out the other side, hopefully, a little wiser, you have gained something from each experience. We have said to you before that you must look at your problems as experiences. When you come through these problems you have learnt to turn them round and treat them as experiences. This is an example of your earth life.

You know you are spirit inside earth dimension. Your spirit is very wise because your spirit has come from spirit for the experience of your earth life. You may be a very wise spirit in an earth body so you may be able to bless here and now, but you may be a young spirit who has not been through these experiences. What I am trying to explain is, if you go through these experiences during your earth life magnify these several times for us from the world of spirit. How many experiences have gone through before you have touched earth? How many experiences you are going through during your earth life? You go home to spirit and you go through many more experiences and all the time you are learning, you are becoming wiser.

We have told you how you learn when in spirit. You learn by blending energies with those from higher dimensions and through this blending and learning you are progressing. When you touch a higher level of understanding you are given a higher awareness, a higher understanding of the higher levels of spirit. This involves what spirit is and what spirit is about, the true essence of spirit that is within you all. When you have gained this knowledge and wisdom you can look at these experiences through a different dimension. When you contact those who come to you for help whether they are of spirit or from earth you look at them differently. You can see differently their problems and experiences. You can see them as from a distance with much love but you can remain slightly detached. You love them and wish to assist them and you give them your love and help but you are a little apart from them. Through this dimension you are able to bless them because you are able to give them they pure, untainted blessing from pure spirit.

Some of you may have had the experience of sitting in a group where there has been someone come from a high dimension and that one has come around the group and has given each one of the group a blessing. From that time on there is something different about your existence, you are more aware, you have opened out, you can touch spirit easier, the cloud that was there before had gone. I am not saying suddenly you see spirit vividly, I am saying you are more aware of spirit and you are more aware of your path of destiny that involves spirit, your spiritual progress. You become more aware of how you are linking and working with spirit, and how you are going forward with spirit. The higher one has given you a blessing and this blessing has triggered something within you that has opened you as if you were a flower in bud and the flower starts to unfurl. The rest is for you, they have given you the blessing, the trigger to open and it is for you then to pursue. Many pursue but some decide to keep their flower closed but this is your own personal responsibility.

You can all bless each other. You do not have to be special to give a blessing but the blessing you were asking of is a little deeper. My friend who does healing, when those come to her for help she asks those who connect with her in spirit to give a blessing to her patients. With spirits help she is able to give this blessing. You can all give blessings but the higher evolved you are the purer the blessing".
Given 16 August 1998

THOUGHT PICTURES

"You each decode differently. There is no sign for one that is the same for another as you each decode in your own way. Sometimes you try to convey a thought to someone else and by doing this you are, yourself turning this thought into a picture to help you to expand on the energy of this thought. Quite often this picture is something that is formed from your own memory, your own reasoning. You perhaps, remember something that was said to you as a child or whatever and you are portraying this. I will give you an example; perhaps someone who is just becoming aware of spiritual knowledge is asking the question as to whether they have a guardian angel. You would probably, visualise those spirit companions who walk with you and make a mental picture of what you think they look like. Someone who is not so far along their path may visualise a guardian angel with wings and a halo because this is a picture that triggers from perhaps a childhood story book or something someone has said to them. A thought is energy and you are decoding that energy into a picture from your own reasoning so you can hang on to this thought for a little longer and try to convey this thought to someone else.

Thought pictures - this is energy you have transposed into a picture so that you can retain that thought for a little longer. You can recall that thought again in future. If I said to you next week the same as I am saying to you now you will recall the picture you made previously. Another example is perhaps a picture of scenery that you may visualise during meditation, a place of peace and serenity. By making pictures it is easier to re-enter that peace and serenity. Each person will create a different picture according to their personal preference. Everybody is different so everybody's thoughts will be different, hence everybody's picture will be different.

There is not such a thing as a thought picture it is something that you create. You may say that when spirit communicates through a medium spirit gives that medium a picture so that the medium knows what they are talking about. Look at it another way, the spirit friend is giving a vibration and that medium is decoding the vibration into a picture. Who creates the picture, the medium or the one in spirit who is giving it? It is a decoding.

This is why you are all different because you all perceive in a different way. Some of you perceive pictures, some perceive sound, some sense, some perceive an aroma, you all decode differently. You are all individuals so why should you not be different? You are not all copies of each other but you are individuals and therefore you are different. No two spirits are the same. Every creative energy is different, no creative energy whether they are encased in a human body or they are free of the human body can be the same. Each has had their own experiences and memories therefore everyone must be different. You may have two siblings who have come from the same parents but they are different, think how you multiply this with spirit families. How many come from the same spirit family but all are different".

Given 16 August 1998

TALKING OF ENERGY

"Your world today is in too much of a hurry, stand back and take in energy because when you rush around you spend your energy. You need time to absorb because there is so much energy around you. When you walk among trees where there is so much energy stored it is vibrant. You walk on path that is well trodden, many feet have trodden that path, many have walked as you and taken in energy, been revitalized with energy. You take but you also give. So around and around in a circle. This is good.

Also look around at sky and hills. You do not observe that there are also creatures in undergrowth. They are dormant when footsteps are around but they are also underground. They are all part of circle of energy. They are alive and vibrant. They also give energy as you give your energy. You commune with nature because you are all one and part of Great Spirit. This is all part of creation's plan. All have place in system. You learn to respect each other. This is good.

I have spoken before of energy so I will not reiterate again but you are aware different areas have different energy. You can be on a hill surveying area this is strong energy of its kind. You can be by seashore with waves rolling in this is also strong energy but different energy. You can be by cliffs at seashore or at flat ground level and both have energy but different energy. You can be in a busy street but there is still energy but different energy. Grass is way below your footsteps but once there was grass there and beneath all your manmade materials there is soil and in that soil there is energy. You have much energy that man brings some is good but some is not so good but there is also natural energy coming up through your pavements and roads because there is ground beneath. Also there are trees in many of your streets. These are your lifeline in your city streets, these breathe and give oxygen. Also there are many of your people in busy street they also have much energy. Your bricks that come from substance in ground are used to build tall buildings these also have energy.

You also have your electricity this is energy that is utilized by man. Man has learnt to control this energy but without control it could become destructive. You understand there is much energy within the vibration of your electricity. Man has discovered sources of energy electricity is one and you think you are very clever because you have created this but it is created from elements and forces that nature has provided. Man has learnt to harness this.

You think for one moment on water. Water flows gently along stream, tranquil but think of the energy in water. How water through your history has been used as a living source to provide you with liquid a life giving fluid but also to work your machines. Going back in your history to times when you had many mills in your land many of these were driven by water. Water is used in industry in your land. It has been used in your farming communities. You know of water that at present is being used to generate electricity. You know of water that is stored in vast quantities for use by your towns and cities. There was a time when there was sufficient without storing so much. You say you have become much more civilized as your population has grown and demands much more energy. You need to continue cycle of water. You use water and it is discarded but it is used again and this goes round and around. You turn on your tap and it is there. You do not think where this comes from. When your ancestors had to gather water and feel weight of water they knew the value of water. Water was a precious commodity because of the effort in gathering the water whether it was gathered from well, stream or from pump they realized how precious this commodity was and how essential it was to their life. It is now so easy for you to have water you do not think where this has come from. You do not realise how much you are using, how you are draining earth's vitality. Yes, you utilize water again and again but what are you doing to that water?

I have come away from path, I was just explaining to you about energy because energy is all around and we traveled from hill to ocean side to city street trying to explain energies under feet, above you, around you and you are part of this energy. You are part of this living vibration of energy, you take and you give. It is impossible for you not to be part of it. You exist in your world so you have to be part of this chain of energy. You have to partake and in partaking you in turn have to give.

This is your natural world but also it is the same as spirit what you take you return. You cannot keep you have to continue cycle of using energy whether it is energy for your human world or energy for spirit. It is a continuous chain of events. You commune with spirit, we share energy with you, you share your energy with us and in turn this energy travels on to others, they in turn send energy to others, and others, eventually energy comes back to you from another source. Not the same source but another source. You are all part of chain.

We have told you of links with others who like yourself are seeking truth but I am not talking just of those that are seeking I am talking of those who do not know they are seeking. They are walking in darkness not knowing that there are opportunities opening for them to discover more and find more to their existence. Your energies that are being circulated are helping to bring a light to darkened world. You remember times when you were seeking, you had questions, you had doubts and uncertainties but gradually you were given answers little by little. Not too much at once because this is not so good. So as you have been taking energies of others who have been working before you, you are now returning that energy to others in turn who are in darkness and doubt. Perhaps they do not realise they are in darkness and doubt because they are content with their blinkered existence not being aware of anything else to absorb. Gradually their blinkers are taken away and they look elsewhere and their perspective is different it is broadening and they are realizing this is an awakening. They, in turn, will learn more of spirit and take on the responsibility of spreading knowledge to others. It is continuous this is why we say to you 'you do not know how far our words and your words travel.'

Your role is to pass knowledge on but you do not go after and chase. Once others take these words they take on the responsibility for themselves. If they wish to use these words it is a base for them to learn and stretch themselves. They also have those from spirit who work with them who will assist them. It is information, enlightenment and a starting point for many. It opens discussion, questions, unlocks the door and gives others an opportunity to say 'I do not understand this, why?' Then there is discussion and others bring in their ideas. What is truth for one is not truth for someone else. It depends where you are on your stage of evolvement and how you understand. Advancement is not reliant on going through one stage before you take on the next.

You are all evolving at different levels and evolving for different reasons. You are in an earth body at this time but more important you are spirit and you just happen to be in an earth body for a short while. If you lived to be 100 years it would still be a short while. Each spirit is evolving at a different level, at a different rate for a different reason. You understand that what is right for one bring questions for others. You have your knowledge and experience that your spirit has brought with it from its other dimension and this knowledge and experience may not be evident while you are in your earth body. You only bring with you the tools you need for your journey through the earth world. These are the tools for your 'walk.'

I listen to words that are spoken on your earth world and as different generations are born to your world different expressions are used. You have an expression at this moment that is being used more often now and it will become more prevalent as the next few years take place because there is this awakening and enlightenment. These words are very fitting for this time as it is an expression that perhaps your younger generation use than the senior members of the community. It is 'You walk the walk.' If you think on what this means — only you can walk your walk. No one can walk the walk for you. The tools you bring with you from spirit are the bare essentials for you to walk the walk. We 'walk the walk' with you but we cannot 'walk the walk' for you, each has to 'walk their walk' themselves.

I leave you with these words and may your walk be fruitful. I have tried to bring this in at the end of my little talk because I started with your walk absorbing the energy of the earth and I have taken you on various walks whether country, seashore or city and tried to explain to you the energy of those physical walks. Now I leave you to ponder on your spiritual walk. I have given you the tools you now 'walk the walk.'"
Given 20 September 1998

This was given after Running Bear's words on the same date. Mafra responds to a question sent in a sealed envelope, this was not opened until Mafra requested. The question being 'As I understand it everything in the universe is made of vibrations, it is the frequency of a vibration that gives the appearance of solidity etc. to our limited senses. It follows that other planets and people can exist sharing the same space and I would like to know of people or spirit entities from other worlds communication through our trance mediums. I have often heard the words listening 'to adjust and understand your world' from our spirit friends.

"Running Bear prepared well for what was to come. He was laying foundation for me to follow. He was talking of energy from your physical world that you live in, the energy and vibrations that are around you. He touched briefly on the energy from spirit and how this was all part of the chain of events.

Your friend asking the question mentions vibrations. Everything around you that appears in your physical world to be solid you know is not solid because of frequencies. You know of atomic structure. Everything in your physical world that you think is solid, of course, is broken down into tiny particles and is involved in a molecular structure that is all the time vibrating. I am not continuing on this subject as it has been spoken of before. Although it is part of your existence and earthly life we are not involved in this so much because we work on a different vibration but I will come to that later.

You are part of your world and you are part of spirit because you are a spirit within a human body and you have brought energy with you of this spirit. A spirit within a human body is ageless, it has been in existence for much evolution. It has evolved through much evolutions and has become wiser and has carried with it its memories and experience and at the moment I am speaking to you it resides in an earthly body. You are part of earth and you are part of spirit but you are also part of a much wider expanse of universe. You know your universe is all the time moving and changing. There is much of your universe that has not been discovered by human man. You are aware of many planets, structures and you know of your solar system and all that contains. Beyond there are many more structures that man is not aware of. I am not here to reveal all these other structures because what is the purpose? You do not need this at this moment in your time.

I must confess myself I have not delved too deeply into this because I have followed the path that is of my interest and my experience I am not of a scientific mind. Perhaps you query the use of the word 'mind' but I am involved in education so I spend more of my energy seeking, searching and trying to work in this field than in the scientific field. There are many that work in the scientific field and this their choice and they are able to work thus.

You are talking of vibrations. Yes, vibrations are different depending on where you are at your point in evolution. Whether you are in a physical condition, or free from the physical condition and being pure spirit. Whether you are a human, animal, part of the earth energy or part of the energy of the other parts of the solar system. We have spoken to you before of a fingerprint, each has their own fingerprint but on a wider scale each collective existence. You are part of the human world at this moment in time so you have that vibration if you were part of another dimension in another part of the universe you would have another energy that would be the fingerprint of that existence.

When we come to earth, I do not mean we come on a journey because we are near you all the time because our dimension intermingles your dimension. Your dimension exists on one frequency and ours exists on another frequency but we are intermingling our energy, we are compatible, different but compatible. This is why we are able to come and commune with you why we are able to merge our energy and why we are able to give you impressions, pictures, sound, noises, aromas. Why we are able to move the object and bring apports. It is because we can intermingle our vibration. You are human in a human world but you are also spirit so you see there is a compatibility. You have taken on earth vibration and earth vibration in comparison to spirit is very heavy, slow and dense. We are able to break through this denseness we alter our vibratory level from the very quick level, rapid, bright, vibrant. It as if we come into a fog. That perhaps more senior of your years who will read these words may remember in times past on your earth when you had a particular kind of fog not the mist you have when you have a hazy morning or evening I mean a very think fog. This fog being so thick that you are unable to get your bearings and you become disorientated, you do not know what is beside you and if you turn round you do not know which way you are facing. It is a similar vibration for us when we penetrate earth's vibration but we have learnt to come through this. When we first experience this we have problems but as always we are given help and guidance by those that have had the experience of penetrating this condition before. As I assist others to come to talk to you, others assisted me when I came for the first time.

We learn how to change our vibration. We slow our vibration down, we slow our energy down until we become compatible with the earth frequency and we can penetrate this and reach you. You also have the ability of changing your frequency. Perhaps you do not realise you do this, you not set out to do this but you are altering your frequency when you are stretching out to commune with spirit.

You also have been taught that when you commune with spirit you shut out your outside world, you leave outside your room that you are sitting in for communication your worries, frustrations and all the problems of your earth day. You have been told 'leave those outside you do not want those.' The simple act of leaving those concerns outside and shutting them away you are increasing your frequencies. You then speak to spirit, to whomever you wish, you may say Divine Spirit, Heavenly Father, White

Spirit or whatever name you wish to call the supreme essence. You are lifting yourself by saying these words. You are also asking for the white light of protection so you are raising your vibration to a vibration that is above your earth condition. This is when you have to be careful because if you do not do this you are not lifting your vibration. You are opening yourself to spirit of any level and some dimensions of spirit are very near your earth dimension so those who may come and commune with you will not be very far removed from the condition you are in already. Some may even be in a lower condition than yourselves. This is because you are opening yourself to any who may wish to be attached. This is why we say to you ask for the white light of protection, stretch yourselves to commune with those from the highest vibration and by doing this you, yourself, are changing your vibratory frequency. You are raising your vibratory frequency as we are lowering ours to join you. Somewhere in the middle we are compatible".

The question also asked about others from other parts of the universe who wish to commune also. There are others from other parts of the universe but as I have explained their level of vibration and frequency is again different. There are those from other frequencies who are able to commune with your world. There are other, perhaps wiser more evolved ones, who do exist. Perhaps not in bodies similar to your bodies but they are living essences that are part of the universe. You must not think that because another part of the universe has some living essence they will be a replica of a human body. They will be a different frequency and if you could see them they would appear in a different form. As some of your people in your world insist that those in spirit always have a spirit body, arms, legs, head, eyes, they sit down at a table and eat and drink existing as you exist. We have explained to you when you go home to spirit you go to whatever dimension you have created for yourself and there are dimensions that are very close to earth level and you will envisage spirit people as earth people.

The more advanced you become the more you realise that you do not need a body in spirit your frequency is different. If I wish to portray myself as Mafra as I was on earth I could show you myself in Mafra's human form. Why would I want to cumbersome myself with that body all the time? So it is the same with others in different vibrations and frequencies they perhaps are in a different form but this does not mean that they do not have intelligence and they do not have a desire to bring love. As you on your earth wish to discover other parts of your earth, you are not content to stay in one part of your earth and you wish to travel from one place to the other so these more enlighten ones who are perhaps in other parts of the universe wish to explore other parts of the universe and they have been able to do this. They may not travel in space ships as people in your world portray when they write stories because we travel but we do not travel in space ships. We are able to travel from one place to another.

I am trying to give information without giving alarm or fear because I do not know where these words are going and I do not want to create facts that are not facts. If you listen and you have an impression of what someone is telling you and you do not understand it fully you make your own picture. You make your own image of what you think is being told to you. If I say the wrong thing now and someone who is reading this will draw a mental picture of something or someone that exists in a part of your universe in a different vibration and frequency and this will cause problems. It may be passed on to others and before you know where you are you have a new creation that is not as it should be.

Yes, there are other frequencies and vibrations that are able to intermingle. It is not something that you have to fear. It is not something that is going to come and overrun earth, you will not be tied up with little green men taking you a prisoner. We are talking of an advanced intelligence, we are talking of much wisdom. We are talking of a level that is above earth level. We are talking of a level that is highly evolved. There are energies that intermingle and are on different vibrations and frequencies.

"I have tried to explain to you how we change our vibration and frequency to merge with you and how you without knowledge and awareness are doing the same thing. It is a natural function, you are doing this naturally. As I have said to you when I spoke of healing I explained it was natural and your merging your energy with us is also natural because you are only merging your energy with another spirit energy. You are spirit first and foremost. All you are doing is discarding for a short while of your earth time your earth condition and your spirit is free to join in vibration those on the same vibratory level. You are taking off your physical overcoat for a very short while and releasing your spirit so that your spirit is free. You will have to return to your physical condition and take on your physical overcoat and lower your frequency and vibration. When you are doing this you are not severing the connection with your earthly body. Your earthly body is still here and the conditions of your earth are still here you are just subduing those conditions for a short while. If something should occur and you need to be aware of your physical condition you are there you haven't gone away. You have just subdued the condition. If something happened in your room, something fell over and touched you and you had to take evasive action you would in your human body and you would make a human reaction. You wouldn't be apart from your human body. It is very difficult to put into words but you are just subduing those frequencies while you are communing with spirit but you are not severing them. It is not the same as when you are asleep because when you are asleep you are bringing your subconscious into work this is different. What you are doing is subduing your human condition to raise your vibration to that which is compatible with spirit that is your spirit's natural frequency.

I hope this goes a little way to answering the question. I know it is not answering the question completely, I know it is not the answer that is being sought but there is a limit to what I can give at this time because I am very wary of giving words that may travel and give wrong impressions and ideas to others. I do not want people to get some ideas that can be altered, changed and bring fear and alarm because we do not want fear and alarm. Everything that occurs is natural, it is with love, dedication and light and we do not want to bring any thoughts into this that are not of this level. We do not want to bring alarm or fear because once you do this you are lowering the vibrations again and by lowering the vibration you are bringing in conditions that are not compatible. We want to bring love and knowledge that inspires, that opens up and brings about awakening, new thoughts and ideas not those that shut down and bring fear.

You are part of a great universe. There is much interaction between your world, our world and the rest of the universe. How can you perceive that your existence is the only existence there is? As Running Bear would say to you look around you, look up and out at what your physical eyes can see which is very minute in comparison with what exists. Just consider what you can see when you look up into your night sky and you see signs of life that are light years away. This is just what you can see".

AN EXAMPLE OF THE DOORKEEPERS ROLE

Following Ararmday's first visit Mafra explains what was occurring with withdrawal of energy.

"He has shown an interest to return and to be become a little more involved so we have given him opportunity. We are there guiding him because he is very enthusiastic and we have to be careful what occurs. He was explaining to you the energy and how we give and take energy. This was good how he explained because I don't think we have spoken before of how this works, how we give energy to someone who is talking and we continue giving energy until it is preferable that they leave the body and return to spirit dimension. Gradually we withdraw energy because it has to be gradual because it would be too great a shock on body if we withdrew suddenly. We introduce them slowly to you, they come and sit here feeling fingers and thumbs, perhaps their face because they are gradually becoming used to a body. We are giving a little more energy but not too much.

If they show a desire to talk we give a little more energy so they can speak and then they fumble to find word and the system of communication. It is easier to just sit here and be in body feeling sensation of body, this needs a degree of energy but when they decide they want to talk it needs some more energy because they have to discover how to communicate. They had a vibration that they change into a thought pattern, so the thought pattern can find a compatible word or expression, or even noise. When E-om-ba came it was a noise. Then they have to discover how to instruct the voice to speak, of course we do not leave them on their own we help but we bring energy at the same time so they can do this. As it is a learning stage we do not let them go too far forward in their first steps because it is difficult for them and we want to encourage them. We want them to leave the body in a state when they were happy and confident so they are happy to come back again. If we leave them too long they become a little fatigued or confused and say 'I do not want to go back again because I was getting in a muddle.' If they just speak for a little while and are confident this is a good time to withdraw energy. We do not say to them 'stop talking come home' because this is not how we work in spirit. We work on vibration and we recognise the vibration, we would not recognise spoken instructions. We would recognise a change in vibration so this is how we work, gradually withdrawing the vibration being used and that one slowly, slowly comes back and leaves body.

This is a way for me to explain what occurs. Of course when I come I am confident so I can go on talking for a long while. I am generating energy because I know how to generate energy but of course when they come at first they do not know how to do this. They rely on us to give them energy. I have the rest of the team here with me, my fellow friends and we are as one. I am here but they are here also merging our energies continuously. When I feel it is time for me to withdraw I can withdraw my own energy but of course this is because I have a little more experience. I am the one who is in control of who comes and who goes.

There are higher evolved ones who are more advanced than myself and if they wish to come to talk who is Mafra to decline their offer? I bow to their superiority. I just ensure the channel is clear and the door is open and they can just walk in. I know my place. It is all in love, there are no disagreements on who comes.

We merge energy and are happy for each other. If one is happy we are happy for them. If one is sad we are sad for them and try to lighten their vibration. We do not draw them down, we do not become envious. If John comes to talk to you and he has given you very clever words we do not say 'he is a lot cleverer than us,' we are not jealous. There is no jealousy, we are happy for each other. We do not say 'that is George he is getting lots of laughs, he is getting a lot of reaction, I don't get that reaction.' We are happy that George gets this reaction, that is his way. It is not my way so much and we are happy for him because that is his vibration. Hannah came and told you about her work in spirit. This is giving you a wider view of our work.

Perhaps you think we are here to stand by and look after you or your group. We do this but it is only part of our work we also have much other work. Of course, we are there for you and will always be there for you. We are always learning, we cannot stay in the same position, we have to learn. Therefore, we will be able to bring more knowledge to you. When you eventually come home to join us you will have much knowledge that we have given you and this will help you. As we share our knowledge with you, you share your knowledge with those you walk with on earth. Those that ask you question you are able to give them words, may not be spiritual words but words that help them with their everyday existence".
Given 3 November 1998

LEARNING TO COMMUNICATE

A question sent from another group who are learning to communicate with spirit - 'We are now able to communicate with our friends and companions through the table. This is very exciting for us all as we do not have a trance medium who 'they' can speak through as yet. I have a question that I hope you are able to answer - Our table friend/controller brought a child spirit to us who was lost in the dark. We were able to direct her to the light, also another child later. Please can you tell me how she was able to use the table or should I say move the table in response to our questions?'

"It is difficult for you to envisage how a child can be lost. A child goes to spirit who has only lived a few earth years, they have not been tainted with the earth conditions as those who grow to a more mature age are affected. Even so when these little ones come home there is always someone there to greet and love them. They may not have their earthly mother and father in spirit or even their grandparents but you must remember they have come from spirit to earth so they have a spirit family and that spirit family is there waiting for them when they return home to spirit after their short stay on your earth.

So you say 'how can they be lost?' Lost is perhaps not a good word. We are again trying to find a word in a language, a tongue to explain a situation that does not exist in your world. If only we could communicate on a vibration and dispose with language but that is not possible. When these little ones come home their ones are there to meet them but sometimes because of the circumstances of their earth life, albeit short. They may come home suddenly or perhaps in circumstance leading up to their passing that was not pleasant and they are bringing these memories with them when leave their earth bodies behind. Due to these vibrations from earth it is difficult for their spirit family to encompass them, surround them with spirit light and to see them safely home.

They are not lost as you would term lost. They are just not awakened. Their spirit family are there waiting for them but they are unable to encompass them in love and light because they are surrounded in a mist. They are not able to see through this mist. They are not able to penetrate this mist, to draw these ones to them. They are not lost, wandering around as a child would be lost on your earth looking for its mother or father. They are in an in-between state, they perhaps cannot understand why their mother or the father cannot see them. They do not realise they are not of your world any more but in the same circumstances they are not able to contact their spirit family and their spirit family are looking at them and saying 'come home to us, you are home with us' but they cannot see them. As the child cannot make contact with the earth family because they are no more of earth, the spirit family cannot make contact with the child because the child has not severed completely their links with earth. They still have these memories and vibrations from earth. I hope these words help you to understand they are not lost just in a cocoon. It is as if they are looking in a mirror and they cannot see through the mirror, it is veiled for them."

The next question was regarding how they are able to move the table.

"These ones that have managed to come to you have help from those in spirit who have been able to make contact with them. They have come a little step further than the child I was explaining to you just now who was in-between. They have those spirit companions whose job it is to greet these young bright souls and bring them safely home returning them to their spirit families. It is these ones that are bringing them to you and acting as their guardian and making their own vibrations known to you by your table. They have to be ones that are wise and are able to communicate with the human world so they are acting as a guardian. They are making the link for that one, paving the way.

If a child on your earth was taken to meet someone for the first time there would perhaps be a guardian or parent there who would say 'this is your Auntie Freda / Auntie Mary' and Auntie Mary would say 'hello, how are you.' That little one would be a little reticent to reply so the guardian would answer for them at first. They would be a spokesperson until the child becomes a little more confident wanting to respond on there on vibration. This is similar to how a spirit child is introduced to you. They would be taught slowly and gradually as they become a little more confident and sure of themselves they are able to communicate with you direct without the intermediary. This is educating the child so that it now knows it is not part of the human world any more because they are having to communicate on a different level. They cannot open their mouth and talk to you as if they would if they were a child of your earth world.

Going through this intermediary way of communication this spirit guardian is teaching this one that the people the child is talking to are of the earth world, they cannot talk to them as they did when they were on earth. They have to communicate in a different way so they are beginning to realise this is the same with their earthly parents. Their earthly parents are not able to communicate with them in the same way. They are realising that they are a step away from their earthly parent and are not part of that world any more. They can visit your earth world and greet you in their own way by vibrations and thoughts. You do not realise that sprit communicates with you all the time on a thought level. These little ones are returning to their earthly homes and they speaking to their parents with their thoughts but the parents do not acknowledge this, they think they are just memories and thoughts in their own minds. This is the only way the child knows how to communicate.

Having come to you and was instructed how to use your table and how to communicate with you. They have learnt that you are of the earth but they are not of the earth any more you are now releasing them to their spirit families and their spirit families can greet them in their love and tenderness. They now can take them to their home in spirit to whatever stage of advancement they are at. They will probably return to you and communicate with you again because you are precious to them, you have helped them on their path. They will want to come and say hello again but perhaps they will not continue to do this. They may do it one or two times and you may not hear of them again. Then perhaps time will go past in your world and they will come back again when they have progressed a little to let you know how they are progressing.

As they went to spirit as a child, even though that child may have encompassed a much wiser soul, they will return to you time and again as a child. They are coming back on that earthly link because they are entering the earth's atmosphere, vibration, the heaviness of earth. So they are coming back on their last link with earth that was as a child. Gradually you may understand if you have the opportunity to hear them talk through a medium they will be talking as a child but the words they give, when you think on, are quite advanced for a child's thoughts. I am taking you now into the future, I am opening the door just a little for you, I am not taking you too far, just giving you a taste of what will come".

Given 17 November 1998

KNOCK, KNOCK IS THERE ANYONE THERE?

Mafra explaining about knockings heard on ceiling during night time.

"The rappings you are speaking of are a movement of energy. It is not necessarily a communication. In your home you have energy that is stored. When you are peaceful and at rest your mind is free and your thoughts are free. You are dreaming and your subconscious is making event occur for you in your sleep but we are not talking of this. This is your subconscious working. We are talking of a higher level. As we are speaking now, you are speaking with your voice and I am using the voice of the medium to reply to you but we are also communicating on another level. When you are at rest you can understand how free you are to communicate on other levels even though your physical body is very much still in its physical state and your subconscious is taking thoughts from your physical mind and going through these thoughts to make sense of them. This is the way your body operates. Your higher senses are free to explore.

This is what is occurring. There is a movement of energy. Your earth is a slow, dense atmosphere. We are communicating with you in this atmosphere. As you are freeing yourself for a short while of your earth vibration and you are communicating with us you are raising your level of vibration, we are slowing ours down. The coming together should be harmonious. It is trial and error, sometimes this does not occur as it should and we have a disturbance of energy that causes this noise. This is the best way I can explain what is happening to you in words. We have to lean to be more gentle. We have to learn to lower our vibration a little more so that we do not cause this disturbance.

We sometimes do this when you are in your room during your day time when we are coming in the evening to talk to you. We are making a disturbance of the energy that makes a sound to make you aware we are here and are preparing for our communication. This is allowed because it is a way of us signaling but we are not still using the same energy to communicate at other times. I am trying to explain something that is on a higher sensory level and it is a movement of energy".
Given 17 November 1998

MORE ON CHILDREN IN SPIRIT

The following question had been sent by a seeker for Mafra to give his views -

'We read that babies and children 'dying' return to spirit as very advanced souls as they have only touched the earth plane. This implies that the longer you are on the earth the soul is deteriorating i.e.

Wonderful when young, pretty useless when old. However, I feel more spiritual every day that passes so I cannot accept that when I am 100 years old my spirit will be 'clapped out.' Your comments will, as always, be very much appreciated.

"We spoke previous before we had this question. We did say that when the child touches earth they sometimes are very advanced souls and they have just come for a short while. That is not implying that your journey on the earth voyage, as you call it, is a downward slope. You are gaining knowledge all the time you are on earth and you are experiencing much. What we implied is that those ones that have perhaps been to earth many, many times and have evolved much in spirit, sometimes there is just a short passage to earth for a reason. Just for a short while to gain a little experience. It does not mean that because they are here on earth for a short while they are not being involved in the conditions of earth. The longer you are on earth the more knowledge you are gaining and you are also meeting many that are treading path with you and you are learning from each other. Perhaps you are learning things that you can only learn in the earth dimension not in other dimensions. You are interacting with each other and you are learning more so the older you grow the more interaction you are having with others on earth so your knowledge is growing and growing.

I try to recall from whence you gleaned the information of souls touching earth for a short while. I believe it was when we were speaking of the creation of spirit. We said that when new souls are created from this high source some come to earth to experience life on earth again, and again, and again. Others choose to evolve in spirit but only come to earth for a short while to gain knowledge. I think this is the context from the previous question. Each has their own path of evolvement. Each has their own way of evolving, developing, experiencing, depending on what they wish to achieve. I will use teaching for an example; if you have chosen this path to be able to teach you must be able to interact with others. To interact with others you need to experience communication with others. You have to experience how others think, how others understand, and by your evolvement you choose a path where you can work with others and understand how to communicate with others, not just by words but by thought and interaction. You do not just listen to others' words and answer them but you try to understand others and try to get behind their words and understand the reasons for these words. They are asking a question but why are they asking that question? This is an example of what you have to learn before you even start to become a teacher. I am just giving this one example. For this purpose you would perhaps choose-an earthly existence where you interact with people a lot more than perhaps you would if you chose a path where you are more withdrawn from others.

Those ones that come from spirit and only come to earth for a short while are choosing a path that takes them in another direction. These directions can be varied; one may be they wish to evolve their knowledge of spirit, to evolve communication in spirit through the different levels of spirit awareness and consciousness, where they can detach themselves from the vibration of earth. They may just, for something in their evolvement need to touch earth for a little while just to get an experience of earth conditions.

We are not saying that those that come to earth and become of great age are going down a 'slippery slope' and when they go home to spirit they will be less evolved than when they came. They will hopefully, have gained much because they have met so many more souls that are walking with them and they have interacted with so many souls. In this way they have gained knowledge from each other because this is how you learn, from each other.

Some choose to learn from going within themselves and their evolvement will take them a different path. They will seek knowledge from within and draw wisdom that way. Each has a different route, different way of evolving. There are so many opportunities, so many paths for you to choose. You may choose one path for an experience then you may decide to choose another path. You have an example of this with Brother John. He chose to withdraw himself from others and take vow of silence during his earth life and then went into deep contemplation and prayer. When he went home to spirit he was used to this solitude, he was used to this isolation even though he didn't have his physical body any more he still continued during his evolvement to not communicate with others but to learn on this other vibration. Then he found he had much knowledge and he wanted to share this knowledge with others but because he had withdrawn for such a long while of his evolution he then had to change his path and alter his vibration a little so that he could learn again to communicate. By returning and speaking, even though it is slowly and calmly, to you he is able to give you his wisdom. He is also giving wisdom through others because he is opening his love to others that are helping you and although he is not talking to you he is giving his knowledge to them so they can give it to you. He is now learning again to communicate.

You can choose a different path. You endeavour to walk a particular route and follow a particular dedicated path of service perhaps, not always, some do not wish to serve. They just wish to exist on their own or mix with others of a similar vibration for other reasons, not particularly for service. Each has their own choice. You each have free will.

Returning to our friend's question. I did not intend him to perceive that the longer you are on earth path the more detached you become from spirit and the less spiritual you become. This was not our intention. Our intention was to endeavour to show you there are different ways of evolving depending on the path you wish to tread. Those who wish to withdraw their energy from intermingling with others and delve into realms and dimensions that are not of earth are able to do this. Others that wish to travel the earth path and through travelling the earth path are able to communicate with others on their journey of earth with them, and learn from each other this way. In return they help each other choose this route. As the children on your earth start in their kindergarten schools at the same time but they all choose their own routes, their own subjects that they wish to pursue. Some are happy to sit at their books and study, others are happy to run around on the sports fields and play games, others wish to take up paint brush and use colours, perhaps others will explore the world of music. They each start in their classroom but they then walk their own paths.

It is a similar story I am trying to give you when new souls are created. Some walk one way, some walk another way. It does not mean that because one chooses one route and other chooses another route that one is progressing at a different rate than the other. You are all progressing at your own pace in whichever choice you have made, whichever dedicated purpose has been chosen.

Continue in your work, I am sure you are gaining knowledge and I am sure you are helping many others. The more people you meet the more you are interchanging and learning from each other and this can only be good. The older in your years you become on earth the wiser you become. In the heat of youth you think you know all the answers, everything is black and white and you can't understand why other do not understand what you perceive to be right. As you mature you then begin to understand there are other views, everything is not black and white, there are other shades in-between. The more you interchange your ideas with others and listen to their views and opinions, and if they are wise they will listen to your views and opinions. If they do not wish to that is their choice, when they are ready to hear your thoughts they will listen. It is not to say your opinion is right or their opinion is right, you come to a compromise in-between".

WHAT IS VIBRATION?

The following question had been sent by a seeker for Mafra to give his views -

Can you explain just what is a vibration. How is this 'lowered' to communicate with us and how best can we raise our vibrations? We are always trying to bridge the gap and any help would be appreciated.

"What is a vibration? We are again down to a language, a tongue, a word to explain something that is unexplainable. We use the word vibration because it is the best word that we can find. The best way I can explain; you understand frequencies in your radio wave lengths that circle your earth. You have a transmitter and a receiver, between these you have these frequencies and you have to tune one to be compatible with others. You have so many vibrations in your air. You have those that come through your radio, you turn the knob and you hear the voice. You have those that you turn on an electric machine and it cooks your food. You have messages used for those that steer ships, fly aeroplanes and other's services. You have to tune into the frequencies you wish to receive so you have to have something that is compatible and you have to choose the right vibration. It is a link, one sending something out and one is receiving and you are linking on a vibration. This is a way of trying to explain.

All the time, everything that is existing is sending out vibrations. You are existing so you have vibration, whether you are in human body or not, you still have vibration because you are existing. As your plants and animals exist, as your very earth exists, so you are pulsating and sending vibration. You have sensed vibration of others, when you are close to others you are aware different people on your earth have a different feeling about them. You come near one person and you shake their hand and you are happy to be in their company but you see another one and perhaps you take a step backwards because you do not feel so comfortable with that one. This is another way of explaining a vibration. You are all the time perceiving, whether you are aware of this or not, you are perceiving others' vibrations and they are perceiving yours.

The question continued as to how spirit lowers their vibration and how you can raise yours to make communication easier. It is not a question of consciously endeavouring to achieve something because if you consciously endeavour you are interfering with the natural flow. Earth's pull and earth's conditions are much slower than the condition that we have in spirit and the more evolved a spirit entity becomes the farther detached they are from the earth condition and the lighter and quicker is their vibration. When we commune with each other in our dimension it is instantaneous, we are not using the thought process that you use on earth. I am not using the thought process even though I am speaking through an earth body but as I am in an earth body the vibration is slower, even though I am not using thought. When we are free of the earth body and we are communicating to each other in spirit we do not have to think as you think, we just link on vibration levels and we communicate with each other. We do not have to think 'Where is that one I will have to go down to his house and find him.' We just think of that one and we are communicating with that one. When we come to earth we are aware we are coming to a slower vibration so we have to learn to slow ourselves down. Sometimes when we first come we find this difficult but we learn.

The question continued as to how you raise your vibration to link with spirit. You raise your vibration by relaxing, by shutting down your earth conditions. You have been trained and in turn you have trained those who are teaching that the most important function when you sit to communicate with spirit is to shut down all your problems, leave all your problems outside your room. So you are sitting here and all the problems you have experienced during your day, and your week are somebody else's problems they are not yours. You have thrown them away for a short while. You can pick them up again later but for this moment they are not yours, you have discarded them and what a weight that is from your shoulders. You then relax, you have been taught how to breathe. I will go through the procedures because it is good to recap. You take a deep breath. First of all you may wish to do it with numbers; you breathe in counting to 5, 1 - 2 - 3 - 4 - 5 - then you hold that breath for 5, then you slowly breathe out to the count of 5. When you have learnt how to breathe you do not need to count it becomes natural. You have to learn to breathe because you forget how to breathe properly. To breathe properly helps you to relax. As you then breathe in you are breathing in and thinking 'calm.' As you breathe out you think 'relax.' By thinking of 'calm' you are calming your mind and conscious reasoning. Slowly you are shutting down your conscious reasoning. Your thoughts are not wandering to what you are going to do later. You are relaxing and living for the moment. You are shutting down your earthly conditions. You are shutting down all the trapping of your human body. Your human body is still there and functioning, it is still living, your heart is still pumping and your organs are functioning. You are still sensing the physical vibrations in your room; hot, cold, noises, whatever but slowly, and slowly you are becoming less and less conscious of your human surroundings. You are then releasing the spirit within you to be free and by being free of your human conditions it is able to raise its vibration to a higher level, to link with its natural condition of spirit, because it is spirit.

It is not a question of 'How am I going to raise my vibration?' It is a question of shutting down your human condition, discarding your human condition for a short while of your existence. You know you have to return to it and you return to it as gently as you leave it. You do not rush, you do not function abruptly. Everything is done slowly, harmoniously, gently. First of all you do it as an exercise but gradually you are doing it as a natural routine without so much reasoning involved. Others shut down in different ways, this is the way you were taught. You were also taught another way where you send the body to sleep; head to foot, or foot to head, whichever way you are happy with. You tell your body to sleep and become calm. Other people have different routines where they close and open their chakras. It is individual preference. You all have your own method but it does not matter which method you use as long as you instil a peaceful calmness and you shut down your conscious reasoning, discarding your earthly conditions for a short while and free your true spirit essence to be part of its natural abode that is spirit. By doing this it is able to raise its vibration and link with those loved ones and companions who are so close to you, who are your natural family.

I hope this has helped. I am not saying the methods I suggest are the methods you should use because each of you has your own methods and way of shutting down your earthly conditions and releasing yourself to spirit. You are only doing something that is natural. You are spirit within a human body and you are just releasing your spirit to its natural abode. As you have spent much time in your earth world and have many pressures sometimes this becomes a little difficult but the more you practice the easier it will become, the more natural it will become. There are those, who unfortunately, take this a step too far, they spend more time shutting themselves from their human world than perhaps is wise because you are part of your human world and human existence. Just for a short while you are able to release yourself".

Given 26 January 1998

THE HIGHER REALMS

A question from a seeker - 'Regarding the most advanced and evolved spirits of the higher realms. Did they inherit the earth in the earliest era of the human race? Had some not had an earth life at all? Did they help us to get established as by helping a child the earth perhaps being just one of their children? Secondly, were we helped in the early stages by friends from other planets or dimensions? Perhaps we can be told of how, why and when.'

"This is a very deep question and I am not sure whether I can answer fully because there are some things that are best said and some things that are best not said at this moment.

The first part of the question; You probably realise in what you call spirit dimension there are many levels of evolvement and many levels of awareness. There are those very advanced ones that give much wisdom to us struggling ones on the lower levels. If you can in a way visualise this, it is difficult to make a picture because when perceive levels you perhaps perceive a staircase, a ladder, a building as you have on your earth with different storeys with one going up higher than the other. What I am trying to explain is that it is not like this. Yes, we are at different levels of evolvement and those very highly evolved ones are a distance from us in their understanding because obviously, we have a long way to go before we are as wise as those ones. It is not levels as you would expect with divisions inbetween. It is more a merging and a blending that we have. We can stretch from higher levels and lower levels of evolvement by linking with those other ones and merging our energies and drawing on their wiser wisdom. If you imagine, perhaps, a beacon of light and the zenith of the beacon is much brighter than the base of the beacon. This in a way would explain to you the levels of advancement, the brighter the light the more evolved, and the more evolved the souls are.

I have tried to explain in a little way how there are different levels. If you can imagine aeons and aeons of your earth time gone back when your earth was just in the throes of its formation. After the great explosion when there was the coming together of the atoms and the gases that made up your world. At this very, very early stage your world was being created, so were so many other worlds and they were in closer proximity with each other. Whereas, now your scientists are telling you that your universe is spreading, it is becoming more distant. In those very early days if you can imagine that all these dimensions that I have spoken of, all these levels of awareness, understanding and learning. If you can imagine that earth was at the base of the awareness scale and those ones from what you call spirit dimension were exploring the different levels of awareness. They were exploring different vibrations, as you yourself explore. Some of you in your world are happy to stay in one place and reside all your time in that one place just communicating with those whom you come into contact with in that area. Others in your physical world are eager to explore and spread their wings a bit farther and explore other parts of your world contacting other people living in different areas. So it is in our dimension there are those of us who would like to stay in the area we have evolved to and are quite happy in that position just communicating with those in that environment but there are other of us that wish to explore other levels of evolvement, whether they are higher or lower, more aware or less aware. This will always be.

In this time that we are speaking of there were those who were eager to explore other levels of awareness and they did transcend down to area that was your planet earth. In its early days they visited but in the early days there was not life as you know it at this moment. There were not physical beings, as yourselves. Spirit would come and would just be part of the energy and be part of the atmosphere of earth. Spirit was intermingling with earth's vibrations, intermingling with the energy of earth and exploring the various energies that had come together. Your earth then progressed and from the atoms that came together all life appeared on your planet gradually over millions of your year, it wasn't instantaneous. Spirit was all the time part of this. They were contributing, they were entering this dimension, they were intertwining their energies. In a way they were assisting in the formation of your earth pattern.

We now go forward some more of your earth years to when there were the beginnings of life, not as you know it, but there was life on your earth. Again, spirit was there assisting. I am not giving the answer to your question of how was man physically created because this something I cannot do. I am sorry but I cannot do this at this point, perhaps at a later date but at this point I cannot give you this information. There was a time when spirit could come and materialise on your planet in a form that was recognisable. Gradually over time your earth became more material, man was one your earth and man dabbled with vibration that perhaps were not so good. Then there came the divide between the two dimension, there was not the intermingling.

We still come are still part of your planet, we come to talk to you and try to share our love and energy with you. We try to transport ourselves by giving you our energy and hoping you can decode. By decoding you are able to perceive us. Sometimes you see us as lights, when you perceive spirit you may perceive lights darting around your room. Those of you that have sat in physical circles you have witnessed this when you sat in darkness. This is us, this is our essence but you can then perhaps, decode our essence form a picture of what we looked like when we had an earth body. In that essence, that pure spirit, is all that we contain, all our energies, memories, and experiences. As you are in a physical body you can decode the physical part of the memory. You can decode what we actually looked like when we had a physical body.

To recap on the question. Yes, in the early days of the formation of the planet earth and other planets, because you asked us about other planets also, spirit as you know we were part of this great adventure. We cannot be separated we are all part of the whole. We are part of you and you are part of us. There cannot be a separation, we are all part of the creative force. We are part of creation whether we have a physical body at this moment in time or not. Whether we have a physical body and live on planet earth or we have a physical body and we are somewhere else in your cosmos, your universe. We are all part of creation and we are all part of that energy from the great creative force.

The energies do change because in the beginning of your world, you cannot know, you cannot understand, but a little has been explained to you by your scientists and men of knowledge of how your earth was created through the elements coming together after the great explosion. The coming together of the gases and atoms. You also know that you are part of the universe and you have knowledge of other planets that in your solar system. You have knowledge that there may be something out farther beyond and your scientists are also telling you that everything is changing, you are all moving farther away from each other. You can see everything is in movement, nothing stays the same, it is all the time changing.

We have spoken to you of how your body should be in harmony and how you all work together as a team when at its best should be in harmony together".

Given 2 February 1998

ADVICE ON SITTING FOR DEVELOPMENT

A question from a seeker - ' When a person sits for development with spirit and they are on daily medication for blood pressure or similar does this medication prevent them working with spirit or does it make it mare difficult?'

"When a person is on medication for whatever there is a reason for this medication so you have to look first at the cause. We have spoken before of treating a symptom rather than treating the illness. There is an imbalance in the body. If there is an imbalance in the body this in itself makes it difficult for the person to relax and to link with spirit. It does not make if impossible, if just makes it a little more difficult. Then that one has been given medicine by doctor to help that one cope with the condition of their body. This should help in one way to bring the body back into balance but it is being brought into balance by the introduction of a chemical that is something that is alien to the body but this is a necessity. It is needed so as much as you do not like taking chemicals into your body for the betterment of your health you have to bow to the wisdom of the doctor because it no good asking doctor for advice and then ignoring the advice they give you.

So you are introducing something into the body that is probably not natural to the body's normal existence. There are some medications that are natural but I think in this case it may be a chemical substance that has been manufactured to help assist lowering the hypertension. When this is first introduced into the body this make a change in the way the body works. The body has to become used to the medication. Initially there is quite a disturbance in the body's metabolism, the body's balance, to become adjusted. This affects how the mechanics of the body but it also affects the thought process, the nervous system and also how you relax because in lowering your blood pressure it has a sedative effect. It is making you relax unnaturally for the betterment of your health, I am not decrying this. It is not a natural way of relaxing. It is teaching your body how to work again. Gradually your body becomes accustomed to this drug, chemical and your body then starts to tolerate the medication.

Coming back to the original question, I am sorry I have gone a long way around but I am just trying to explain to you what occurs when someone takes medicine into their body. Also, of course, the patient could be taking medicine for a while then they are changed onto another medicine and then you start this process all over again. Initially while your body is becoming accustomed to the introduction of this chemical into its system it could make and affect with the communication with spirit because the sedativeness of the medicine goes against your natural closing down procedure. When you link with spirit you go through a process of closing down, each one uses their own method, whether it is breathing, sending their body to sleep, contemplating on picture in your mind of a flower or scene, you could be repeating a mantra to yourself. Each one has their own way of relaxing. You may find this difficult at first with the affects of the medicine but gradually your body adjusts to the medicine and becomes used to the medicine. Then you are more in control again of your thought process and of your shutting down process, you take charge of your body again. When you are in control of your body you are able to shut down and in so doing release your spirit from the trapping of your human world and it is then free to link with spirit.

I hope this has answered your question. We do not want to decry medicine because it is given for a purpose and it would be wrong for me to tell you to ignore what your doctor has told you and ignore the medicine they give you".

Given 9 February 1999

SPEED IS RELATIVE

Responding to question sent by a seeker 'Assuming that man will discover how to travel faster than the speed of light do we, at that stage, change the vibration level so as to become undetectable to the human eye, that is invisible?' Mafra answers.

"You are speaking to someone who used to travel down the Douro in a boat that was quite slow in comparison to your travel today. I understand, of course, that man has progressed and learnt to leave the pull of your earth's gravity and travel into what you call 'space,' into this void that is a vacuum to discover other parts of your galaxy. Yes, of course, in time to come when those of you here will not be worried about material substances man may possibly discover other form of transport and other means of travelling. I am drawing on knowledge from those that have chosen the scientific field for their evolutionary ladder.

With this advancement and knowledge of how to travel farther away from your planet earth there will also come knowledge of inter dimensional activity. I do not want to go too deep into this because it is something for future of your world and I am not here to tell future. As man advances there will be advancement in some scientific field to be able to create means of transport. Also man is also developing in another direction he is developing this aptitude to explore other dimensions. Experiments are already taking place in your world but these are not open to public surveillance at this moment. There is knowledge that within this space around you there are other dimensions. Man has discovered that there is a breakdown of quantum physics, there are discoveries taking place regarding quantum physics which involves a breakdown of subatomic structures. It will be sometime before this knowledge is accepted. There are experiments and research taking place at this moment.

To unleash this knowledge into your world will mean a lot of rethinking of doctrines that have been handed down in your books of learning over many centuries. They will have to handle this information carefully because there will be much opposition. Going back a few centuries in your world, when you read your history books, you can compare this a little to when your explorers were trying to tell your men of letters that the world was not flat it was round. There was much disagreement and people wondered how this could be a fact. Of course, this is something in your history but it is just an example of how you have to rewrite facts and how an indoctrinate fact is difficult to eradicate. It has to be several generations before these facts are accepted as truth.

Into the future a little glimpse. Man is discovering quantum physics. How subatomic structures are broken down, how what you think is solid is not solid. The limitations you can see with your physical eyes are not there. You look to a horizon with your physical eyes and you see scenery laid before you but within that scenery, you are looking at with your human eyes, there is much more that you are not perceiving. It is in another structure, in another dimension. There is not heaven above the sky, there cannot be heaven above the sky because your spaceships have travelled there and they have not seen angels sitting on clouds playing their harps. You have had proof that there is existence after your mortal body is now more. So where is this existence? It has to be somewhere.

You have had proof that we are near you, we know what goes on without being nosy but we intermingle. We learn with you and you learn with us. We intermingle and exchange vibrations but you cannot see us unless you are developed and are opening your psychic eye to us. Those that have developed their psychic eye are able to witness us. They are not witnessing us every minute of the day. Those that are trained correctly are opening themselves to spirit and close down. That does not mean when they close down we are disappearing until they open their vision again.

There will be times ahead when this knowledge is accepted and this knowledge that is within you that is now dormant is able to be free and you will be able to explore much more than you are able to at this moment. We have said to you that each generation that comes to your world comes with a different vibration, a different ability, so you can understand why those more senior years are not able to perceive this. You have not come to earth to experience this. Those that are born later into your world, those that are to be born into your world, will come with different abilities and skills for their walk on earth than you had. Perhaps, my friends, you may wish to return to earth at that time to experience it again in a different body and vibration.

This will an opportunity that will be open to you if you wish but I am not predicting future. You will return home when your voyage on your earth has come to its conclusion and when you return to your spirit home you then have opportunity and free will to decide which path you wish to travel. It is not for myself to tell you.

I haven't answered your question completely but I hope I have given you some thoughts to think upon".

Given 23 January 1999

A QUESTION OF REINCARNATION

Mafra responding to the following question. 'When we return home to spirit will we be given the opportunity to reincarnate in a different life form on another planet - in our quest to be perfect?'

"I will continue from the previous question "Speed is Relative". I have just spoken that when you return home you have opportunities offered and you have free will to choose your own path.

As regarding another planet. I will not talk of a particular named person, I will talk of an entity returning home to spirit. When a spirit comes to earth they take an earth body and they go through their cycle of earth life and then return home to spirit. When you return home to spirit you are welcomed into your spirit family and you are met by those loved ones that you hold very dear and those ones that have guided you through your earth steps who knew you before you took that earth body. You are welcomed home. As you have been on earth for a certain amount of years you have to adjust. We have spoken before of the different levels of evolution and when you first go home perhaps you go to a stage that is very similar to your earth world. For your adjustment you are given a time to adjust where you are in a vibration that is very near the vibration you left behind. You go through this stage of adjustment. It is similar to your earth but it is lighter, quicker vibration and gradually it is a time of becoming adjusted. Realising you are no longer of earth. You may be given opportunity to return to earth to view those you have left behind and your earth conditions. Those wiser ones will acknowledge that they are home in spirit but there are those that do not realise this and they have to be educated that they are somewhere different.

After this time of adjustment you are then given opportunity to rise to a different level of vibration that is farther away from the stage that is near to your earth. This does not mean you cannot return to earth to greet or view those that are walking the earth path but it means you are raised to a different, quicker, vibration where you do not have the trapping of earth that you had before. You meet with those senior ones from your spirit family, I do not mean senior in years, the guardians, the more learned ones. If you wish you take their advice as to what opportunities are open to you and what path you wish to explore. There may be something in your last existence that you go through the experiences you had, whether you have achieved all you wished to achieve or whether there is something you left unfinished and you wish to explore a little more. You are given opportunity, if you wish, to return to earth in another earth body or you may wish to explore other avenues in what you call our spirit dimension. There are so many paths you can follow, too many for me to explain to you. If we just say 'healing' there are so many routes in the healing vibration you can explore.

Although you are in spirit and you have accepted that you have come away from earth you are still vibrating to similar frequency to your earth frequency. To go from that frequency into another planet would be incompatible because the vibrations are so different. Those ones that come to you that are highly evolved, they do not use the same kind of communication that we would use to talk to you. They are so evolved they can talk and communicate with a different frequency, at a different level. They are more detached from your earth than Mafra or the rest of the team that talk to you. They are very learned and are away from earth's vibration. If the condition is right they can visit earth and communicate with you. As they have evolved so much since their time on earth they are more free to explore other vibrations. They can visit you here or there are others that would wish to explore other parts of your universe because they are not so closely linked with earth and their earth condition. I come and talk to you, I have been in spirit many of your earth years but I still recall my earth existence, I still give you my name. I have given you my conditions on earth, I have explained to you where I lived, where I worked, my companions on my earth journey, occasions that occurred in my earth journey because they are still very vivid and very clear in my memory. It has been a long while since these highly evolved ones had a physical connection with earth. Some perhaps may not have touched earth at all. They do not have the pull of earth as perhaps, we still have, even though we are detached we still have our memories. Those more evolved ones do not have this same connection so they are free then to adapt their vibration to other vibrations. Whereas, for us it would be difficult and would cause imbalance.

Having said all this. We have said to you that when you are on earth you have free will. It is the same in our dimensions, you always have free will. Even though you are guided and shown different ways to explore you still have your free will to choose your own direction. If you find that direction is not so fulfilling as you wished you have the free will to change and go a different way. Every creative entity is an individual and what is right for one is not right for the other. You may just need to explore one avenue for a short while to gain some knowledge in that avenue and then you change directions and go in another direction to learn something else. This is what evolution is, it is learning, exploring and gaining knowledge. There again, you have free will.

You may not wish to evolve but stay where you are, on the level that is near earth and experience a near earth vibration. It is your choice and free will. There are those there that would offer you advancement to learn a little more but if you wish you can decline their offer until such a time when

you become a little discontent and you wonder what else there is to discover. Once you have the incentive that you are wondering and wanting to discover that is the time to move on. If you move on too early you are not ready so you are not taking the best advantage of that opportunity. You have an expression in your world 'you can take horse to water but you cannot make him drink.' It is the same, it is all down to individuals and their desire to progress. It is the same as the students in your world those that have the desire to learn achieve, those that study but do not have the desire are not so fulfilled at the end of their education. This does not happen just in your world it happens wherever you wish to progress. You have to have a desire from within to achieve whatever".
Given 23 January 1999

TYPES OF TRANCE COMMUNICATION EVIDENCE

Reading books of the past trance mediums' guides used to come through with evidence like family members, nowadays mediums when in trance only bring guides who bring philosophy never any evidence any more why is that?

"This is a good question. Yes, we understand what you are saying. A little background why we have come. Trevor has explained to you we are part of a teaching group. You are probably aware because you are knowledgeable people that there is a time of great enlightenment. There is an upsurge of inquiry, wanting to know why this? And why that? We are trying to bring those to you who can answer these questions. This is why this group and other groups tend to answer questions.

Now Coming back to your question. You say those in the past brought relatives. There are also groups now that this occurs in. There are times in the history of your country and other countries when many went to spirit within a few years because of unrest and warfare. Also there were many illnesses that your doctors were unable to remedy, many children went home to spirit very early because childhood illnesses were unable to be treated as you are able to treat your children now. The conditions of your earth, your working conditions were not so amenable as now, so many went home to spirit younger in their life span than your life spans now. There was much grief and anguish for those that were remaining on earth. The religions of the lands at that time were one of fear. Not so many were enlightened, not so many were encouraged to think outside the restrictions that they were indoctrinated in when they were brought up as children and young adults. There was much grief. Those ones had gone never to be contacted until they themselves perhaps would leave their earthly life. Can you imagine all this grief, all this sorrow.

Spirit was trying to bring some comfort and solace to those that were struggling to exist. Your loved ones are with you, they have not gone to sleep for a long while, they are with you, they are close to you and they were bringing this evidence to try and bring comfort because that was important. Also to bring enlightenment that, as we say now, one goes home to spirit but in those days it was more that one had died. The word 'died' brought so much sorrow, such grief, so many negative thoughts. Spirits were trying to bring enlightenment, trying to bring some light, some encouragement, to look broader than the aspects that they had previously been taught. Gradually as these groups, churches, became known and these mediums of old became known more and more people on your earth became aware that death, that terrible word, was not the end. That their loved ones did still exist. Not only did they still exist but they were near to them, they were as near to them as when they had body but of course, they could not see them. There was someone there that could give them evidence their loved ones were close.

Now your world has moved forward and you are encouraged to think more. Yes, religion has its place because there has to be a belief, there has to be a respect, belief in something greater but you are not blinkered. You are free to keep an open mind, to look at other avenues, other religions and to take from these religions what you wish. What you feel is right for you. Now your population has hopefully, become a little more knowledgeable spiritually. Perhaps you may doubt whether spiritual progress has been made in your 'cut throat' world. If you wish to pursue spiritual knowledge it is there for you. There are avenues, you do not feel so much encased in your beliefs of religions of previous years. There is much more knowledge for the seeking. It is the stretching out and seeking which assists in gaining this knowledge. We can bring you knowledge, not only myself but all those others in our realms that are seeking to assist and bring knowledge to many, many groups over the world. Until you are ready and asking the questions, it is as sowing a seed in a field that has not been prepared. You are ready for it and you are given a little bit of knowledge perhaps from your church platform this week and this gives you something to think about, then next week another medium may visit with a little bit more knowledge, so gradually you build up this awareness, Also, the mediums from your platform are still bringing you evidence that your loved ones continue to exist, they are with you, they have not gone away and you will not see them or sense them until you meet again in another world.

Years ago the evidence that was given through trance mediumship in circles and groups not platforms involved a lot of personalities. This because of bringing evidence that they did exist. They were not dead, they had survived and there was another existence. It was a time when this was needed because of the conditions of your earth. It is still need today but you now you have more freedom of thought, you are able to explore yourself without prejudice different thoughts, different religions, different aspects. You do not feel you are trapped in a religion where you have to follow strictly to what someone in authority is telling you. You have freedom and more enlightenment.

That for ones that have lost loved ones it is important for them but you are able to go more now to churches that have open doors and people can walk in. They are not closed and meetings are not held in secret. At one time it was against the law of your land to hold a service where people could come in freely, sit and be given messages from their loved ones. The mediums of those days worked in fear of being taking into custody and locked away. It was therefore, important that when spirit had an opportunity to bring evidence that the loved ones could come and talk because this was only selective opportunities. Whereas, now you have much more freedom. Your churches have open doors. The laws of your land have changed, in your land unfortunately not in all. In many lands you are free to hold services with mediums giving evidence of your loved one existence.
Given 13 March 1999

DIFFERENT ATTITUDES TO HEALING
Mafra speaking about different attitudes to healing.

"You must understand that all of you come together for a reason. In a healing situation you all come together to try and assist those that come to you with illness, to revitalise and ease their illness. This is the reason you have come together.

You have come together from various walks of life. You are all personalities and you are all different. You have all come from a different background, a different history and you have come to healing in different ways. You have had different teachers and you must respect that each one is different. There is no right or wrong because you heal with love in your heart not for your self satisfaction, your own ego but you heal and give your love to assist those that are going through a situation that is causing them problems. Whether it is physical, mental or whether it is a condition of the earth that causes anxiety, fear, bereavement. They come to you because there is an imbalance within in them for whatever reason and you as healers, have been trained, in different ways because you have had different teachers, to link with that one to try and bring a balance to the condition of their body.

As a trained healer you understand that all illness is a result of an imbalance. You will tackle this in one way and another healer will tackle it in another way because they have been taught differently. Different healers refer to energy centre, chakras and their positions in the body, maybe being perceived in different places. Do not become involved in disagreements because you have all been taught differently but the end result is the same, you want to assist. Please try and recognise each other, that you are all individuals and you all work in your own way. As long as you are working for the good of others, with love in your heart that is the most important asset you can bring to your service to others. They cannot convert you to their way of thinking and you cannot convert them to your way of thinking because you are all individuals and have all come from a different background being taught differently. Please accept each other as they are. They are different from you and you are different from them. As long as you can unite with your various methods and ways without causing a problem. If they were doing something physically to the patient that was not right you would then step in and say 'you must not do that because you are going against the Code of Conduct' but they are not doing something as this. It is just their method. As long as they are working within the rules of your organisation and are working with love in their heart try and voice, perhaps, to them that you understand they work differently from you but ask them to please accept that you have been taught differently and are happy with the way you work. Say. 'I am happy to work my way and you are happy to work yours let us work together to try and help these ones.' It is good to agree to disagree.

    We cannot walk your life for you and no one else in your earthly existence can walk your life for you. It is your way and your path. If you are happy and your patients are happy with the way you work it is not for others to criticise you. If others are working differently you can perhaps teach by example. You can continue as you work in y our quiet way and they can watch and observe, still work their way but together because all the time you are communicating on another level also. You are teaching by example and if you are uniting in love you are sharing energy and by sharing you are teaching without them knowing. It is for good.

    There are so many problems and disputes because someone tries to convert another to their methods. I am not only talking of healing but the world in general. When these disagreements involve major problems of course this is a different matter. You can teach a lot by love rather than argument".

Given 2 May 1999

PROTECTING THE MEDIUM

Mafra explaining his role as the protector when a different level of energy communicates through the medium following an instance when a new communicator accidentally knocked the medium's arm against a table while she was in trance. This caused a reaction although not pain.

"There was no problem. This is why we say to you be careful when people are close to the medium because the body is extra sensitive. We bring to the body our vibration and it is so different from your vibration. We have to use an earth body but we are altering the vibration of the earth body because we are the caretakers of that body for a short while and we bring our own energy that is so different. If we did not we would have great difficulty talking to you because we would not be compatible. We have to lower our vibration to a slower, denser vibration that is not so quick as in our own environment but we are still compatible with a human vibration but a little level above it. In our natural environment we are sensitive to vibrations all the time, of course not in a body, but we are sensitive to others that are calling on us for different reasons. They are thinking of us and sending their vibrations to us in order to ask questions. We in turn are doing the same. We are very aware of other influences because we do not have the physical shell that you have.

When we come here we bring with us a similar vibration, although it is lower and more dense it is similar, so we are protected from any influence towards us. The baser thoughts and influences from earth do not effect us because we like yourself have the white light to protect us from these problems. You cannot protect us from something physical because we are, at that moment, in a body and when we come into contact with something physical we then react because we are not compatible. That table may appear solid but it is not solid because it is made up of molecules, subatomic all the time moving. You are also comprised of subatomic matter that is constantly moving and you vibrate in a compatible frequency so that when you touch the table you are compatible. We vibrate at a higher frequency so we are not compatible. Therefore, when we touch it suddenly without adjusting that frequency there is a reaction because it is a different vibration and it impinges on the medium because it is not their natural element. You are in your natural element here in the human world, existing alongside other humans together with items and objects that are of your earth world. You are vibrating in a similar frequency but we are not. If we are not prepared and come into contact this causes a reaction. There is nothing to be worried about.

This is why we say to you there should be no sudden lights because again this would impinge and cause a reaction because it is in a different element to what we are accustomed to".

Given 27 April 1999

PROGRESSIVE EDUCATION

We were introduced to a new companion called Gwyn(th), a gentleman who when on earth was a teacher in Harlech, who is helping us with our teaching work. For the first time he came to speak to us on June 8th 1999. To start with he communicated in Welsh and then adjusted to speak in English. He spoke of the technique of getting the message over, and the transcript of his words are given below in the hope that it may be of use to others who undertake public speaking.

"When I was in Harlech I did not know your tongue. I taught boys to have sense of purpose. I communicate with you on higher level no language. When I communicate there is no need for words. I can help when you teach they are your words not mine but I help with energy vibration above tongue. Be strong in delivery of words with purpose. Purpose behind words. Keep attention not your attention but the attention of those listening. Use voice up and down not all at one level, raise and lower to keep attention. Delivery of words to keep attention. Be articulate, demonstrative and authoritative with purpose. Fill those listening with enthusiasm so that they want to be part of what you are speaking of. Emphasise vowels. Give meaning and life to words. There is no need to shout but give expression not monotone, vary levels of speech to keep those attentive. Involve them in your words by asking them to contribute their words. Encourage. Fill your lungs with air before you deliver speech! Put expression in your words, up and down, alter tone to keep attention.

We bring thoughts that you can transpose into your words we do not put words into your mouth. They are your words, you are able to assess situation of those present. You are able to find words that those present understand but we give you the vibration for you to transpose. If words are given with feeling they take on life, energy and it is energy that can deliver. Others absorb and can carry energy forward themselves. If you mumble in boots all in one tone there is no energy in words and those that listen do not absorb but if you throw words to them with energy words take on energy and mingle with their vibration. All speech has energy. Energy can either flow forward and be absorbed or if it hits wall (non acceptance) it will bounce back. You can only deliver for others to take on.

I valued energy when I was on earth. Energy from mountains, from rocks, from sea, from hillside and green pastures. Energy from buildings of stone with the energy absorbed in these stones. Energy absorbed for those that can feel.

Good. I am please that I have come."

Talks about seeing the true person behind the facade during the Christmas/New Year holiday period.

Time to reflect and to look back but not too far. Time to put your thoughts in order, plan your move forward into your new year. Time to look around and observe all that is going on around you. You do not have time to look around when you are rushing here and rushing there. You have taken a step away from your busy life but the world still rolls on.

Take notice of what goes on around you, listen to the noises of the birds, look at the scenery that you see. It is not so good at the moment but there are still things to observe. Notice the changes of the season, colours around you and feel the energy around you. When you have time to look and observe you begin to feel the energy. Become attuned to the vibrations around you. Absorb the energy. You take time away from your home to go on trips and voyages where you look at scenery and feel the energy. Well, do that at your home and treat it as a holiday. Look at things around you as if you are a visitor. Notice things that you would not normally see. Take time to stand in your garden, look around and you will see plants that are poking through. You will see bare trees but in those branches you will see the beginnings of new life. Watch your animals and birds watching what they are doing. Observe the sky, look to the heavens at night time and observe the stars and moon. Observe the sunrise, perhaps there is no sun but the light returns and your sky changes with different hues and colours in the cloud formation.

Take notice of what people say and how people act. Observe human nature, it is an education! We had boys in our school, they would go through the school, they would learn their lessons, they would leave school and go on their way. Sometimes they would return as adults grown to maturity, very wise, very educated, very worldly wise but if you looked and studied you would see within them the boy that was in the school. Yes, age alters everybody. The lessons of life do not stop when you leave school but you still learn all through your existence but within that man you see the boy. You become able to hide what the boy cannot hide but there are signs if you look of the boy within. So it is with all of mankind whatever their colour or their race within them is the child, the innocence of the child, the naivety of the child and the wisdom of the child. Yes, time changes with the coming of hurts and pain and you learn to put a defence around yourselves so that others cannot see within. If you observe others you can see the child within still mischievous and perhaps still naughty! Still exploring and discovering but still wise. Do not lose that wisdom that comes with you.

As you walk you change your ideas, you are influence by others but keep your wisdom that is within. Of course, explore but keep your own wisdom because this has come with you and will return home with you. When you see others that you know, others you do not know but you watch and observe them, perhaps they are ones with power and authority, just remember within them is the child. I could tell you some stories of some of my boys when they became men and the positions they held but I could see the boy within them. I am sure John (Lyon) will tell you the same.

I recall what I taught in my school at Harlech. I taught the boys to be strong and to be truthful. It is important to be truthful to yourself and to others. The boys did not always come from Harlech. They would come and board in dormitories. We had houses and the houses had dormitories. We would have different houses but I do not mean houses like your house. Each boy when he entered the school would be designated to a house and they would stay in that house during their time at the school. They had responsibility to that house, it was an honour and they would not disgrace that house. There would be rivalry between the houses and this was good because it provoked team with the house but rivalry one to other. There were many contests between the houses, not always sport.

This is in the past but it was good because it taught and built character. It was educational that you had to put your trust in others also. You could not be individual because you were part of others and there were times when you had to rely on others. This is a lesson that goes all through your life. You are an individual but you are also part of others. There are times when you are a leader and there are times when you have to stand back and let others lead.

You are wise because you know of eternal existence and you are all part of a much bigger team but you all play your part. There is a difference. If a boy disgraced himself he was thrown out of school but you cannot be thrown out of eternal existence. You have to brush yourself down and start again.

Go forward as my friend tells you. Do not despair of problems that are around. You were told that there would be many that would not enjoying the festivities of the Christmas season and so it came to pass. Many were in situations that were not so good. Do not despair but keep hope. Keep the lantern of truth shining bright. As you walk forward carry this light for others to show the way. Blessing be with you".
Given 28 December 1999

LEARNING BY OWN EXPERIENCES

"It is an education listening to others because everyone is different. You have what you call circles but no two are the same because you are all individuals and you all bring something to that group so no two groups can be the same. Is that not the same in all walks of existence? You can have a row of houses and within those houses there are families but each house is different, each is different in the style, the decoration but also in the vibration. When you walk within the doors each house will have a different vibration.

You can see how the world is made up of vibrations. This is why it is important to teach the young people because they are the ones that are making the vibrations for the future. As each generation goes through their existence and they finally leave the planet of earth, as you call it, the vibration of that country changes because they are not there anymore. They leave behind a semblance for those that are to follow and they build their own vibration on the vibration that has been left to them. This is why your land changes and your countries change because they are made up of the vibrations of the people that exist within those lands. As each new life comes to that land a new vibration comes and it is the responsibility of those that teach to guide that one so that they have responsibility for their actions because they will build the vibrations of tomorrow.

Teach well, teach by example because this is important. Each generation looks at the generation before and turns the other way to find their own way of doing things but eventually when they are not the new generation any more they will take from those that went before them some of the examples that were set. Each has to find their own path. They cannot walk exactly in the path of their forebears. They travel their way, experience their own obstacles but their path winds and turns and before they know where they are they are treading the same path as their ancestors but in a modern world. Doing the same actions but in a different way. The young do not want to take responsibility because life lies before them, it is an adventure, they do not want to be tied down with the responsibilities but want broader horizons. Let them discover, let them experiment, then they will come to the path of wisdom because they have learnt for themselves. You can teach, you can show examples but you cannot instil wisdom because that is gained by your own experience. All need to experience for themselves because if they don't there is now growth because it is muted. This does not mean that you cannot guide and give your thoughts when they are asked for. There are ways of teaching without driving with a stick. A carrot for the donkey.

Within you is the wisdom of those that went before so why should not those that come after also have this wisdom. They will find it in a different way. It is the same for all that tread the path, they have wisdom but they need to uncover it. It is in the sharing that you learn because others learn from you but you also learn from them. There is a very old expression that you have probably heard, 'the teacher learns from his pupil'. It is so true but of course we do not tell them that, do we? We keep that to ourselves".

Given 22 January 2000

Education needs to be progressive changing the format to suit the vibrations of today but encompassing the truth that is eternal.

"There must be new ideas and new ways of teaching not to keep going back to old ideas. To go forward, roll forward and keep changing and altering but still you have your truth but you present it in a different way. You will perceive that those that come to are all the time changing. You have groups where visitors come and talk year in and year out that same ones come and say the same words but we are bringing to you different people. I say people because that is a way of explaining. We are bringing different energy because this is part of your work, you are encompassing different energy and you will be meeting different people whom all require a different approach. When you meet these people you are able to draw the energy that adapts to their energy. It is not just one kind of energy but it is multifaceted.

One of your helpers is Hanns and his work involves blending and balancing energy. He rolls off formulas and technical information but he juggles vibrations. He adapts to what is needed and he can help you to draw different vibrations from different teachers for what is needed. You have many groups of people whom you are teaching but they will not be all the same, they are all different. Everyone comes from a different background with differing knowledge and vibrations. Therefore, the answer to each question must be different. When I try to assist you with questions that are sent needing answers I try and answer that question for that particular person. It may not be the same answer that I would give to another person who asks the same question. Inside the answer is the same but I try to clothe it in a different way, approach it in a different way for individuals. This why you have so many come to you because they are themselves all different. Hanns helps here because he helps to balance.

This is our way of working. It is something very vital and very much alive. Some methods of teaching can become very repetitive and flat. We want to keep it alive, to keep it moving on and moving forward so that words that are said now are meaningful for those that read these words later. There again, we want others to carry the word forward for those that are coming later. We do not want them to keep reading our old words but we want to teach teachers. We want our words to hit those that want to become teachers so that they can take our words, adapt and change our words to suit another generation yet to come. They can carry on the work that we are starting. The teachers that we are training will be able to help the future teachers. It is ongoing all the time going on. We do not claim our group are going to talk to you and you are going to listen to us and continue to teach by the same method but we want those that listen to take our words and continue by develop their own teaching.

You cannot continue to teach in the same way as others did in the past because it is a forward world. Everything is going forward and if you try to go backwards you are doing nothing. You are not doing any good to your own progress. You would not teach your children in your world the same way as you were taught when you were a child. Why should the then all the times look back on how mediums performed in the past. They performed at that time for those people existing a that time but your world has moved forward. Your earth world has moved forward but also energy that spirit has brought to your world has altered and is not the same. We have told you that each generation brings their own energy and as each generation matures and leaves your world they are withdrawing energy from your world. They leave behind for a while some of their energy because that is how it should be for those that are to follow. In time when the next generation has gone home gradually the memories of those ones that went previous are dulled. Although perhaps bricks and mortar still stand, their generation has contributed something for the time they were there and others have had to carry on with a different energy. Taking a little what their seniors have left for them and adapting it. You have a building that has been built hundreds of years ago, many fine buildings in your land and my land, but they are not being used for exactly the same purpose and way for which they were first built. They have been adapted and changed. The architects have designed them and builders have erected them and the stones are still standing but the way they are being used today may not be much different but there is a difference. Perhaps the heating is different. If it is a church perhaps the way the service is held is a little different or the way you dress when you go into that building may be different. As the senior ones leave your world to go home to spirit what they are leaving behind is being changed and altered.

It is the same with your religion, truth or whatever description you use it has be to carried forward. You cannot protect it in a glass case and keep it the same for ever and ever as in a museum. You have things in your museums that have been there for hundreds of years perhaps but they have become faded and tired. When you look at them you remark that they are old and dusty and not interesting. You have books that have been written by your scribes that are beautiful but you cannot read them today because they would mean nothing to you. The beauty and skill is still there but they were meant to be used and you are not using them. You are making an exhibition piece from them. Do you want your religion to be an exhibition piece not to be used? You want to carry it forward. Perhaps you want to keep it as a resemblance of what it was but you want to carry it forward as something that can be used and adapted for each generation that is to come. Nothing is forever and if those that will not accept change or can not accept change will cause a problem for their own progression. None of us are so important that we have the right to stop the progress of others. None of us has that right".

A LOST TRAVELER

When visiting Southern Ireland we sat for a short while and a visitor came through who Sister Celeste described as a traveler. This is a new term to us can you explain what you mean as traveler? Mafra replies.

"I of course was there but Sister Celeste stepped in to assist because she brings a blessings and sanctifies where you are sitting so she had taken the responsibility. Traveler was the word was spoken but what is a word? It is a description. It was a soul that is traveling not knowing where they were going. They did not know they were in spirit or what had happened, they were traveling. They had not got a home or a destination and it just happened that the vibrations in that particular area and your linking with a different area, place and situation that merged their energy with your energy for a short while. We bring these people to you, I do not like the word people as a description, these forces to you and sometimes you are able to assist them because there is work you can do to assist those who are seeking. Sometimes linking and being in your presence and those of us who are with you assists those ones but in this situation we could not assist that one. We tried but it is not always possible because of conditions that are beyond our control. It is just good to say, 'Go your way in peace' and hopefully at some point in that one's existence they will be at peace and will be able to be more aware. We do bring people to you that you can help because as you are of the earth vibration it is sometimes easier for us to bring the to you in order for us to help them because of the link with your earth condition. In this case it was not possible. We were unable to balance the vibrations and there was too much pull one way so we stepped in.

The medium was brought to a level where she was able to bring herself back and take charge of herself again. She was aware of what was happening. This is why you are trained well being responsible for yourself. We are here to assist but in a situation as this we were giving as much help as we could but in order to break the link completely we brought her back so that she could positively say, 'No I do not want this presence'. Then we were able to take that one away. As we are dealing with the unknown vibrations we do not know how far we can assist. You know yourself, in your earth world sometimes someone come to you for help and give them your help but they are adamant they know the right way and do not want to listen. You just have to say, 'Go your way' and perhaps another time in another condition they can be helped. We not put any of you in any problem situations. We are in control. This is why those that sit without experience and knowledge are opening themselves up to many vibration. We know that you ask for the white light of protection and we endeavor to give this but in our work in helping others we do involve ourselves in other vibrations that perhaps are not so compatible. There is a need to help others. It is all very well us learning and you learning, stretching out learning more and more wisdom but it is good to help others also. This is what we try to do. We try to draw up others and sometimes it works but sometimes it does not work. If it does not work we are in control and can cut the situation off. They may have taken away something with them that will help them sometime in the future. We do not want to become involved in their conditions because this may leave an imprint so we tell them to go in peace.

So my friend you were speaking of conditions in a few of your weeks. I want to give a few words. I understand from vibration I am absorbing from yourself that this group is searching and seeking but also there is within that group a smaller group who want to delve a little deeper. A group that are used to sitting together and wish to develop their own abilities a little more than just sitting and listening. So you are doing a few hours of teaching and then a break, then a few more hours of deeper instruction, more practical. I am not telling you what to do but you do not want to repeat yourself. What you are doing during the major part of your day to what to are doing later. You want to come fresh to this group, you do not want to come repeating what they have done earlier. Of course, it will be repetition but you will want to dress it in a different guise. I would advise that when you can what you are going to do in your smaller group first because this is the group that wants to work rather than listen. If you plan how you want to involve them, I will give you an example; if you want to teach them how to shut themselves off completely, how to work towards going into trance or into awareness you may perhaps wish to take them through the shutting down process. Whether it is your usual talking into the garden or whether it teaching by shutting down their physical body as you were taught, that is entirely up to you, my friend. If you do that you do not want to do it previously in your other session because they will be going through that procedure twice in a few short hours. If you want to do that you must think of something different to do with the larger group. If they want to become more involved and more spiritually aware it is important that you teach them to shut down and put aside other thoughts. You are there teaching them but they may not want to do it on their own. They may already be aware of this but it is good as instructions to teach them to do it properly. Then from there you can gently lead them into whatever they wish to develop. By that time we will have had time to communicate and listen to them which is very important, listen to what they want and guide them through that process. If they wish to become more spiritually aware you can say to them, 'Well, what do you see, what do you perceive?' You know how to gently guide them and lead them out not to be self conscious. They have worked together as a team before so there will not be a problem.

People do not want to just sit and listen but want to become more involved. So during your day before other session try to think of something that involves them. Of course you must say to them that when they speak to spirit they must shut themselves down but do not put them through the procedure. They will then be aware of spiritual protection and being aware of their surroundings and shutting themselves away. Involve them as much as you can because this is how you learned when you were learning. You would become frustrated when someone spoke to you and you were not able to voice your thoughts and opinions. You understand how others want to learn by participation, working with each other. Perhaps putting one person with another person or one group with another group so that they are bouncing off each other. Try to break down barriers and intermingle the group. This is just a suggestion. I am happy to assist. We will be there linking with the helpers of those who are sitting with you and we will try to assist on our level. We are a team. There is no dictation we should do this or that, we work together and try to assist where we can.

As others learn more by working together so you also learn by teaching how to communicate with others, how to involve others. If I said to you that you must do a certain thing you would not be learning yourself. You would be taking instructions. I am offering the opportunity to use your own thoughts as to how you wish to work your time but just giving you some ideas".

Given 13 July 1999

THOUGHTS ON THE DEVELOPMENT OF RELIGIONS
Some thoughts on the development of religions from Mafra.

"I will talk of the enlightenment of your religions. If only your religions could join together and enlighten likewise there would be much progress. Unfortunately, they are still segregated and there is much division. They say that they join together but there is still much bigotry and many egos. If only there was harmony within those that guide and teach religion but each is afraid. It is fear.

You speak of the one called Jesus who came to your world and there has been many debates recently of whether he should be worshipped or whether he should not be worshiped. The name Christianity has been echoed many times. Unfortunately, you link the name Christianity with the man called Jesus. The man called Jesus came to your world to bring much wisdom, he was a healer, he was a visionary, he was a teacher and he performed many of the actions that you perform. He was a very advanced soul that came to your world to teach.

After he went home to spirit others realised that he brought much wisdom to they world and they wanted to carry that wisdom forward but unfortunately over many, many aeons of your time his words have been distorted. A religion has grown that is not a religion of humbleness and sincerity but is full of egos and fear. He did not teach fear but love. Love of his Father and love for his fellow men and women. The name that his religion has grown into is one of fear. Do not decry the one that came and brought the wisdom because it is what has happened since".

The forthcoming eclipse of the Sun in mid 1999, is seen by some religions as a very bad omen, in particular the Hindus in India. Is because of the history of eclipses of the sun or the residual affect of the sun worshippers?

"There are religions going back a long, long time and there are religions that worship the sun. There is fear in these religions. I have spoken of fear in Christianity but there is also fear in other religions. Those that led and those that still lead those that follow any religion wish to have control and they envisage they have control by making those followers fearful. It has unfortunately grown. Ideas develop into thoughts. You are aware that thought go out into the surrounding ether and once they are there they take on a life of their own and become part of the Universal Mind which many call draw from. It depends on what level of advance you are to what part of the Universal Mind you can draw from. Those ones with more wisdom can draw higher knowledge and higher wisdom but there are many that are still searching and seeking but because of their teaching they have fear. They then link with these other vibrations of the Universal Mind that are not so enlightened and the more thought that is given the more this spreads.

There is of course energy in the sun, moon and planets that encircle your universe and your ancient ones knew of this strength and energy and how this does affect your world and your vibrations. Your flowers open and close, your crops grow and harvest, your tides come and go, there are storms and floods and it is all part of control. Man cannot harness this energy because it is outside of man's control.

Fear is very dangerous. If only you could do away with fear and create more love this would help the energy to be channeled in the right direction. There is much energy coming to your world because of the eclipse vibrations but it important that it is channeled in the right direction not channeled with fear because with fear it will rebound and cause problems. It is wise and prudent to encompass this with love not fear. Welcome it as an energy force that can do good.

Man is man and there are those that wish to sensationalise on aspects to draw attention to themselves and to their professions and this spreads fear. Send out your love and we will work with you to tray and diffuse negative energy as we have done in times of unrest where there have been many thoughts of fear sent out. There are many from higher realms that are working and are continuing to work to diffuse this negative energy. You have had this occur already in this cycle of your year. Much fear has been sent out from peoples' minds and we have linked with those from higher realms that are dedicated ones working to diffuse this negative energy and to bring a balance. It is an imbalance when there is too much fear and this is negativity. We are still working and all we ask is for you to send love to assist us and those ones from the higher realms.

You say that you can do nothing on your own because you are only one small part of existence but you joined together with many others can make a big difference".

HELEN DUNCAN - HER THOUGHTS

Following communication through the table identified as Helen Duncan, Mafra was asked to confirm communication and then proceeds to give words from her.

It was nice that Helen Duncan was able to make herself known through the table.

"She has come to give energy. She is pleased that there is interest in what has gone before but not because she wants any glory or any praise. She wants people to think, to realise that there is a purpose behind everything. That what there has been is linked with what is now, and what there will be in time to come. We all take our place in a progressive way and while we are on earth we do what is ours to do and then we hand on to the next generation. What has been sown by those gone before the energy is still there for the others to work on and to develop. They can then hand this on to next generation, and so on, and so on.

She is happy that, although her life had its good and not so good times, the energy she was able to leave is now being carried forward for others to build on. If the problems that she experienced and that helped her to learn can help others to learn she is very happy for this to be revived. Not to be revived so that she can sit on a cloud and glory in her name being mentioned. That the truth that she tried to spread when she was on earth to so many; that their loved ones live on, they are taken from them for a while but not only will they meet again as is taught by many religions, but they are with you here and now. There is not a separation; they know what you are thinking, what you are doing, they help you in your existence on earth. You have your own path and destiny that they cannot alter but if they were on earth they would be walking with you helping and what is the difference? They still are interested in you and they are still there to give you strength and guidance if you should need it. You do not have to wait for the great hereafter.

This is the message she tried to bring to those that were mourning and those that were sad. So many at that time because of the conditions of your world during war time. So many were separated so quickly without the last good-bye and they regretted this. What she was trying to teach them was; there is not the last good-bye, there is no such thing as the last good-bye. Life is continuous whether you are in a human body or you have discarded your human body. If this knowledge can be brought to others she is very happy for it to be so.

Of course, there is much more deeper learning and knowledge but also you must not overlook that the initial teaching to those that are bereaved is very important. If they wish to pursue this and ask deeper questions about what is the truth and what spirit is like, so forth and so forth, so be it but do not overlook the importance of bringing comfort to those that are bereaved. This is something that she tried to do when she was on earth and she still believes it is important to do it now.

She is happy to come and join you and give you support. She thanks you for the interest you are showing in this work".
Given 8 August 1999

KEEPING TYPES OF COMMUNICATION SEPARATED

Is it acceptable to do distant healing before a physical communication work in the same circle?

"If you separate vibrations. You are a healing group and your first thought is for healing before you go onto other paths. This is what brought you into the awareness of spirit so healing is your prime ideal. If you shut healing out you are going against the true love that is in you but there is time for energy for all kinds of communication, mediumship and love that you send to others.

If you are saying that you need to shut out your healing thoughts because you want to do physical communication you are causing yourself an imbalance because you are denying yourself what is natural to you. You are shutting the door.

Yes, give your healing and love but then consciously shut down that vibration and move to the next stage of your evening. Do not overlap. I am not saying shut down and open again in prayer because you open in prayer at the beginning and close with prayer at the end but be in control of your energies and how you direct them. If you wish to start with your healing send your love to those because we understand that you wish to work with healing energies. Then consciously shut down your healing thoughts because you have sent your love and finished that task. Consciously be aware that you are changing energy and moving on for physical energy. If you wish to make a change in your energy by altering the music or the way you sing to raise vibrations you are acknowledging that you are changing the purpose of communication. Be aware that you are closing one kind of energy and opening to another kind.

If you shut out something that you desire to do so much for the love of others you are causing an imbalance. For some that sit for physical communication this would not be a problem because their prime reason for sitting would be for physical communication and it would not distress them not to send healing. I am not saying that this is right for them or wrong for them because I am not here to judge. This is not your way of working and if you shut down a way of working that is for you it means that you are working in a condition that you are not happy with. If you are not happy you are drawing the wrong vibrations to yourself because you have an imbalance".
Given 8 August 1999

MUSIC IN THE SPIRIT REALMS

Can you tell us about music in the spirit realms and how we can continue our love of music that we have in the world?

"Music is energy. Music and colour work together because they are both energy. If you were sitting in a concert hall and you were hearing so many instruments being played and were spiritually aware of the vibrations you could perceive so many colours. As the music is played as it leaves the instrument it is an energy and energy is colour. If you saw a paint box of colours on your earth with so many colours of the spectrum however big your paint box it would be very minute compared to the colours of spirit. With your physical eye you can only perceive so much. As with your ears you can only hear a certain range, you know that your animals can hear a different range of sound than yourselves.

USE OF GREEN LIGHT

A sitter remarked that they had heard that the use of green light for physical phenomena instead of red light had produced better results in the seance room.

"Traditionally your groups have used red light because that has been handed down one person to another. In days gone by the physical work needed the energy that was created by the sitter but was also assisted by light of the red glow. Each colour has its own energy. I know that we have used the words 'new energy' and this has been criticised because we have said to you that there is new energy. As you change in your material as your circumstance so does your energy. We are not working the same as groups that sat many years ago. We have said to you that there is new energy.

I would say that there has been a change of energy. Green has a different effect. In circles of your past years ectoplasm was created from a human source for materialisation and we have said to you that spirit are now working to find a different way of working because of the vibrations of earth and the contamination of your earth. It is good to try to find an energy that is more compatible with your modern vibrations. Some groups will be happy to use red light and will get good results but others can try other colours and green is a vibration for today in your world. It is a vibration that is more compatible with the energy you are emanating at this time. You are using energy that you are creating but you are also using energy that is around you. Your are much more aware now of energy that is within your world. You are able to tap into energy that is here now for your everyday existence and you are able to adapt that energy for use in your everyday existence. Therefore, you have become more aware. You have taken a step forward and are perceiving that there is now not only energy from within but energy from around you. The green light would help if you are aware of energy around. If you wish to sit as those that sat in circles previously and work in the same way by sitting and creating physical phenomena through the use of ectoplasm then please continue to use the red light because that is good for that condition. If you wish to develop another kind of way of working which spirit are working for at this time utilising energy that is around you to create physical phenomena you will be happier working with a green vibration. This is because it is not a new energy but an energy that has always been but you have not been aware of it.

Spirit are working to try to bring about a closer link between spirit and your human world by using energy that is there and always has been there but you have been unaware of it. You looked at the world around you but you were only aware of what you could see and feel but as you have progressed in your material world you have learnt that there is energy that can be utilised for your everyday existence. You have learnt of electricity, you have learnt of various waves that are part of your existence for communication, for cooking. Therefore, your brain in functioning in a different way. You are not so introverted and thinking on a single level. You are now aware of energy. You look around you at open space but you are aware that in that space there is energy. You cannot see or touch this energy but you know it is there and it can be used. It is just finding a way of linking this energy to your vibration and unleashing the energy. As you have done this in your material world so it is possible for spirit work as well. You know it exists, you know it works because you send healing. You do see your healing thoughts leaving and going to their destination but you know they go. You are aware of this action. It is just another way of linking the energy that is around you rather than the energy that is within you.

Practise, try green, try red and see what results are better for your group. It is an adventure, it is exciting. You are on the threshold of new discoveries and new ways of communication. You are all part of this experiment so try not a bright or dark green but a soft green. Energy changes and the energy of green is going to be more prevalent as you go further into your new century.

I have tried to explain why we were giving this information not just to give the information. It is important that you understand why changes are happening. So many times in the past people have been told and they have followed instructions without any thought. This is not what we wish. We wish you to part of the adventure, part of the discovery. We wish you to put your vibrations into what is occurring as well as us because you are the human link, we are the spirit link. You are spirit with a human body but you are on earth and are surrounded by human vibrations so it is a coming together of us both. This is what you are working towards for communication, bringing our dimensions closer together. They are together it is just the awareness of knowing we are together".

BLESSING FROM FATHER DOMINIC

May the love of Spirit enfold you, protect you and walk with you,

May the light of Spirit shine before you, illuminate your path with a radiance of love,

May you walk in harmony with those companions that have chosen to serve with you along your path of enlightenment,

Go forward with love and joy in your heart in the service of your fellow brothers and sisters.

A FINAL BLESSING TO YOU ALL

Blessings be with you.

May the light of spirit surround you, may your path be peaceful,

May you share the experience of those who have walked before with knowledge and wisdom and brought light to your dark world

May you share this light of Spirit to those that you meet.

May you share the love of Spirit with those who are seeking.

May you give strength and encouragement to those who are struggling.

May you give healing and upliftment to those who are suffering.

May you walk for ever in the light of spirit and raise your face to the beauty that surrounds you, and the love that encompasses you, and those who share their love with you from our realms.

This is a blessing for yourselves and also for your friends who listen to this voice.

Peace and blessings be with you.

These words were given by one who called themselves Urazan and used to close our public meetings and is therefore offered to whoever reads these words.

THE COMMUNICATORS

MAFRA is Eileen's protector or door keeper who not only controlled proceedings but responded when asked answer questions on spiritual matters. Mafra (pronounced Mafwior) was his surname and he was a Grandee gentleman with a port business in Oporto Portugal (but at the time part of Spain), the time was before Columbus and he supplied the court of King Louis of France with port . He was proud of his brand of port which included the local brandy from the Franciscan Monks. In January 1996 we visited Oporto and crossed the river Douro to the area of wine lodges known as, Vila Nova de Gaia, and there we were able to place ourselves in the spot where Mafra described the location of his business on the waterfront.

During May 1997 we paid a further visit to Oporto and travelled up into the area in Douro valley where the grapes for the port wine are grown. While in Portugal, Mafra came to talk with us and told use a little more of his earthly life. He lived in a large house in Oporto in a main square near the Royal Palace and the Custom House, evidently the house is still there, but considerable altered today. The house had many servants and during the winter months the family came to the City from their home in the country. Mafra had his business on the other side of the river and crossed by boat, because the rope bridge was too rickety. At the time of the English war with France he was officially banned from using French brandy in his port sold to the English market, however to ensure the high quality of his port wine he obtained the best brandy made by French monks, but that was his little secret!. He was able to speak English and Latin.

BEDA was the first communicator to make herself known and comes to bring us joy. Her mother was French and she was born in 1606 . She was married to a Count ('Chi-coffer-chiev' this was spoken by Beda but we could only guess at spelling) who at some time the ambassador, for the area we now know as Russia, to the French Court, around 1630. She was therefore a Countess, and was part of the aristocracy She was very fond of dancing which she performed folk dancing with a group to entertain at the various functions held at the time. She tells us that it is her influence that makes the table "dance". *Reference books refer to Tsar Mikhail the First of the Romanov Dynasty engaging a dancing master Ivan Lodygin. Also the revival of a type of dance called Trepak involving much stamping of the feet. It therefore seems that folk dancing by the aristocracy was the "in thing" around the 1630's. The family moved to Russia and Beda passed as a young woman probably due to the severe climate.*

BROTHER JOHN when on Earth was a Friar many years ago at the Greyfriers Abbey in Coventry, he always comes through with the hands in the praying position.   His role in the Abbey was to pray for peace for as long as he could remember, as such he had taken a vow of silence. Other friars attended his physical needs, provided his food and took every worry from him. He entered the friary at a very young age and used to go and visit the sick and if they were very ill bring them back to the Abbey Hospital for special attention. Then he was drawn into the Abbey learning the chants, eventually he took further vows to allow him to concentrate on prayers for peace . Others told him what prayers were required and he became totally isolated from the world outside.

JOHN LYON was the founder of Harrow School for Boys and is a distant relative of Trevor's on his Mother's side of the family. He is another powerful communicator providing teaching on a wide range of topics. He helps me personally with logical thought and educational activities in my employment. His image and that of his wife are depicted as brasses in the Parish Church with stained glass windows in the school's church.

KIMYANO is a lady from Japan, brings colours for help with healing the body and mind which includes things like depression.

RUNNING BEAR as the name suggests is a North American Indian who brings strength which should not be confused with power. He helps with strength of conviction and is an extremely powerful communicator. He lived in the area we now know as New England and again he lead us to his home by a river running through the forest. Running Bear is Trevor's doorkeeper.

ROSA this lady was skilled in the use of natural remedies and lived high in the mountains of what we know today as Andorra. She helped people who would come to her home for advice on medical and other problems and she gave help as the "wise old lady", they in turn gave her food and other essentials of life. She lived in what she described as a hovel with her many goats. Her name comes from a type of rose that grows high in the mountains that is called Rosa in the local languages. It was not till we travelled in the area that we asked the travel guide the name of this wild rose looking bush that the answer rosa was given and of course when we next spoke to Rosa she confirmed that she had prompted the question.

GEORGE or to give him his full name George William Davey who is Trevor's paternal grandfather, passed to the higher life in 1941 after being knocked off he bicycle by a car during the " black out ", during the Second World War. Now George, to put it in his own words did a bit of "ducking and diving". He was a mechanic by trade and worked in garages on car maintenance, but he was also on the stage in a semi-professional way. He toured the clubs and public houses as a comic and sing along man, around the Tooting area of South London. Once he tells us he "got lucky", and he was on the variety theatre in Kingston. He communicates with a great deal of humour, often singing whistling and accompanying himself on the spoons his stage signature song "Daisy, Daisy give me your answer do" (Daisy, or as he calls her Dais' was his wife who he talks about with great affection). George and Daisy had five sons. Leslie Charles Davey, being the middle one, of the family. George has the ability to communicate on any level of understanding, often acting as the go between for others to communicate by passing on their messages, all with a generous measure of well meaning fun. His work in the Spirit World, is helping people who have recently passed to come to a realisation of their new circumstances and opportunities that await them.

CHURCHMAN OF MALMESBURY at the time of writing we do not have a name for this friend . He tells us that he was a country parson in the Malmesbury area who then went on to become a tutor in philosophy in a college for the Church of England trainee vicars in the South of England.

ALBERT EDWARD FRUIN MSNU passed to spirit in 1969, being Trevor's Mother's Father. He was a medium , speaker and healer while on Earth, together with having a very active involvement in the work of the Spiritualist Lyceum Movement. He was also a transfiguration medium over many years. He is often with us and we sense his presence, also he normally opens up when we sit with the table for communication.

RUTH FRUIN wife of Albert Fruin is a regular communicator who apart from coming for a chat is good at explaining the way people think.

WILLIAM JOHN CANE passed to spirit in *1949*, being Eileen's Mother's Father. He was a originally a driver of horse drawn trams and then became a storekeeper for the predecessors of London Underground. He was one of the first communicators that we had through the table, and brought support for Eileen.

JOHN THOMAS EYER passed to spirit in 1936, being Eileen's Fathers Father. He was a Policeman firstly in Bow (London), then in

Isleworth (West London). In his case he shows himself in his policeman's cape and brings protection when undertaking during psychic work.

DORIS RUTH DAVEY *MSNU*, passed to spirit on the Tuesday 12 March 1996, although she was in a state of a coma from midday on the previous Saturday. On the evening of the 12 March 1996 she made her self known in a circle we were attending at the time, (we are given to understand that this was a "piggy back", communication with another spirit friend showing her around). Within a matter of weeks she was communicating directly under her own "steam", bringing a knowledge of her progression, who she had "met" and with words of guidance to our sitters. Together with a very clear indication that she knows exactly what is happening with her family and other matters that interest her. It should be explained that my Mother had a very clear understanding of spirit and had no fears or qualms about going forward to her new phase of life, she would have liked a little longer on the Earth plain to finish off the many jobs she had in plan, but it was not destined to be.

DOCTOR this man was a medical doctor and surgeon who had his surgery near Bath he trained at Oxford and became a doctor c1750. He has not been able to give his name so far. It seems that he had a country "practice", and dealt with most problems himself although he was happy to have the help of lay people to tend the sick and deal with childbirth.

LESLIE CHARLES DAVEY *MSNU* in this case Trevor's Father who passed into the higher life in 1986, following the side effects of Alzheimer's Disease. In his working life which he somehow managed to fit in with his extensive church committee and church platform work, he was a Group Station Master on the London Underground. He is a regular communicator and is still involved from the Spirit Side in church matters, giving a nudge to those making decisions.

SISTER CECELIA while on holiday in Malta in late September 1996, we were maintaining our usual Sunday night sitting in the relative quite of our hotel room when this communicator made herself known, for the first time. She told us that she was a nursing sister working with the "Order of the Hospital of St John of Jerusalem" or as we know them the Knights Hospitallers or Templars. She worked in the hospice in Valletta tending the sick who had been brought to Malta from many other lands. The medicines they used came mainly from Greece This would have between 1530 and 1800, probably towards the latter period as the Hospice still stands in Valletta and the Knights moved to Valletta from Madina to be on the coast, some years after becoming established in Malta. She told us that her language was a mixture of Latin, Arabic and Greek, today the language of Malta is still a mixture of many other languages with some native

Maltase words. Sister Cecilia tells us that she worked with Eileen's father, (who was a healer), assisting with matters that involved the nerves, their control of the body rather than nervous conditions of the mind. She now assists us with healing work with the same speciality as she helped Eileen's father. As we had been near her place of work / involvement while on Earth she was able to make the link.

SISTER CELESTE she tells us that she was a serving sister in a Catholic Church in Paris near the River Seine (St Denise). Her function was to look after the Holy Fathers, look after the church including the candles, undertake vigils when the deceased was laying in the church overnight before funeral service. Her main role was to prepare and sanctify of the church before mass. She did this by praying with her rosary in various parts of the church. Her role with us is to prepare the room we are sitting in prior to communication with spirit. She does this wherever we are communicating with spirit. Her service is one of love and duty carried out in a humble manner.

CHEE FO SO' *(Phonetically spelt , translation said to be Wise One)*

This communicator was the elder of the village in a Chinese Island, Chang Fu Su (phonetically spelt) This island was said to be very beautiful with many flowers. His role was to listen and speak few words. He was a healer and dispensed Chinese medicine. He had the power to look at body and see where the problem was and direct energy to that point. This knowledge had been handed down from his father to him and has been handed down through his son to his ancestors today. It is unclear at what time he was on earth but he tells us that the silk trade was good but the opium trade was bad. Today he works with us our healing work.

E-OM-BA,*(meaning wise one)*, This man when on earth came from the land we now know as Ethiopia, but know to him as Abyssinia. He was the warier of a tribe that roamed looking for fertile land. When on earth he tells us they had knowledge of spirit, they acknowledged spirit, they danced for spirit to welcome spirit. They used this to create energy for spirit. The following were his words, "not bad spirit good spirit, difference, we gave thanks to spirit for gifts from spirit we linked with spirit for our good, crops, we not go hungry, we would dance special dance for food. Spirit would send blessings for us, respect spirit. We spoke to spirit through a wise one, go deep into meditation, we would dance, create vibration , he go, spirit talk, spirit of ancestor, mighty one, strong one, give words of wisdom".

His role is to bring wisdom. Although he tells us he has joined our group for mutual learning.

Subsequently, Trevor's grandmother (Ruth Fruin), told us that E-OM-BA worked through her husband with his healing activities and public speaking. E-OM-BA regularly transfigured on Albert Fruin's face while he was demonstrating transfiguration. A would bang his staff on the floor to indicate his presence in the home circle. It's a matter of the continuous system of working through ancestors.

JULES, This man had a family vineyard near to the city of Marseilles in Southern France.

He was a devout Roman Catholic and worshipped in the large church in the centre of the city.

Clearly he was an educated man and tells us he sold his wine locally. He joins us to learn and progress.

GEORGE "MAN OF LETTERS", This gentleman introduced himself as another one of the band of spirit friends who come to learn with us, but he also has a role in recording events. He has told us a little about his life when on earth. He had a business in Winchester in a large house with steps up to the door. He undertook the work of a solicitor, swearing oaths, covenants, business transactions, transfer of money and as a Commissioner of Oaths. He used a quill pen to write. His style of clothing was to wear high collars, long coats and foot leggings to protect his shoes. At the time he was in the body men had long hair, as did he. He travelled about by horse drawn coach. He tells us it is good to keep records. He takes account of what occurs, there are no records like ours but a certain amount of order is necessary to ensure everything is in it's due course. Everything is for a purpose, happening at it's appointed time, he oversees what occurs. He is learning also, as others talk he listens, as Mafra co-ordinates.

SOPHIA, This lady is a helper, who helps with our thoughts transmission towards others. She lived in Italy when on earth. Ensuring that we are on the same vibration when linking with the mind, rather than by speech. Prompting can be done by the mind without conscious reasoning.

BROTHER STEPHAN - Brother was a fellow friar at Greyfriars, Coventry at the same time as Brother John. He helped with the sick creating their own medicine, they grew plants in the friary garden. These were preserved for use throughout the year and were administered to people in the surrounding area. They treated injured people and ensured that their family were taken care of whilst the injured person was unable to work. If the father of the family was injured and had to rest until the injury was healed the brothers would ensure his family did not go hungry and their farm. small holdings or businesses were looked after. It was just not the process of tending the sick but looking at the whole family. There were also sisters if the mother was ill, the sisters would assist with the running of the home, these sister were not from Greyfriars but from another religious settlement in Coventry. There were also sisters who taught as in Gloucester there were sisters in the school. It was a service to the community not just within closed walls. They would not take payment for their services but they were looked after. They were self sufficient in their grounds, they had vast grounds where they grew vegetables and livestock but those whom they looked after were not asked for payment. When thankful they would give us what they could afford in the way of their produce and if the brothers did not need it they would pass it on to others who were experiencing hard times. They would look after their buildings themselves, there were brothers who would do brickwork and carpentry. They were self sufficient. There were people who would come and give to the church in gratitude. They were thankful to the brothers but they would show their gratitude through the church and in turn the church would be able to use their donations. Some of the wealthy residents of the area would give monetary donations to the church which would enable the brothers to erect new buildings or create another room for patients to come and stay. They relied on these donations for such works. There have always been those who have more than they need and there has always been those who have less than they need and the brothers felt it was their duty to administer where it was needed. Those that had money would look after their own servant but would give to the brothers to enable them to look after the remainder of the community. Their donations were not for the brothers but for the glory of God. There were other settlements within the town not just Greyfriars. Greyfriars was on the edge of the town and had much ground this was a friary, the big church in the town had it's own monastery different from Greyfriars. This monastery did not serve the community, they attracted more nobility.

Records and accounts were kept but these have been long lost. Account was taken of all that came and all that went. No profit was made but they had to account for themselves, especially after the change in circumstances of the Church of the Country. This was the time of upheaval with churches, churches were closed, so those that were still in existence had to keep good records to show that they were of service to the community. They had to prove their worth, to give education, succour to the sick. Records were kept and these were examined by those who were in high authority who came to Coventry.

It was a time of great change and many of our other brothers in other communities were not able to exist. This was why Joseph and his brothers came to Coventry, others went across water for some years returning later, some went to Ireland others to France and other countries where they settled in communities and came back later. Some stayed in their new homes and did not return.

Greyfriars in Coventry had a closed Order, Brother John was in the closed Order, but to keep this as such they had to have a community service otherwise it would not have been possible to exist. This was part of the reason for the closed Order, prayers were needed very much in the country at that time. Many would not have known of those who had taken higher vows. Many of the monasteries throughout England were very wealthy before this time but much of their valuable assets were taken from them by the Crown. There was much secrecy, much was hidden. King Henry VIII was the instigator but it went on for many years afterwards. When Mary was queen we were able to survive again for a short while but then when Elizabeth became queen the country was Protestant again so there was much unrest from one to the other between the various monarchs. Queen Bess ruled for many years, once she was on the throne there was not much growth. During her reign they looked out from the country to other lands. Whatever befalls the land the human race goes on and your brothers and sisters still need each other. Much changes but nothing changes. There have been upsets and upheavals throughout history but all races come through. It is good to know there is a stronger force behind us all whom you can call upon. As the friars had a deep belief and were able to ask for help and assistance all mankind is able to do the same and is made stronger for doing so.

ROSEAH Introducing herself to us for the first time, " I come, I'm here now, I have come for a short while, to experience the body. I have often sat with you and listened with you, I have worked with you, I have so much to learn, there are many of us you know, who come and sit, not sit as you sit but come. I have come because I want you to be my friends. You see I have no one on earth that I could talk to, because they are of a different belief, and I am not able to talk to them, so I am happy if you will let me talk to you. By talking I learn, and I share, so you see I talk to you with voice but I am also talk to you on another level, and this makes progression easier for us all. I was on earth a long while ago in your time, and I have been finding so much to learn in what you call spirit. It is wonderful what progress there is for everyone, once they   accept that there is more than just sleep. I believed we slept, I was of Church of Rome, They now say I must give you name so you know, Roseah, it was a name I used when I had body, it is a name of years of your time gone by. I go now, someone says you must not confuse me with someone else who has a name similar, (Rosa) not the same not same vibration. I must tell you one thing, I was a Sister. Blessings my friends, I have friends yes"

HANNS Introducing himself tells us that he was a German chemist who is a visiting helper, not permanently attached to our particular group,